Other Books by W.P. Jaspert

Encyclopaedia of Type Faces (with W. Turner Berry & A.F. Johnson), London ISBN 978-1-084493-670-7; *State of the Art* London & Brussels ISBN 0-9597071-0-4; *Popo* (in German) London ISBN 0-9547383-0-6 and some revised technical or translated books published in London, England; Brussels, Belgium; and Würzburg, Germany.

He still works and also contributed at one time to some forty technical and other magazines and newspapers in Britain and overseas.

AS MY final hours will be approaching I think of the Roman elegiac poet Albius Tibullus, who died over two thousand years ago. I have made this transliteration of his moving poem:

"Let me gaze upon you
When my last hour comes
And when I shall die
Let me hold you
With the waning power
Of my hand."
(*later addition:* And when I am gone
Shroud me in some book papyrus)

Te spectem, suprema mihi cum venerit hora,
Te tenam morens deficiente manu

Think or Swim

Dancing the Conga with Molotov and Other Reminiscences

WERNER PINCUS JASPERT

PRIVATELY PRINTED

Published by juntincappers@aol.com
First published in London in 2011

A CIP catalogue record for this title is available from the British Library
ISBN 978-0-9568736

Designed and typeset in Plantin by Steve Brown,
www.stevebrowndesign.co.uk

Printed in England by icreateprint.co.uk
London NW6

Contents

Acknowledgments

THIS NARRATIVE is dedicated to my children and grandchildren, family and especially the three wives and the three mistresses in my life.

Bareda Ann Clark, my third wife, implanted the idea for these notes. Robert O. Bradley pestered me to "get on with it". Roy Coxhead helped me greatly and gave me new ideas. Roy and Terry Sewards also suggested some good – I hope – catch phrases. Steve Brown put them into shape. Kitty Forge rescued the draft of the book and keyboarded the content on to her computer for me to continue. My sons Willem and Augustus helped with editing and tried to point out duplications.

In these reminiscences I recount, not necessarily in the proper time sequence, how my life was affected by outside happenings.

Writing these notes I have come to realise that without my friends and the family I could not face life. I deliberately do not name or pinpoint their additional help. One friend made me come out of my self-imposed shell and brought me to regular lunches with former colleagues. I was also taken to museums and theatres or just to dinner. It was company and talk I craved. When I was too weak to carry heavier loads, one friend faced a journey of several hours just to take my laundry round the corner to get it washed. He also offered to share his life savings with me. The friends and family in Britain and abroad made me live again. I say Thank You to them!

My life has been shaped by my close-knit family and my brother Jürgen, my few but close friends, and – of course – by the women in my life. These notes are about the past and a full life. Some people called "uncle" or "aunt" in the pages are not actually related to me, but were a great influence on my childhood. I miss intimate companionship and activity around me.

Throughout these reminiscences some sayings and quotations are recited. Many have greatly influenced my life and thinking.

I sent a first draft of these notes as a courtesy to Barri Clark, my third wife, who contemptuously returned the pages unread and wrote that she had heard it all before. My vanity was hurt, but this dismissal had a good side to it, too. A bit of money was thus wasted on postage; more was saved in copying costs.

If I have confused any facts, it was not deliberate; my faulty memory is to blame. Some of my recollections may seem like the tales of Baron Münchhausen or those of Walter Mitty. They may sound like tall stories, but they are fact. Once I luckily got out of trouble I had to thank my gift of the gab, coupled with my blonde Germanic looks.

I rarely use my first name of Werner. It has the irritating connotation of "warner" or "watchman". On my birth certificate only one first name was given. For various reasons my father often called me "Pincus" and I gradually became known by my second name as W. P. Jaspert. Amid the growing anti-Semitism around me I asked whether I was Jewish. I was assured that I carried an illustrious name, then of the Roman general from Illyria, supposedly the only foreign officer in the Imperial Army.

I tend to annoy people by often thinking that I know what is best for them. Unfortunately those new anti-terror security restrictions insist on the given first name. Waiting in airport lounges I fail to turn up when my little used first name is called over the public address system.

These days Big Brother is always watching you. Before 9/11 even the most totalitarian regimes slipped up. Under the Nazis my mother, of all people, was asked by Josef Goebbels' propaganda ministry to handle classified news and policy information, as she spoke good English. Despite all the bodyguards around the Soviet Politburo member Molotov, I could join him in a dance. Security guards were stationed at Harwell, the British atomic weapons place. I visited my first brother-in-law, identified myself with a Press card and was admitted through an unguarded door in the fence – in those less-obsessed days – unaccompanied by personnel. I could have walked anywhere and – had I understood them – sneaked a look at secret papers lying on unattended desks. On another occasion I was allowed into the (British) air ministry. East Germany's last and later imprisoned Prime Minister travelled unaccompanied with me to Sweden. There he talked freely and almost like a West German living in a freer society.

All this was before the present obsession with security and interference with privacy. I could cite numerous other examples.

Now I live alone and am trying to get used to this. I am lucky because I still love reading a book almost every day. Some nonfiction takes a bit longer, though. I also rediscover books I read in my youth. They are almost new books to me now. I disdain television (which I could have free), radio and newspapers. I dislike the outside world entering my home and my peace.

I love being surrounded by pictures and books, even when I go to my daughter's home in Spain. Some two thousand years ago Cicero said: "To give a house a library is to give a house a soul".

Throughout the reminiscences some sentiments of fictitious characters from various works of authors from Homer to modern times are quoted. I can only hope that I have remembered or paraphrased more or less accurately. The chronological sequence of events described here may be somewhat confusing. Some duplications are deliberate because they show important influences on my life.

I am especially grateful for the Librarians at the British Library in St. Pancras, London, who greatly helped in finding the quotations from Latin.

I dedicate this book to my parents, Willem and Isolde Jaspert (née Anger) the paternal grandfather, many uncles and aunts, as well as good friends. The children made the effort worthwhile. They all taught me respect and gave me a fierce belief in fighting for the right of everyone to have freedom of speech and thought, even if objectionable to me. Some people have a rather astonishingly limited vocabulary and seem to know only four-letter words. I pity them and often suggest they should learn the five-letter word "fudge".

Introduction

MANY OF the people mentioned in these pages I have actually met. Some, however, I read about only. Some sentiments I disliked or disapproved. Views expressed are therefore opinions only. This thinking was or is about their attitudes or thoughts – if they have had any real ones.

For over fifty years I had lived at the same address in "leafy Hampstead" with the firm conviction that I would end my days there. Alas, "old man's disease" struck. I committed adultery and truly stupidly married in California, only to be quickly divorced by my new American wife, using the "Hollywood-Style" Californian matrimonial legislation. She paid for the divorce. In my ignorance I, too, paid Californian court fees and then also to get the divorce registered in England. A costly business all for the benefit of the legal profession. I had to surrender the US immigrant's Green Card. I long for my old life. Reading is a great compensation. I have no television. It bores me. Newspapers at one time were my life blood. Every day at my ripe old age I spend several hours writing. I also walk most days for three or four hours to exercise my legs. I still dislike organized sport or regimented exercises.

After my second marriage I moved from London's Hampstead to St. John's Wood, a favoured suburb in north London, in my late seventies. At the same time I started commuting regularly between London and Los Angeles at roughly a fortnightly pace. That earned me plenty of air miles. Back in London I recently moved to a canal-side sheltered home nearby. Life seems like that which a friend whimsically calls the life of a *boulevardier*. In fact it is the day-to-day struggle of someone who is no longer affluent, physically impeded by a stroke, but supported by a loving and caring family and fortified by friendship. Five friends brought me back to living life: Philip Burton and his wife Muriel, Roy Coxhead, Michael Freer, and Denis Havard. There are others who made me re-embrace life. My first two wives are in good contact with me again. They both gave me lovable and loving children.

I look back on a childhood in Nazi Germany, and even today, almost three quarters of a century after the evil around me first had an impact on upon me, I suffer almost every night terror and frightening half-awake nightmarish dreams in which I without hope confusedly fight events.

Events in the outside world affected my brother and me. As friends of the parents' suddenly disappeared and we learned that they had been arrested, Jürgen and I prepared ourselves for such a harsh fate by resolutely eating bread and water, while Mama kept cooking us proper meals.

I generally sleep soundly, but wake up with nameless fear when I return to the real world.

I recall three marriages, a smattering of extramarital liaisons, plus a youthful enjoyable and welcome affair before I came to England. There may well be a unique record: wartime service with the opposing German and American forces. I am probably the most widely travelled printing journalist and well-known for my writings on print developments and personalities for over thirty publications and some books worldwide. Literally thousands of articles were published. I also used pen names, such as Seamus O'Pinhas, which even found their way into newspapers, and an anagram of my name for the now defunct *EuroPrinter* magazine. That anagram also offers my e-mail "screen" name.

Pride in my family is important. There are probably under a thousand Jaspert families around the world. I have found that many of them – by this I mean those I have met over the years – are in what is nowadays called "the media". Some, in America, are related to my grandfather, whose brother emigrated there in the nineteenth century. In the middle ages a Jaspert established a branch in Spain. The country then ruled the Low Countries. Now my brother, one of my daughters and some cousins live in Spain.

I hate being made to do things and regimentation. That is why I do not like almost masochist organized sport. All my life I have managed to shirk it, although I like activity such as slow long distance swimming, walking and – in the old days – even hurdle jumping. Being tall made that easy.

The times of affluence are over. The divorces were costly. Only one former wife burdened me with maintenance settlements. There are probably more expenses to come, most of them to pay lawyers. There is money enough for some years for small indulgences. My wanderlust will mean that the children will get only a pittance, some good books, passable pictures and furniture. Jennifer Clark, the daughter of Barri, my third wife, will lose out through no fault of her own. Barri's maiden name, by the way, claims to trace back to the Welsh admiral Sir Arthur Limpus.

I like living near the centre of London. In the Italian shop where I took my regular morning caffè latte until recently I was greeted as '*dottore*', which I liked, though fully aware of the blatant flattery. The Spanish fishmonger greeted me and picked really fresh fish for me. His wife from Colombia offered to cook for me when I was abandoned by my third wife. The Greek printer and stationer around the corner was considerate and interested in my welfare. The same goes even now for many shopkeepers, the hairdresser, and the dry cleaner. In the pub I enjoy the occasional large glass of wine and sometimes take friends. One night, when a pavement cyclist tried to attack me, a very tall Lebanese sitting with some friends outside a street cafe was watching the altercation. Suddenly – like a genie out of bottle – he jumped up and told the would-be assailant rather quietly to move off, which the man did at whirlwind speed. Everybody seems to know me.

To state it again; I hate living alone, though I am not really alone, and have good friends and loving, attentive and caring children. All but two live far away. Evenings and weekends are a time of desolation, lightened only by the glass of wine in the pub, where they know me and greet me almost as an old friend.

Some red wine, I was glad to read, acts as a tonic and helps the heart, thus winning praise from patients suffering high blood pressure. Doctors, I read, have long praised the benefits of red wine (some no doubt liking it very much themselves). Years ago I learnt that at one national health hospital in Britain nurses dispense glasses of red wine every night to some patients. Research seems to have shown that two daily glasses of red wine can reduce the chances of a stroke by some twenty per cent, by even fifty per cent in the case of heart attacks. The idea of giving patients this bonus drink and help them on the way to recovery is the idea of Dr William McRea, a heart surgeon who claims antioxidants in the red wine are the key. Wines such as Pinot Noir, Cabernet Sauvignon and Shiraz are thought best. Sadly, Dr McRea recommends cheaper wines. Mature and vintage wines lose antioxidant over time. White wines seem of little benefit. The grape skins holding the clot-fighting antioxidants have been discarded.

Life is trial and error. Robert Hale summed it up when he wrote, 'If I had known then what I know now I would have made the same mistakes sooner.'

But let us go back eighty years or more …

A Lapsed Calvinist's Lament

NO ANIMAL would behave in such inhuman ways as nations and their leaders. Cruelty surrounds our lives. At heart I am a Calvinist, though not actually believing in things religious, though some beliefs have traces of realism. So I feel strongly, in a Calvinist lament, how wrong the world is in its righteous cruelty:

I was a child then – and then a teenager.
The horrors of the Nazi era went on around me.
My parents and the family cared for Jews and ideals.
Our father was murdered in a concentration camp.
The good side fought a war and won.
We survived and thought the world
would be a kinder place.
We have learnt our lesson.
Now we know: nothing has changed –
Korea, Rwanda, Palestine, Kosovo, Iraq.

Beginning

I WAS born on the 21st of March 1926 in Frankfurt, south of the River Main, a circumstance which became important when later, in Munich, I was able to deny that I was a Prussian (every country has its ridiculed tribes). The regions south of the River Main once were all part of Bavaria.

I had largely liked my Montessori kindergarten nursery. I appreciated early that I was encouraged to develop my own nature. I was encouraged to express myself and even be moderately unruly. I avoided any form of compulsory sport. I continued this at school in Switzerland and in the military services and learned to shirk. Some non-competitive sports activities, however, came easy. I actually liked rugby, hurdle jumping and swimming. I found these activities non-challenging and easy. I shirked other sporting activities and took to again growing radishes. I rarely failed to ogle the day girls doing their gymnastics. The acquired skills in avoiding competitive sport later enabled me to talk my way out of problematic difficulties during the war and in peacetime situations.

Earlier in Angola Papa was attacked by a leopard who jumped on his back and tried to kill him. Maurice Sidney Ryan, a strong and tall Australian, jumped on the animal's back, got his arms around its neck and choked it. My father's life was saved. Papa and his brother ran out of money and got jobs as engine drivers. Any European then was considered a jack-of-all-trades. They managed to crash their engines head on. Papa jumped from the locomotive's cab, but caught his hand in some metal rods. Mama must have been a very determined woman. The available medic wanted to amputate his entire arm. My mother staggered the long way to the "white people's" hospital in town, carrying the grown-up man. One finger only was shortened.

How times have changed! I spent the first years of my life in Angola in darkest Africa. I loved my black houseboy. I also played with my golliwog (the soft toy red-coated black character). Now these dolls beloved by children are practically banned as politically incorrect. I recently bought such a plaything. It adorns one of the walls in my home. Does this make me a racist?

Dorothy Parker, the American writer and wit of the *Algonquin Round Table* wrote about the 1930s: "They were progressive, these days. We thought we were going to make the world better. I forget why we thought it, but we did!" Shades of today! Looking at events these days around me, it seems most of one's intentions and aspirations have come to naught. Politics has become the epitome of cynicism.

Accidents will happen. As a child they add spice to life. Uncle Franz Perneder had bought a tiny car and wanted to show this off. He took me for a drive. Cars then were still something of a sensation. Franz, a nominal uncle, rammed his car and I crashed into the windscreen which broke into splinters and cut my upper lip. I was taken to hospital. When I woke up from the anaesthetic all I could think of was that I was missing the Sunday lunch – chicken! That was something special in those days. A few years later the parents went sailing in the Baltic from Germany to Lithuania. We capsized. I clung to the boat which went keel up and was taken to emergency hospital with severe sunburn. The nurses were kind, I thought them beautiful. Once back at school, the other boys admired the exciting sailing adventure and aftermath.

Going to primary school in 1932 was an exciting adventure. In Berlin's Zehlendorf district the Nazi storm troopers had already arrived before Adolf Hitler gained power. That meant anybody those villains imagined looked Jewish could be beaten up and humiliated – grown-ups or children alike. We were a normal mixed bunch of small school children – Aryans and Jews alike – who did not care about the newly discovered distinctions between the races. In a protective move mounted police collected us from outside our homes and took us to primary school on horseback. That made going to school truly exciting. My brother was only four years old. I was six by then.

My somewhat Flemish (but German national) father and partly South African mother – she was born after her father lived in that country – decided that I could no longer attend school in Nazi-dominated Germany. I thus went to school in five countries, ending up in neutral Switzerland, after Berlin, Prague, Vienna and Budapest, always followed by the Nazis. My brother was later sent westward through occupied France, travelling with diplomatic immunity *sans* inspection (where he lived with my uncle Bernhard's family and their advanced and streamlined Tatra car from Czechoslovakia).

He ended up in Spain and still lives there. Today I know that my parents made a supreme sacrifice in sending me away so that I would not be eternally poisoned by Nazi ideology and the cult-like ideas they instilled in an almost totally besotted adoring populace. My parents suffered: their beloved children were far away!

We children had to learn the importance of independence. My brother was four years old. I was six by then. Jürgen and I decided to visit our grandparents – over three hundred miles away! We set out on our pedal scooters for the railway station and boarded a train. We felt all was well arranged. A conductor came and asked where our parents were. Truthfully we told him that they were in Berlin. He asked whether we knew the telephone number and we willingly gave that to him. At the first stop we were asked to step out. The station master called my by then anxious mother and told her that she should go to the main terminal, bring some money for the penalty charge and take us home. Mama did not even scold us. Corporal punishment did not exist at home.

When my parents married, so my mother Isolde told me, they were invited to spend the honeymoon on one of the Mumm family's Sekt (sparkling wine) estates in Germany. My father Willem, so my mother claimed, overindulged in the wine and neglected – though only temporarily, fortunately for my brother and me – his husbandly duties. His liking of bubbly remained, though it was thereafter only moderately indulged. Mama also told me that when they stayed with the paternal grandparents they were sternly admonished to keep the bedroom door open at all times. They obeyed!

We lived in Berlin. I went to primary school where Andreas Herxheimer, now an internationally renowned pharmacologist, became my friend. Seventy-five years later we are still friends. He lives in London, whereto his late parents emigrated. Before then his father was a professor in Berlin.

Grandfather August Jaspert was a headmaster. The school is nowadays named after him – and so is one of the many streets of Frankfurt. He was also a Deutsche National Party follower. I recall him as a member of the (dissolved by Hitler) Prussian Landtag assembly and the founder of what is still, I believe, the largest children's holiday village in Europe. His youngest son Werner was one of the last editorial staff of the *Frankfurter Zeitung* before the Nazis closed the paper down. He was the first mayor of the suburb of Oberusel after the US occupation authorities arrived. He got one of the first publishing licenses then, and so did his younger brother Reinhardt in (the British Zone) Berlin. Werner's son Michael married Colette, the daughter of an escaped French prisoner-of-war whom my uncle and his family sheltered briefly in their garden at the end of the war. My mother's sister, Tante Gert, was Franz Perneder's partner for many years. Gertrud Anger took a boat to South Africa when the partnership broke up, but, alas, returned just before the Second World War disgusted with the appearance of Apartheid.

Aunt Gertrud Anger (who later married Fritz Wolf – an Austrian ex-concentration camp inmate – who was released to serve in a punishment battalion exploding mines) sheltered a Jewess, with whom she shared her meagre rations. My mother Isolde took in the Jewish, and later Erika Kasten (her husband ran the famous

Gurlitt Gallery and after the war founded the art gallery in Linz, Austria), to enable their daughter to be born in secret. At the age of fifteen, though terrified, I assisted at the birth.

Separately our father Willem and mother Isolde, (née Anger), took Jewish persons (or their valuables sometimes) to sanctuary in Czechoslovakia and later Switzerland. They also helped others to escape, such as a relative of Sergei Eisenstein, the Soviet filmmaker.

In Berlin, my father Willem Jaspert published books by Jewish authors who befriended me. Karl Brinitzer and Egon H. Strassburger, who used pictures of my brother Jürgen and me in his book *Kinder*, were some of them. Their books were later, when Jews were barred from writing, published by my father's publishing house under pseudonyms. The authors thus had access to badly needed small funds. Risky acts of bravery by family members were taken for granted by me as a small boy. Already in 1934 Papa had protested to the Nazis about the erratic banning of authors, which caused consternation abroad.

When I neared military service age the Nazi consulate in my school's town St. Gallen requested the Swiss cantonal police to escort me to the German border and I was made to leave Switzerland after friends sheltered me in Zurich. Once escorted to the German border I went first to hide but then gave myself up to the German Navy. Paul Rosbaud, the science spy for Britain in wartime Berlin, advised my mother to persuade me to do this. It seemed preferable. An uncle had been a vice-admiral and this may have helped me before deserting to the Americans together with the grandson of a famous German First World War hero.

In the early 1930s we had a dog, Mirku, a large shaggy Hungarian sheepdog. He was most affectionate and slobbered over children and visitors alike. He was wary and knew the danger of the road. Consequently, he had to be carried over the asphalt, a task usually left to us small boys (five and seven years old) and made even more difficult in rain when we all got soaked, the dog vigorously shaking itself all over the carpet once home again. He was killed in the road and properly mourned. We also had at another time two Scottish terriers who protected us fiercely against all strangers, even the beloved grandparents. In later days they reminded me of Black & White whisky. I like dogs and am happy with them. The children later had Jasper, a gentle golden retriever. He allowed Bella, a black rabbit, to jump over his nose and followed him only with his eyes. We thought Bella to be female. The rabbit turned out to be male and aggressively pursued the squealing and suffering guinea pig.

Cats worry me. Dogs I like. Cats like me, and I am frightened. I think they are mystical and somewhat weird creatures. Muriel and Philip Burton's cat years ago – I hallucinated – appeared to walk on the ceiling.

It wanted to sit on my lap and I was horrified and sat stock still. Cats also creep between the legs onto the crotch and cause embarrassment. So do dogs!

Once, having dinner at friends, Brigitte Steinhardt's cat jumped on my back and made me spit out spaghetti in a thick tomato sauce. That ruined a nice shirt and I was glad of wearing a bow tie, as always properly tied, of course. I cannot tie conventional long neckties. They easily fall into soup bowls or dishes.

Papa ached from severe migraines. When they occurred curtains had to be drawn, day turned into night, and all noise had to stop. I was reminded of this later when Jack Yates, the painter from Sheffield, had such migraines. One day a soft pear dropping onto the floor provoked him into agonised moans and stopped him from painting. I liked his pictures of nudes and Welsh scenes. Many of them are now at my daughter Beatrice's home in Spain.

Mama suffered from painful gallstones, perhaps a result of her malaria treatment with quinine, and was given morphine to alleviate her pain. I suspect that she also for a time indulged experimentally in cocaine when she was an habituée of Berlin's Jockey Club in the late 1920s and early '30s. She was never an addict, although there were always morphine suppositories in the medicine cupboard. The time in Africa had exacted its toll on the parents. Mama suffered the after-effects of malaria. I got away with sunstroke, though my friends used to tease me about that, knowing that the sun made me do something rebellious at school or behave eccentrically in later life.

My late and for some time penniless Mama deserved an easier life. She was left maintenance money after her second divorce from my father. The parents had married again. Mama and Inge, my father's thus third wife, each got half of the restitution money after the war and then only because I sent Chancellor Adenauer a multi-page telegram when he had come to visit London. Before the war Mama had a reasonable income, but after the murder of my father she had to rely first on Papa's brothers and then on her family, and then on my brother Jürgen and me. We supplemented her income, though Jürgen never earned remotely what I earned.

The high life my mother knew was privileged I know, but it must have been a terrible fall from grace to experience real poverty for ten years. I used to send her each month in Berlin £10 wrapped up in a magazine by putting a staple over the metal strip of the banknotes. At that time I got ten pounds sterling weekly as salary before tax and insurance, so the paltry sum sent from London was considerably more than a week's paid out wages. Now my children say, "Dad, we shall look after you", and that is very sweet. I know I have looked after my children not badly, but I do not think this sort of charity (though lovingly given) is what I wanted to happen to me.

I was pleased to hear cousins and friends say that they could always talk to my mother, better sometimes than to their own mothers. That makes me very proud of her. But I did not do the things for her I wanted to do: take her to New York, for instance. She did not want to move there because she was so annoyed about America. She said that was not the country she wanted to go to. She and many immigrants before the war were interned on Ellis Island and people came on Sundays to look at the people in cages.

One of the American immigration officers, looking at her nose, said she was Jewish. The US State Department stubbornly clung to outdated immigration quotas for Germans. Hitler had made Jewish nationals (of course not my mother) stateless and their passport carried a large "J" stamp. Mama's passport did not carry such a stamp. Mama had at first travelled to across the Atlantic to check out America. She had misgivings. Arthur D. Morse's *While Six Million Died* describes the disturbing attitudes of the American authorities at that time. Despite Mama's fears she travelled repeatedly to the States to do her Christmas shopping in New York City and Chicago.

Willem Jaspert, my father, was tired of banking when he returned with my mother and me to Europe. He was made publisher of a company owned by Hugo Stinnes and published many books, some written by himself or under a pseudonym. One, written jointly with his elder brother Fritz, was notable for the Angolan various native language dictionary section.

When I was six weeks old my mother, accompanied by her sister, Gertrud Anger (Wolf) and my best-loved aunt, Elisabeth Jaspert, had taken me to Antwerp. Mama and I boarded a ship bound for Angola. There my father and his brother Fritz had gone to study native languages and culture. Angola was then also a penal colony. Natives ran many police stations, post offices and local government. Mixed marriages were common.

I did learn some African dialects; I still remember the keyword *olombongo* (money). I loved the black houseboy and played with young rescued jungle animals.

My paternal grandmother, Anna Jaspert, loved me, but thought me a little heathen when we had returned to Europe. How real life changes establish genuinely held beliefs. About a dozen years earlier my grandmother had called me a little heathen. I missed black people around me and had had sunstroke. I had not been baptized. The grandparents soon arranged for that. As for the sunstroke, schoolmates later laughed at me because of that.

Africa has exerted a pull even on our present generation. My two sons worked there as volunteers or Foreign & Commonwealth Office aspirants. A cousin went to the Congo as a consultant engineer. The maternal grandfather was a District Surgeon in the Cape Province. My mother's sister, Gertrud Anger, went to South Africa where some of her cousins then were ministers in the apartheid government. She returned to Europe just before the outbreak of the Second World War. My aunt married Fritz Wolf, an Austrian who was sent to a concentration camp, freed only to serve later in the German Army in a punishment battalion. He was captured by the Russians who soon released him as an Austrian ally.

The parents of Walter Anger, my maternal grandfather, lived for a while in White Russia. They were fur traders, I believe. He had met Dora, my maternal grandmother, in Saxony at the time he was organist in Leipzig at the St. Thomas church where the composer Bach once reigned. Some of his music still exists in the Preussisches Staatsarchiv library in Berlin. After Leipzig and concert tours in Europe, he went with his wife to Aberdeen, where he qualified as a doctor. He suffered a stroke just before taking up an appointment in the then German-controlled Samoa.

Walter Anger, my maternal grandfather, changed from being an organist to the study of medicine at Aberdeen. While a crown servant in South Africa, he holidayed on St. Helena. He brought back a splendid walking stick which I still have. His house in Port St John's still stood in the late 1990s – the last time I visited there – on a slope near the mouth of the river. After he died suddenly before taking up a new posting to the Pacific Islands, my grandmother moved to Saxony, where my mother was born.

In the days of apartheid, the quasi-independent country had Indians and other races freely mixing on beaches, in hotels and restaurants. People of non-white races came from Durban and other places to holiday and enjoy themselves. Family legend said that at one time Walter Anger owned half of Main Street in Cape Town. Whatever: after his death his widow returned to Europe and was advised to invest the remaining money in German securities. All was lost in the massive inflation of the 1920s.

By the age of nine years I knew some originally English literature. Dickens' Mr Micawber and Uriah Heep (whom I much later encountered in real life, living in Basel), Kipling and the Jungle Book with Mowgli and Rikki-Tikki-Tavi, and Hugh Lofting's Dr Dolittle and his animals. I loved Frances Hodgson Burnett's sentimental snobbish Little Lord Fauntleroy and the Mississippi adventures of Mark Twain's young heroes. These were books translated into German and mostly published by Williams & Co. in Berlin.

Goulash of Genes

ON THE paternal side, I also trace my ancestors back to Belgium's disputed and German-speaking Eupen-Malmedy region. The farm carrying the family name is said to still stand there. I believe that only one family member, who was a London dry cleaner, lived in England. But there are several others in America, Australia and everywhere in Europe. Many are journalists and writers. August Jaspert, my father's father, was a representative of the free city of Frankfurt. He had been a forester and became headmaster of a school. There is also a street in the city's Bonames district named after him there. After the First World War he had founded Wegscheide, Europe's largest holiday village for needy schoolchildren. It is still in full use and his children and grandchildren were welcome guests. He was an outspoken man. Early in childhood I looked up to him. At the funeral of great-great aunt Eulalia he had noticed that I was fidgeting and deeply embarrassed. He took me by the hand, went behind another tombstone and unbuttoned his trousers to demonstrate what to do. I followed suit and was much relieved. Despite the obvious sacrilege the gods had not shot a sudden bolt from the heavens.

As a deputy coming to Berlin, Opa had free travel. He took his wife and me on a city train, stood on the seat and addressed passengers in a stentorian voice and told them that they were being led by a madman (Hitler). Anna, my grandmother, tried to quieten him down to no avail.

Both maternal and paternal grandparents were musical. The four brothers in my father's family had formed a quartet. Sometimes Mama's sister joined in playing the violin. Her partner uncle Franz also played that instrument. The main ensemble, though, was by the brothers and Mama, who played the mandolin. Papa sat at the grand piano, uncle Äd handled another string instrument and hardy the cello. Werner played the flute and the second piano, sometimes Mama attended to that. Werner Jaspert had worked as a conductor for some years. Later he wrote books on composers. My maternal grandmother had known Clara Schumann and Johannes Brahms. Mama and Papa also played four-headed pieces on the Bechstein and Grotrian-Steinweg grand pianos. We thus had a small orchestra. Neither Jürgen nor I are active, though we learnt to play music as children. My children had music lessons, too, but also did not maintain the interest.

Papa was a great admirer of Gustav Mahler. I still have one of etchings of a portrait of the musician.

There were scandalous stories of Alma Mahler which we did not comprehend. One tale, however, amused us again and again: the painter Oskar Kokoschka went to performances at the opera with a life-size blown up plastic doll. Gradually we came to believe it. Rosbaud vouched for this. Later in London and after Rosbaud's death his widow's nephew removed a painting by the artist to Switzerland "for safekeeping" or as a so-called gift to his daughter.

Both my brother and I had pocket money from an early age. I think it was quite generous for those days. By the time I was seven and a half years old, savings with the Stadtsparkasse (city savings bank) had grown – augmented by little gifts from grandparents – to more than a grown-up labourer's weekly wages then. Mama was suddenly short of cash. I lent her that money. I felt a bit resentful at the time. Later I was proud to have been able to rescue her at some embarrassing moment. She did not even think of that "loan". I learnt to save. In Switzerland I had very generous pocket money. In later years – once the children had begun to arrive – I opened savings bank accounts for them. When they came of age the money was theirs. Two children used it to pay deposits on their mortgages. Two other children wasted it on their husbands or on "frivolities". One has still to use it up. Even today I keep all small change for the younger grandchildren's accounts.

Jasperts and Angers have *wanderlust* in their blood.

A brother of my mother's father settled in the United States, where both Jasperts and Angers are now primarily engaged in the area of journalism. There is, of course, Africa. Four generations of the families have lived there for years. Some of my children have done so and since then spread to Spain and Switzerland and also to Mexico. Australia has also played a major role in other branches of the family, who are spread throughout Europe. The children also travelled to North and South America, India, South-East Asia, the Far East and the Philippines.

I have got knobbly knees and elephantine ankles. The latter, according to legend, were twisted around soon after birth. I was told – perhaps jokingly – that the feet were pointed backward, but a quick-witted doctor almost immediately turned them round. This seemed a reasonable explanation. It satisfied me, however bizarre an instant cure it may have seemed. This strange tale may also explain my personal makeup and the reluctance to walk in step. All my life I seem to have resisted authority. Photographs of me, in the book *Kinder*, record my being out of step or having unacceptable behaviour even at the Montessori kindergarten (which I, incidentally, appear to have loved). it conforms, in a way, to the British Broadcasting Corporation's famed *Goon Show* and one of its theme songs: "I'm walking backwards for Christmas, and the whole world is walking with me" The BBC show was addictive and I felt in tune with the madcap things going on all the time. It was compulsive listening. One evening my first wife's parents telephoned from Sheffield. The interruption meant that the programme became incomprehensible. Only years later did I get a tape recording of those lost episodes. Well, surely not the whole world was at one time walking with me, but perhaps some elements of it.

We went sailing along the coast of the Baltic. Near the East Prussian and Lithuanian coast the boat capsized. I clung to the belly-up hull and got badly sunburnt and was hospitalized. I thought the nurses beautiful and gloried in my rescue dramatics. Earlier I also learnt to appreciate female beauty when, on a Sunday one of my uncles to me for a ride in his newly acquired car. We had an accident and after hospitalization I still carry a scar on my upper lip. I complained about missing the Sunday roast chicken lunch then.

Life in Berlin seemed peaceful. True enough, we were taken to school by uniformed police on horseback. I thought that exciting, but protection was necessary. Nazis and communists fought pitched battles in the streets. If children were around, they were not spared in our bourgeois district.

The Russian film director Sergei Eisenstein, of *Battleship Potemkin* fame, visited the parents. He stroked my head absently. Later Mama risked her life smuggling gold to Zurich for one of his relatives in Berlin. After the war Mama was penniless. That man, then in New York, did not respond to appeals for help. Luigi Pirandello had his beard pulled by me while I sat on his lap. The American cowboy actor Tom Mix came to see the parents. There is a photo of me sitting on my uncle's balcony of the house in Berlin-Dahlem, wearing his gift of a large white cowboy hat and pretending to smoke a peace pipe. Papa flirted with the actress Brigitte Helm.

I am proud of my family. There was just one exception to this spirit of liberty – nay freedom – they all shared: an uncle was a follower of the Nazis. The evening of the 30th January 1933, the day Adolf Hitler usurped power has stayed with me forever. I was almost seven years old then, visiting my paternal grandparents in Frankfurt, a free city which was quite proud of its history of Jewish advancement. My grandfather's gymnasium school taught classical Hebrew, too. Grandfather, my father and his older brother had learnt Hebrew and – of course – Latin and Greek.

When they were young boys in Frankfurt, the four Jaspert brothers formed an exclusive club, the *Löwenbund* (Lions' club). This, of course had nothing to do with the businessmen's clubs of today. My father published a novel about his former secret society – and the idea of a closed association was taken up by us children, with Andreas Herxheimer of the distinguished medical family being invited to join. We would not admit girls and stayed a three-members-only society. We solemnly attended the burial of a budgerigar, had toy car races in Berlin's Tiergarten near what we called the *Löwenbrücke* (four large iron sculptures of lions held the bridge's chains) and even had minutes of meetings. The club died a death by natural erosion. We dispersed and left the country for Prague and soon after Vienna, England and Spain, while Andreas, now Andrew, went to London. We started growing up, even if perhaps a bit too early.

We often moved. After Reichskanzlerplatz the family moved opposite the modern building of the Shell Oil Company on the banks of the Landwehr canal in Berlin. Then we moved to a posh place, also on the canal, near the army's head office in Bendlerstrasse. Generals visited us, men like Ludwig Beck, Helmut von Moltke, Manfred von Brauchitsch or Field Marshal Erwin von Witzleben, and other officers. These men were proud of their country and disliked the Nazis. Sadly their sense of duty made some of them obey Hitler's orders all too frequently. But – and people forget this all too often – there were officers who decided not to carry out orders which they felt were too immoral and also protected soldiers under their command who did not want to commit cruel and inhumane acts.

Karl Gördeler, one of the "20th July" Hitler assassination plotters, became an acquaintance of my mother.

One of the childhood highlights were uncle Hans Richter's visits from Kiel to Berlin. He was a *bon vivant* and took us with him to see the practically nude chorus girls at the Wintergarten variety house and such places. The glamorous girls liked us small children – despite all the grown-up men around. The dancers were all powdered and showered my brother and me with balloons floating down. Everybody tried to catch a balloon, but the girls favoured us and grabbed for my brother and me dozens of balloons to carry home, Charlie Rivels – the clown – delighted us. Soon after came "not for minors" films with Jean Gabin in *The Foreign Legion* or Paul Muni having exciting adventures in civil war China, etcetera when I was still a child and already in Vienna. I was fairly tall; all dressed up in adult gear and managed to be smuggled into the cinema by Tante Trude.

In the make-believe world of childhood, fantasy and fact merged. I really thought that I could levitate walking on park railings.

At school I ran into problems. The Nazis' youth organization seemed glamorous. Initially I wanted to join the *Jungvolk*, the youngsters' section of the Hitler-Youth. After four weeks of membership I asked the parents to take me out of that odiously regimented organisation. The parents demurred. They feared repercussions, but eventually let me resign. I believe that was the first time my father's difficulties with the Nazis became clear. On his own, Papa wrote letters to the propaganda ministry describing the problems of knowing which books by whom were to be banned – the list grew all the time. At school the class teacher, Mr Richter, violently objected to my friendship with 'that Jew boy' Andreas (now Andrew) Herxheimer. Mr Richter wanted to teach everyone a permanent lesson that a Jewish child should never have the audacity of being close to an Aryan, especially a true Nordic type like myself so obviously suiting the Nazi ideal. So we hobbled in the schoolyard still smarting from the caning and with red streaks on our short-trousered legs and bottoms. Some schoolmates jeered at us. One of the teachers remonstrated with the caning sadist, but was soon pensioned off.

I told my father of this humiliating treatment. He came to the school soon after and asked for Mr Richter. Having had him pointed out he came up, introduced himself and – though he was a relatively small man – jumped up and punched the teacher who, to the universal glee of the children, fell. We were arrested and taken to police headquarters. That was serious. Under the Nazis even children could testify against parents and siblings. Kurt Daluege, the police chief interrogated me. I was proud of my father's action and proclaimed so very loudly. Papa called me a stupid boy.

I had gone to a Montessori kindergarten and grew up in a liberal and open-minded family surrounding. Yet, when I was seven or so years old, I envied some of the other boys who were in the *Jungvolk*, proudly wearing uniforms which seemed to me to personify the dignity and pride of the military officers who came to visit my parents when we lived near the army headquarters.

Sometimes I wonder, though. Was all that independence that made me self-sufficient at an early age worth it? I lost the comforts of my loving parents and close relatives around me, though I knew that I could rely on them. They brought reassurance and visited me wherever I would be. I owe them my conscience and independent thinking. No doubt that makes me difficult to live with.

At one time living in Berlin we had a flashy neighbour, though we admired him as children. He drove a classic blue open-top Bugatti tourer and sometimes gave my brother Jürgen and me a ride round the area near the zoological gardens.

Many years later we had a Bugatti-driving neighbour again in London's Hampstead. He also gave me a ride in the much admired blue car. Then – lo and behold – this self-same man one day parked outside my new home in London's St. John's Wood.

On seeing me he offered a ride again! The gods look kindly upon me!

Why were the warnings neglected? Robert Dell, foreign correspondent of the *Manchester Guardian*, published *Germany Unmasked* already in 1934! He documented the Nazi's totalitarian and racist ideas. People like Frank Buchman and his Oxford Group (also known as Moral Rearmament) and the British establishment flirted with the Nazis.

Arthur Koestler as a refugee published his novel *Arrival and Departure* in London. No careful notice was taken of his fictitious account of the killing of Jews or sterilization of gypsies. Then, even after the Second World War was nearing its end phase, the Foreign Office, ministries and the cabinet, also the US State Department, knew, but obstinately refused to act or admit real knowledge of the atrocities committed in Germany, although they received many warnings years before from their embassies in axis countries.

Adolf Hitler in one of his Machiavellian moods realized “that despots are lucky because people obey them without thinking”.

Flying the Nest

STARTING SCHOOL in Berlin I "fell in love" with a girl called Beatrice. I thought her truly beautiful. She was the daughter of an architect. More than thirty years later I named my second daughter after her – and the young one is also beautiful. She looks a bit like the actress Lauren Bacall. That, at least, is what I think. Beatrice seems a bit flattered, but is not ostentatious about the supposed similarity.

People seemed to be quite religious in Austria. They invoked the saints of the church frequently. Going to school in Vienna I was puzzled that their faith made them obvious of the fact that *quid licet bovem non licet Jovem*. It amazed me that they fervently called on St. Florian to set fire to the neighbours' house, but should spare their home. Did their parish priests approve of such sentiments?

Despite my fall from grace at school and the odious teacher, I became the envy of my schoolmates in Derflingerstrasse. Bernd Rosemeyer, the auto-union racing car driver, took me for a spin in his famous car on the AVUS circuit. My fame soon eclipsed.

Rosemeyer's wife, the aviatrix Elly Beinhorn, took my brother on a flight in her small plane above Berlin. Later he accompanied Will Stehmann flying to Vienna. At that time that was something of a sensation.

One of my schoolmates was the son of the somewhat elderly poet Eduard von Stucken, who impressed me by his appearance and elegant home. His paleness frightened me. It seemed ethereal and ghostlike. It lent him an aura of mystic authority.

The composer Feruccio Busoni's son Mario – who now lives in Manhattan – played with me when he was a baby. I was already a small boy. My father owned one of Rafaello Busoni's paintings which had won the painter the Rome Prize. The canvas filled the whole space of a wall in Papa's sitting room. Sadly, the painting was destroyed in an air raid. Rafaello illustrated many fine books in Germany and then in America. Mario himself is gifted. I own a beautiful carved statue by him.

My mother was rather awed by Andreas' father, Dr Herbert Herxheimer of the distinguished medical family (there is even a Herxheimer effect or "herx" so named after Andrew's great uncle). My schoolmate came to play or eat rice pudding, which was delicious and made to a recipe handed down by my maternal grandmother. Come late afternoon, our telephone would ring. Andreas was still playing in our home. My mother picked up the receiver and Dr Herxheimer would ask "is my son Andreas still there?" The reply came instantly: "Andreas left a few minutes ago". Andreas was still in our home. He hastily grabbed his things and ran to his nearby home, barely waving goodbye, but never neglecting to shout Thank You!

Andrew Herxheimer is now a rather famous doctor and pharmacist. He is concerned with public health. He celebrated his eightieth birthday at a splendid international gathering in London's Kenwood House, attended by around eighty to one hundred people, who had come from as far as Australia, Canada and Japan. He travels more than I to meetings around the world, lecturing and seeing relatives and friends. I am very lucky. He remains my friend even after more than seventy-five years.

Among his many notable and also international achievements is his involvement in *Dipex* (also healthtalkonline.org), the database of people's personal experiences of illness, which covers at present such subjects as hypertension, cancers of the prostate, breast, bowel, lung, testis and cervix, as well as epilepsy. He is also actively involved in investigations to gain more understanding of end of life issues, such as Alzheimer's disease, heart failure, etcetera. Lately he started researching the effect of a new language on refugees. I believe he and some colleagues were prime movers to bring drug information in the form of printed inserts in dispensed packages of medicine to the general public.

As befits a person of his wide spread of interests he has been an advisor to governments, medical journals, and in teaching and the study of drugs. He cares deeply about patients' rights and information.

In the mid-1930s the time came to leave Nazidom. One evening Papa came home whistling a sort of family signalling tune and announced that there is no way for the children to be influenced by things going on in this country, adding that Trude (who was his mistress) has consented to take me and keep me safe. Mama agreed and three days later I left Berlin, to return only sporadically.

Trude took motherly care of me. We moved in at first with her aunt and uncle in Prague. I was told of Czech history, saw the Charles Bridge, Hradchin Castle, the magic old town and the Jewish cemetery, reminding me of the *Golem*, of whom I knew through the film and story by Hans-Heinz Ewers, whom Papa had introduced to the family and, of course, us children.

Trude loved me like an own son and loved Papa all her life. Mama amazingly did not seem to resent her. Trude had no hate for anybody as far as I can make out. This respect was instilled in me, too. It was clung to in spite of what happened later, when Trude was treated like a piece of flesh and in face of Mama's sufferings. I think sometimes real life would be too hard to accept without a stubborn belief in values.

Ernesto Bobek, Trude's brother was a Jewish Nazi, if there is such a thing. He used to rant round the house singing *Fascietta Nera*, the Italian Blackshirts' song. He escaped with his family to Argentina. He remained anti-Semitic! Once, in Barliloche near the Chilean border, he left a restaurant complaining about too many Jews there. These people had fled from Pinochet to Argentina (or from the rain into the trough).

Visiting Trude Bobek, who had so wonderfully looked after me in Eastern Europe, in Buenos Aires I met Jacobo Timerman in the Plaza Hotel. He was soon to be imprisoned and tortured by the Junta. The other outspoken newspaper voice apart from his *La Opinion* was Andrew Graham-Yooll, of the English-language *Buenos Aires Herald.*

The initial stage of my wanderings away from Germany and the Nazis was in Prague. Anti-German feelings were rather high already and I left school there despite having been made very welcome by my "aunt's" family and continued to Vienna. Unfortunately the Nazis soon followed and arrived when my mother was visiting from Berlin. She was pushed and kicked about and forced to raise her arm by Austrians who made her do the Nazi salute. Mama decided I should move on to Hungary, although I had secured a good place at a famous school in Vienna. Alas, the Nazis were soon making their influence felt in Hungary, too.

Catholic Austria made me realize that the help of

saints of the church could be called upon (perhaps!). I recall the saying "O thou, St. Florian – spare my house, lay fire to the neighbour's home!" Piety indeed.

I was quite excited, nay proud; I was my own self at an early age. For a while I stayed in luxury hotels, then with mostly nice people. After hotel life, looking after myself, but going to school and really learning quite much. I became somewhat disillusioned for a while. An episode of those times haunts me. I was playing in the hills of Buda (the old town district), when suddenly a ragged looking man cried out, whispering at first. He wanted help from us children. We were frightened. He was an escaped serf from the south of the country, he told us. We were upset at his sad story and gave him some of our measly pocket money change.

The German consulate caught up with me and insisted I move away from the Jewish Tausz family and stay with a "reliable" family – Nazis in fact. After dinner they sat around, making me sit with them while they sang Nazi songs. Today they would probably dispense with such nonsense and watch senseless TV instead. My father rescued me when he found a school in Switzerland (the Institut Rosenberg) and the funds to keep me there. My education was superior. Homer's *Odyssey* was one of my favourite books and I begged to learn Greek. Papa insisted on Latin first. The fantastic tales of E.T.A. Hoffmann were intriguing me. They continue to do that today.

Papa felt that Switzerland would provide a haven, though this did not quite prove so. At that stage I was still trying to fit in. At the boarding school there I wanted to be one of the crowd and amateurishly took up forbidden smoking, a habit some boys had flashily adopted. Smoking, even then, was banned unless the parents gave written permission once one was over fourteen years of age. Permission came. Some years later when with the US Quartermaster corps, I took to smoking Lucky Strikes. Then it was reported to the medics that I fainted at morning call. A doctor examined me. In seeming friendliness he suddenly handed me a packet of cigarettes and asked me to chain-smoke the remaining fags. I promptly fainted – and the medic told me that I would be court marshalled if I fainted again because of self-inflicted injury and of smoking. I feared Fort Leavenworth in Kansas and stopped any thought of ever smoking again. I was lucky and did not have to fear the later discovered ill effects of the noxious weed.

Among classmates was a nephew of the Viennese prelate Count Clement August von Galen, whose outspoken comments on Nazi acts worried those disgusting people.

The son of a German duke had a special arrangement on Saturdays. The older boys were allowed to go out. His chauffeur had an apartment in town and must have lived a fairly lush life. Come

Saturday, he would collect the boy, drive him to town in a Maybach (the top of the range German limousine then) and bring him back a few hours later. Those were his duties all week, rent and wage paid. Later, after the war, an English pupil with whom I have sporadic contact nowadays had his chauffeur come up in a Bentley.

In adult life, I started working for publishers. It all began with F. Bruckmann in Munich, Germany, and then in preparation to coming to England with the Springer Science publishing group there, learning much about mathematical and chemical formulae typesetting. That knowledge was transferred to London's Butterworth-Springer (later Pergamon Press) and printers Acfords of Chichester. I went for a year to *Graphis* magazine in Switzerland. There followed an interregnum of some general work, print related, with a city firm of export-import traders until printers Cox & Sharland made me Associate Editor of their magazines. There was some publishing activity with Blandford Press in London (who also published my first book – still in print today after numerous reprints). I went to America the first time with printers Jarrold & Sons, of Norwich, followed by part-time editorial consultancy with the London *Sunday Times* and *Financial Times*. Then there were many years of part-time editing of the now defunct *Worldwide Printer* and its Spanish-language sister magazine in

America, later published from The Netherlands and then Germany, where I also collaborated on *Deutscher Drucker*. At some time, as a freelance, I contributed to over thirty magazines and numerous newspapers all over the world. That activity has much shrunk, but still continues to a much reduced extent. Time is spent writing for newspapers and some magazines. I now spend much of my time writing more books – in English or German.

At Christmas time, and when it was snowing Papa would invite one or two friends and take us all "men only", to the Grunewald forest. A good Christmas tree was located, decorated and wax candles lit. We all danced round the tree and sang Christmas songs. Rafaello Busoni had come and impressed us. He managed to write his shortened name *Lello* while urinating on the snow. We tried, but could not imitate him. The letters of our names did not lend themselves to such skills.

Jürgen and I on another occasion tried to move a stone boulder apparently; it had not yet become embedded in the soil. We got it to move a few inches and thus had rediscovered leverage. Papa commented that we had achieved the feat with force.

During the war, in Switzerland, I was at times very popular at school. One of the main suppliers of butter to the Swiss Army admired my mother. He kept sending flowers and huge boxes of pralines to the school to pass on to her during her visits. She did not want these gifts and my fellow schoolboys eagerly munched the luxury chocolates. That contributed to my popularity. The other schoolmates showed little interest in the floral bouquets. The flowers were given to the school nurse.

In Hungary, the late Tante Trude Bobek, whose beauty I was able to appreciate even as a child was harassed by the police overlooking the alien community, who pressed her to grant one of their officers special favours. She fled and reached England, worked as a cipher clerk for an embassy and eventually joined her family in Argentina. Later she moved with Elena Mazzola and her daughter's family to French-speaking Quebec in Canada.

To prove that the Jaspert clan was Aryan, Papa traced our ancestry back to the late Middle Ages and claimed he had found a Flemish ancestor: Jasper von der Burg. That name was probably a bit of a satirical joke invention.

The Nazis loved (fictitious) links with Teutonic allusions and heroes. Mama visited the supposed ancestral homestead in what had become Belgium. Papa at first had approved of the Nazis to the annoyance of his father.

Disillusion soon set in. The Nazis were obsessed with cultish fantasies and inhuman dreams of racial purity leading to revolting and fanatic cruelty.

As Nazi-dom's tentacles began to extend into all spheres of life, my parents felt that my youth had to escape the poisonous Nazi influence. First they thought of keeping me relatively in the country, aiming for Salem School near Lake Constance, but I did not go to Hahn's place. The parents realized that Germany was no longer a country where I could grow up to become a free person and sent me East. At one time they planned to move to England, talking of a prestigious school in Cambridge. The war interfered.

As the war was on it became difficult for the parents to keep in touch with their friends in America. I took a few letters to mail in neutral Switzerland. At Feldkirch, the border station, my luggage was searched and the letters found.

I was detained. I pretended that the letters were for friends in Switzerland. My Germanic looks helped and I was let go. That happened again. Early in the war, Franz Winninger, painter and author, had given me a letter to his Jewish girlfriend in Palestine. It was found, but the examining officer felt that I, still a youth, had my bags packed by others and been duped. Note was taken of the parents' home address.

One other matter stands out in my memory of that time: after Papa's death my quite religious paternal grandmother Anna was visited by the local vicar who expressed his condolences, but stressing that Papa now "rests in peace with the Lord". My grandmother told him that the imaginary God was not all-seeing or would not have allowed the murder of quite a young man. Anna Jaspert turned the vicar away. Since then I have been to church only rarely, twice for weddings and also only to some funeral services or to listen to Christmas carols.

I was impressed by the writers with whom my father congregated at Berlin's Romanisches Café and thought the parents' late nights out at the Jockey Club somehow mysteriously glamorous. Many years later I, too, managed to become familiar with prestigious gatherings. During my times spent in the United States, Edward McSweeney invited me to address the American Legion at New York's Metropolitan Club and many lunches there and at the nearby Racquet & Tennis Club.

Life is stranger than fiction. Among us schoolboys much ribald and mildly salacious comment was generated by a fictitious medication called *Nello*. This imaginary suppository was supposed to hide bodily winds by giving them a fragrant smell, in a refined version this sound was accompanied by classical music, such as Boccherini or Vivaldi.

These days a company called Fart Neutral in California actually seems to offer practical help and solutions to various gastric gas problems – all in the interest of saving the planet!

One of my favourite children's fiction readings was

Erich Kästner's *The 35th of May*. He describes the city of the future, when on a moving pavement a soberly clad executive pulls a telephone from his briefcase to say he would be late coming home because of work. Konrad, the hero of the book, and his uncle Ringelhut had invited Negro Caballo, a roller-skating circus horse, into the uncle's flat upstairs. The clever horse delighted in picking pots of geraniums and dropping them on the heads of passers-by in the street below. Later Konrad and his uncle rode on the horseback to the South Sea on the equator, claimed to be a steel band circling the globe. There they met chieftain Rabenas, who shot toffee apples from his penknife, and his daughter Parsley. Having a coloured father and the white-skinned diamond washer woman Lehmann as mother, it seemed only natural her skin was chequerboard. I truly believed that the offspring of mixed races would have such skin. Decades later American GIs ridiculed that persistent and silly delusion which was based on Walter Trier's illustrations.

I find mobile telephones deeply irritating, so I recount this experience with considerable glee: I was with friends in a hotel bar in Kowloon, Hong Kong. The bar had a huge plate glass window. A posh, chauffeur-driven Rolls-Royce rolled up. Out stepped a small businessman clutching a hand-held telephone and escorting a truly stunning lady. They entered the bar, took seats and the man kept shouting into the instrument, neglecting the woman. Finally she rose, left the bar and went out to the car. The driver rushed to open the car door. She ordered the chauffeur to move off. The gentleman in the bar, still shouting into his telephone, rushed after her and the car – too late! He was left standing and clutching the mobile. The whole population of the watering hole watched the scene and burst into a chorus of Schadenfreude laughter.

Negro Caballo, the roller-skating circus horse in *The 35th of May*, managed to climb up the steps to chat to uncle Ringelhut and his nephew Konrad. At London's Knightsbridge Barracks a ramp led to the upper floor stables. Horses could be seen from the street. In Fulham the horses drawing milk floats looked at you out of the first floor windows. To me these were childhood tales come true, but not all the Kästner prophesies came true.

I learnt about life from Trude's father Jaromir Bobek. He showed me great kindness. He took me to the Vienna Woods on hikes and tried to explain to me the sad story of the Austro-Hungarian emperor's daughter and Radetzky or the role of Prince Eugeniusz in saving Europe from the Turks. The vast social housing estate at Ottakring and its significance were explained, and much about tolerance.

The Nazis occupied Austria. Viennese crowds cheered the invading troops. My mother happened to be visiting me at that desperate time. We watched the marching invaders. Bystanders lined the streets and hysterically welcomed the troops with the Hitler salute. Mama refused to raise her arm. People standing next to her tried to force her arm up. She fell and I could not help. I was a frightened and helpless small boy.

The parents decided to send me to Budapest. I did not speak Hungarian, but found a place at the German school in Damjanich Utca. The move away from Vienna lost me the place at the exalted Albertinum School in Vienna.

While at school in Budapest, Baron Konstantin von Neurath, of the German Foreign Office, visited the premises. As I obviously spoke German the headmaster thought it nice to have one of the pupils do some of the interpreting. Alas, my knowledge of the Hungarian language let me down. The official interpreter quickly had to take over.

At this school one of my classmates was Denes Biro. I sometimes wonder whether he was of the ballpoint pen family settled in Argentina. Another classmate was a pretty girl I had a crush on. Her father owned a chain of cinemas. I gained access to badly understood films meant for adults only, as I had done in Vienna the year before.

Papa wrote to me from Berlin and sent a copy of a book on Miklos von Horthy, the Hungarian regent. He thought it would do me some good to meet important people. So I went to the residence and presented myself with a copy of the book in hand. I was invited to coffee and some cake at the palatial place in Buda.

Far away in the south of Africa some relatives of my maternal grandmother were close to the government and had almost wanted to side with Germany. General Jan Smuts prevailed and South Africa became an ally of Britain. After the Second World War that demented system of apartheid or segregation was introduced. Perversely, some beaches carried signs warning people that these were not for whites. Mama was sent care food parcels from South Africa, but refused to accept them despite real starvation. I was hungry and could not understand her action then.

Koko, our childhood friend, was a Blue Amazon parrot. Gentle and often affectionate, it used to sit on a low stool and often had dinner with us, mainly sardines or nuts. We were certain he had superior intelligence. When Adolf Hitler gave a speech, which was broadcast and almost compulsory listening, he would loudly scream and cackle. We rushed to close the windows and cover his cage with a blanket in case the neighbours reported us for laughing at the Fuehrer. I loved Koko, who would nibble a finger softly despite his formidable beak. Koko would have come to England, but strict quarantine made that difficult. The parrot lived to a ripe old age. For my sixtieth birthday my wife gave me a magnificent present: another parrot. I got too upset to accept it. The bird was returned to the shop. I felt guilty.

I envied my mother's sea journeys by giant liners. Planes were catapulted to fly back to Europe and take passengers' mail. I wish I had kept the letters' envelopes and special stamps instead of just showing them off to schoolmates and then throwing them away.

Real envy came when Mama travelled on the Raymond Loewy designed *Twentieth Century Limited* to Chicago. All I got in Vienna was an airmail postcard picturing the modernistic train. Years later I bought a replica model of that train. Mama was interned by over-zealous immigration officers and locked up on Ellis Island. They suspected her as being Jewish because of her rather large nose. She was of north German stock. Idiotically, they accused her of trying to enter the country permanently. At the weekend, New Yorkers came to gape at the "exotic" internees. Finally Mama was freed. Josef Szigety, the violinist, put up the bond. On return to Berlin my mother was emphatic: America was not a country to go to. It was not the "land of the free". Had she not been temporarily interned, perhaps we would have gone to America and my father would have lived.

My first encounter with American music was Paul Whiteman's *Rhapsody in Blue.* Mama even got a recording of this. Then came *Porgy and Bess*. I found that less impressive, but when the war came, hundreds of jazz records arrived. A friend of my mother's, Hans

Schöller, was in the German Army and happened to be among the men who ransacked Radio Luxembourg. There was a vast record library. It was doomed and to be destroyed as "degraded". Schöller as an officer commandeered an army lorry and thus saved many records. Some found their way to Berlin, where I hungrily listened to them. One of my cousins was brought up strictly on classical music. He envied me that lively music. I heard "real black music" and also the Lecuona Cuban Boys. I can still hum some of the tunes.

My mother used my father's passport to get a relative's of a famous Russian film producer's solid gold fake fountain pen to Switzerland. After the war Mama was penniless. We wrote to the man and asked for some help. He did not deign to reply. His address was valid, though. We checked up through friends in New York City.

Such is life: one of my father's brothers, himself a publisher, had guarded a Jewish art book publisher's photographic archives throughout the war. Admittedly, after the war, he used some of those photographs. When I contacted the refugee from Berlin and then living in London, thinking he would be pleased that his archives were safe, he wrote that he was suing my uncle for the return of the photographs. There was no need to do that. My uncle was in any case preparing to return the pictures to their rightful owner. I was disillusioned with the man, who I had fondly believed to be quite grateful and would perhaps even employ me.

The fascist propaganda event of the air squadron's flight from Italy across the Atlantic impressed me, though I resented that Mussolini got some admiration.

I did not quite take it in at the time – film was discovered as a powerful tool of propaganda, boosting evil regimes. On holiday in Berlin from Budapest the Olympic Games were held in the already known as contemptible Nazi capital. I had met two young army officers in Budapest and when they told me that they had been selected to go to Berlin to represent their country in the fencing contest, I suggested that they could probably stay with my family. My mother invited them, but told them it was the wrong time to come because of the implicit acceptance of the Nazis' corruption of everything decent. Nevertheless, the two men arrived in a Fiat Topolino to compete for their country. My parents ranted about Leni Riefenstahl, the contemptible woman who made the *Triumph of the Will* film glorifying and adulating Hitler's Games. The Nazi-adulating filmmaker later became a war correspondent and watched, albeit in horror, as uniformed soldiers carried out a mass execution of Jews. She watched (a DPA press agency photograph of the onlookers exists) and never resigned from her chosen post or publicly protested at such atrocity. Did she ever feel sorrow at what was done to her fellow humans? In Donna Leon's fiction an Italian journalist is presented who resigns his work, telling his editor: "I just cannot stomach the pictures of piles of corpses; casualties in some civil war". That is why I no longer read newspapers.

I still feel haunted and have to cry when I recall those photos of a (Jewish) mother, clutching her also naked baby to her chest while a German uniformed soldier aims his rifle at her – ready for the kill. The pictures of children in the Warsaw Ghetto raising their pitiful arms in surrender are equally harrowing.

Among the favourite fantasy adventure stories of German children were the imaginary exploits of Baron von Münchhausen. Adults liked the stories, too. My father discussed an idea for a film based on these tales and talked of them in his circle of acquaintances. The Nazi propaganda minister, Josef Goebbels, heard of these ideas and ordered one of the first colour films ever to be made (in glorious Agfacolor) by the UFA Studios, who used a script by Erich Kästner, who wrote under an assumed name since some of his writing was banned under the Nazis, though his children's books were widely available. The popular actor Hans Albers starred as the hero of the tale.

Some of Ernst Barlach's pictures were also frowned upon. At home we had a large lithograph of a prophet. It was destroyed in an air raid. Now I have a small picture by him bought for me by Theodor Anton at an auction in Germany. Today some two hundred primarily original prints are framed and grace the walls of my home. I also have a few paintings, but most are already with my children and grandchildren in England and somewhere in Europe. A "real" Matisse print is with one of my former wives in America.

Kristallnacht

I WAS just over twelve years old and visiting Berlin and the parents. On the way back from mine and my brother's old school – surprisingly my father came to accompany us home – we passed the 'Jew' ice-cream parlour near our home. Outside their shop stood a stern looking brown-shirted SA storm trooper and wanted to prevent us from entering. Papa told him that "the children would get their promised cones". In the shop the subdued husband and wife proprietors welcomed and served us. They were crying. They handed us the ice cream cones. I still cry!

The Nazi example was in a milder, equally humiliating and longer lasting manner repeated by the apartheid system in white supremacist South Africa. I was ashamed when visiting the country where some remote family members on the maternal grandmother's side lived.

The Year of the Refugees was proclaimed. Should this not read "Two centuries of refugees"?

Erich Maria Remarque in the 1930s wrote *Arch of Triumph* about world war in perhaps initially self-imposed exile, which turned into serious and dangerous years. He saw that what had started with the Russian émigrés became even more serious and deadly when the Gestapo and KVD got into the act. The Spanish under Francisco Franco and in Italy the former socialist Benito Mussolini and his henchmen followed the ghastly German example. Fanatic Hitler committed suicide. Mussolini was hanged upside down. In the French Revolution, Robespierre, who had started the Terror, was finally executed. Will this sort of horror go on forever? The past two centuries saw a migration of people which puts the Goths and the Vandals in the shade. The perhaps contemporary eternal migration is not just for economic reasons, but for fear of persecution, in Africa, Latin America and Asia – even North America. That latter migration had started with the Vietnam War and seems to have increased under the zealous George W. Bush and the short-term power of Donald Rumsfeld under whose ignominious leadership the torturers of Abu Ghraib were trained, and who proudly announced that "the war in Iraq is really about peace". This notorious former Secretary of Defense also felt that "death has a tendency to encourage a depressing view of war". Presumably some people positively enjoy war.

The Shape of Things to Come

HAPPY SUMMER weeks were spent at the Wegscheide children's village my grandfather August Jaspert had founded near a deserted army camp at Bad Orb. The place was used by Frankfurt city council to give children a good holiday and learning to manage life's necessities at the same time. Later some of my children went there, too.

As a deputy he had some travel concessions. I was thrilled to travel with him in luxury between Frankfurt and Berlin on a Zeppelin-like propeller-driven silvery railcar.

Meanwhile at home Papa's glamorous exploits sometimes misfired. He and his brother went to Stöckler's restaurant and had an enjoyable evening. Papa admired the pepper shaker and slipped this into his jacket. Came the time to pay and leave, the proprietor himself saw the brothers to the door. They shook hands. The proprietor hastened to speak to Papa and handed him a salt cellar with profuse compliments. Papa took it and could not help blushing.

I had wanted to learn classical Greek. I loved the

tales of Troy and Homer's *Iliad* and *Odyssey*. Solon's maxim *Know Thyself* became an important part of life. First I had to study Latin – and loved it. Greek came later.

As children and under constant bombing raids in Berlin, one of my father's brother's family's entrusted us teenagers with escorting the mother-in-law, Hermine Waldmann, to a safe retirement home where she would be protected from the Nazi's shameful euthanasia programme. On the way south the train we were travelling on was strafed by Allied aeroplanes. We escaped by dragging the elderly lady under the train and across the tracks, always darting to the other side of the embankment the train was on, to thus escape the firing from the turned around returning planes. Later I learned from a pilot hero friend that strafing small moving objects frantically scurrying about, like ants, seemingly aimless, was exciting and even fun for perhaps Walter Mitty types. Obviously the officers briefing air crews must have "recommended" the practice. Seemingly all believed that all is fair in war.

Extreme events produce new responses in peaceable people. My mother gained temporary fame for her photo reportage of inmates of a mental home in a well-known pictorial weekly of that time. A friend of my mother's was Charlotte Leuenberger in Zurich. As a teenager I admired her American-style kitchen in the building on Utokai facing the lake. Later I found out that this Swiss woman had been on the side of the *Maquis* resistance fighters in occupied France. She was temporarily exiled from neutral Switzerland. There were other brave people like André Nuijten, a Dutchman (later of the *Nieuwe Rotterdamse Courant* daily), who had braved the North Sea waters to get to England in a small boat and join the RAF – Royal Air Force. Different was Paolo de Lucca. He lived at Varese and knew the mountain paths across the border to nearby Switzerland. He had been a senior at my school there, too. During the war he served in the Italian Air Force. He fought and shot down allied fighters. He carefully followed the parachuting and baling-out airmen, landed his plane perilously close by and rescued the enemy pilots to escort those able to walk to internment in the neutral country. In his post-war visits to England as sales director for the Nebiolo type foundry and printing press makers, he was accorded a hero's welcome at RAF Hatfield.

For almost a year I worked for a City of London firm in export-import. I think some of their business deals were illegal. One of the bosses was Edward Ruff, a Swiss. During the war he had set up a meeting in neutral Sweden with Germans trying to save the continued post-war existence of the Heidelberg printing press company. The trading company had good contacts behind the Iron Curtain. Among other principals were the US-based Smythe bookbinding machinery company and its British associate Smythe-Horne. The then largest book manufacturing plant in the world was in Soviet Leningrad (now St. Petersburg), using this western machinery. Ruff later married a daughter of the production manager of Mohndruck, part of the Bertelsmann printing and publishing group. This is today one of the world's largest media companies.

My dislike of organized sport must stem from the brief flirt with the Nazi youth movement and boarding school days in Switzerland. Not only did I feel almost insulted by the obligatory morning runs. The sports teacher was a German and organizer of the German schoolboys' Nazi activities in the neutral country during the war. I managed to get out of these activities by pretending for years that my injuries after a pillow fight and days in hospital prevented taking part in regimented sport activities. I affected a slight limp. Instead I grew radishes on a gardening plot. Schoolmates seemed to like them. My popularity rose. That sport teacher was Karl Sommer. Shortly after Papa's murder he wanted me to be flag carrier in eastern Switzerland's May Parade of Nazi sympathizers. He felt that being tall and blonde; I mirrored the image of the Nazi ideal of an Aryan. The headmaster came to my help and cited my apparent disability.

Sommer's wife was rather beautiful. I and other schoolboys secretly watched through the windows of the gym hall when she and the day girls did their exercises, until our voyeurism was discovered.

Walking, swimming almost weightless in water or hiking were natural. Excelling at hurdle jumping had been easy. I was tall. No great effort was involved and it was therefore noncompetitive. That infuriated the physical education teacher. He did not find out that I had succeeded in avoiding the daily morning run's strain. I lined up with the other boys, but almost immediately and when all were abreast of the gym hall, broke ranks and sneaked into the roadside bushes. When the panting mob of returning runners approached, it was child's play to sneak back into the stream of tired runners.

Imagine my surprise and consternation when I saw this Nazi after the war in London. A stroll through Green Park had taken me to Parliament Square. I recognized this man. He appeared to have come out of the House of Commons. Bizarrely he seemed to have escaped de-Nazification. Presumably he had hoodwinked the Home Office people that he had spent wartime as a refugee in Switzerland. He was recruited and came to Britain to lecture POWs on the boons of democracy! In his sports instructor role, and as the Nazi presence in St. Gallen, Sommer, among his nonpolitical aims, had wanted me to get the school acclaimed for my hurdle jumping and long distance swimming stamina. These were natural skills. I was simply tall for my age. Swimming in later years, I happily carried some of our children on my back crossing mountain lakes and in the surf of Pacific shores.

My dislike of any organized form of sport was lent support more than half a century later by a message on bus shelters in the twenty-first century telling passers-by to "after 'exhausting sport' have energy replaced by a power beverage"!

My father, who in his younger years was keen on fencing, but not other sport, had only briefly flirted with driving. That I came to loathe, but have always enjoyed the benefits of motorized transport in taxis, chauffeur-driven motors and even stretch limousines in America and Britain.

When I was about fourteen years old my mother felt I should begin to learn about grown-up life. While still in Berlin when Papa was passing through one of his *1,001 Nights* phases – as my mother's brother, uncle Bernhard Langer called it – there were some inklings of sex. Papa was now around. Mama resorted to two books which I read with the assistance of our English master from New Zealand, Angus McBean. *Lady Chatterley's Lover* and *Ulysses* were thus, after *Beowulf*, which I had picked up in a second-hand bookshop, the first books I read in English. These books introduced me vaguely to adulthood, but I did not really comprehend their content, though I felt the ancient title easier to understand. Old English was almost like German; Andrew Herxheimer introduced me to lighter reading by sending me John Buchan's *The Thirty-Nine Steps*. The book arrived in Switzerland during the war and came via Lisbon.

Papa's Death

PAPA HAD been arrested one morning in March on his way to his office. For some days nobody had a clue where he was until Paul Rosbaud telephoned Mama. Papa had been taken away by the Gestapo. His older brother uncle Äd donned his First World War uniform and insisted on seeing him. He was admitted with some reluctance. Uncle Äd had taken me along. Papa was dragged up from the cellars in Prinz Albrecht Strasse. He was a wreck and in such low spirits that he told us to go away. The Gestapo interrogator told us Papa could have gone free (a trick perhaps) if only he had been "sensible" and disclosed who his accomplices were. There were none. Papa was sent to Oranienburg-Sachsenhausen concentration camp. Within a month we received the death certificate of Prisoner 37483 and his ashes. The commandant of the camp sent different explanations for the murder: Suicide; attacking a Guard; Shot in Self-Defence and Shot While Trying To Escape. We preferred the fiction of his having attacked a guard. After we received the various death certificates and the confused statements of Papa's death, we were also allowed to collect his scanty belongings. Among them was a gold full hunter pocket watch which I wore as an adult. It was later stolen. I traced it and tried unsuccessfully to buy it back. A pawnshop had paid a miserable £50 and then auctioned it for ten times that amount.

Even now, more than almost seventy years later, I shut my eyes when a train passes the former camp and I am on my way to childhood haunts in Brandenburg Province or the Baltic coast. The Nazis in their frenetic, demented and cultish thinking, turned to murder without blinking an eyelid.

Jürgen, my brother, was not told of the facts of the death. Years later he came to Berlin and I was back from Switzerland, I was the one who told him the terrible news. He suspected it anyway. The world does not acknowledge that additional to the horrendous extermination and the holocaust, the Nazis also killed around a million German and Austrian Aryan so-called opponents, gypsies, homosexuals and – of course – Eastern Europeans, soldiers and slave labourers.

As a boy I had sometimes tried to speak directly to God. He never answered. Former US President George W. Bush seemed to have been luckier and appears to have established a direct wireless telephone link with the Almighty, if some of the man's statements are to be believed.

Mama's brother, the Nazi-sympathising black

sheep of the family, knew some corrupt SS bonzes. Our family very quickly had raised some twenty or thirty thousand marks, which was quite a lot of money in those days, to buy my father free. They all fell for a con trick. The money was accepted, but nothing was done to help and Papa was dead within four weeks.

Landlocked Switzerland, like most of Europe during the Second World War, also had rationing. The canny Swiss, however, sailed merchant vessels under their own and neutral flag. My mother came from Berlin on a visit. Mama had wangled herself an exit visa from Germany. She knew the Swiss diplomat Paul Hochstrasser, in Berlin's Haus der Schweiz building on the Unter den Linden Boulevard in Berlin. Hochstrasser let her use the consulate's telephone to call my school. Hochstrasser had persuaded the headmaster to free me from the machinations of the Nazi sports teacher, who had wanted me to lead, clad in white socks and shirt, wearing black shorts, the special St. Gallen German Nazi marchers in the Workers' Day parade on 1st May.

Elegant Mama was walking with me along Zurich's Bahnhofstrasse shopping street. She admired the fruit shop then near the main station. Even tropical fruit was on the shelves when such delicacies were dreamed of luxuries over the border barely an hour away. She cried when she came to my school's town and saw the pastry shops there. I was much upset by seeing her nostalgic suffering and even to this day usually refuse to eat pastries and desserts.

One of the highlights at school had been the Sunday lunch with a gorgeous fruit salad served in large bowls. Our tables were presided over by a teacher. I happened to be Head Boy. I sat next to the teacher, who had the infuriating habit of picking out choice morsels from the fruit bowl and then passing it to me to serve myself and then hand it so others. One Sunday I lost my temper. I emptied the fruit bowl over the teacher's head. I was promptly relieved of my exalted status and my name expunged from the wallboard listing head boys. As an added punishment I also had to sit for two weeks underneath the dining room's grand piano and did not get any desserts.

I listen to recordings with great pleasure and go to concerts. There my past catches up. I refuse nowadays (though I have been to his performances) to anything Herbert von Karajan conducted. His Nazi past offends me. And yet, I do not apply such stringent criteria to literature. I appreciate the translations of Fyodor Dostoevsky's books by Dietrich Eckhart, who was a Nazi idol.

In Poland, the Nazis uncovered the bodies of the Polish officers massacred on Stalin's order in the Katyn Forest. We believed this was a propaganda trick of the Nazis, and were horrified when the terrible truth of the atrocity was confirmed. The Nazi monsters had actually told the scarcely believable truth.

I followed the progress of the war by sticking coloured pins into a large map over my bed. It looked sombre. The Nazis just conquered East and West. It was *Springtime for Hitler and Germany –Winter for Poland and France*, as a song sung in the later film by Mel Brooks *The Producers* had it. Hitler appeared to conquer the vast spaces and Lebensraum of Russia – but then he failed at Leningrad, Moscow and spectacularly at Stalingrad.

I could not be shaken in the belief, ridiculed by the other boys, that the glum situation depicted thus shown would finally change and give the allies victory. My half-Jewish friend Wolfgang (who sometimes called himself Lupus) Steinhardt thought me somewhat stupid. I revenged myself and beat him up, till the headmaster warned me. We were equals in mental arithmetic contests, but he easily beat me in science subjects. I was ahead of him in Latin and English. We stayed friends till he died quite young still. His mother, in an act of supreme self-denial slept throughout the war with an SS-bonze to protect her son (of a deceased Jewish father and a Christian mother).

On Christmas holiday in Berlin, Paul Rosbaud was told about this when I visited him in his office near the Landwehr canal. I was despondent. He cheered me up by taking me to a large world map. Half the world was shaded in red for British. There, too, were the vast

Soviet Union and the powerful as yet uncommitted USA, as well as Brazil. Rosbaud convinced me that sheer size alone would triumph in the long run.

I found out much later that Paul Rosbaud was almost recklessly brave. Right in the middle of Berlin – and in the middle of the war – he managed to raise the Union Jack on the Springer office building his publishers had on the Landwehr Canal. The flag was quickly pulled down, of course, but Rosbaud was apparently not traced by the Gestapo. Throughout the war he audaciously befriended Polish and later Russian prisoners.

A Swedish friend of my mother's ran a concert agency from Stockholm and travelled reasonably freely in Germany even during wartime. I was impressed with the Scandinavian flamboyance. Felicitas Keller not only looked impressive. She managed to have good relations with the Nazi cultural authorities, who liked her arrangements for "German culture" bookings of conductors, soloists and orchestras. Surreptitiously she also managed to help some Jewish or dissident performers to travel abroad and escape.

How My Life Was Shaped By Jewish People

AT EIGHTY-THREE years of age, I realize how my youth and growing up have been influenced by Jewish friends and mentors.

I had been at school for almost two years in Berlin, but spent an after-Christmas holiday visiting my paternal grandparents in Frankfurt. The grandfather, August Jaspert was founder of one of the largest children's villages in Europe, headmaster of a school now named Jaspert-Schule, and the school curriculum even included Hebrew. After all, Frankfurt was a centre of Jewish culture.

My father and his brother also studied Hebrew as well as Greek and Latin. Grandfather was also a city councillor and a deputy in the Landtag Assembly. I believe that a street in Frankfurt is also named after him.

I was with the grandparents on 30th January 1933. August Jaspert, my paternal grandfather opened the window of the flat and sat by the piano. He loudly played the *Loreley* song, intermittently belting out "music by a Jew – Felix Mendelsohn-Batholdy; words by a Jew – Heinrich Heine". Grandmother Anna tried to shush her husband, aware that Jews were not Aryans. Grandfather disregarded these dangers. He was brave, outraged and probably foolhardy. It is with pride that I recognize this courage and humanity are today acknowledged. A street and his former school are named after him. Only a few months before Hitler had come to power, we children had enjoyed the thrill of being escorted to school on horseback by mounted police. Even before Hitler had come to power, SA storm troopers fought pitched street battles with communists and Jews and "capitalists" in the more affluent suburbs of Berlin already then. Blatant persecution had started.

My Jewish friend Andrew at primary school – still my friend today in London – and I were routinely caned, stretched out face downward and lying on a school desk in front of the whole class, by the Nazi teacher Mr Richter, who punished me for making friends with a Jew, and Andrew for the audacity to inveigle himself with an Aryan. The older Mr Klauke protested at considerable risk to himself and was prematurely retired.

I grew up in exaggeratedly privileged surroundings. I had jackets and trousers made by tailors Steinhardt, of Unter den Linden – the posh shopping street in the centre of the city. Even when the war had started my jackets were made up of Scottish or Irish tweed, English flannel was used for the trousers. When the tailor asked me how I wore my trousers I failed to get his meaning. Some shirts were tailored from raw silk.

Both Mama and Papa helped smuggle Jewish friends – some quite famous – to (the then) Czechoslovakia and later to Switzerland. I was proud of them. My mother's sister put up a loyal Nazi front. When visiting Tante Gert we were never allowed to go upstairs. My mother, however, probably knew – and trembled. I owe Tante Gertrud Wolf-Anger an abject apology. I had for a time thought she was a Nazi follower. She only pretended in order to save her friend and herself. She was also married to a former non-Jewish concentration camp inmate.

I was launched into adult life at age sixteen. The year before Papa, an Aryan had died in a concentration camp. Few people know that the Nazis killed almost a million Austrians and Germans. Soon after Papa's death came my premature launch into adulthood. Mama had given secret shelter to a young Jewish woman engaged to the manager of a famous Berlin art gallery. The woman gave birth to a little girl, who is still alive and lives in Austria. I assisted in the birth of the child and almost rigid (these days and nights trauma) and fear had to press a hand over the mother's mouth to stop the natural expression of pain. These events still haunt me. Fear was everywhere. Small red posters on prominent hoardings proclaimed the execution of racial offenders having had sexual relations between Aryans and Jews.

Conditions in Nazi Berlin were thought to be unsavoury for a young boy's upbringing. So my parents decided to send me abroad. A Jewish woman – my beloved Tante Trude – went with me to Prague, where I stayed with relatives of hers… a Jewish family. At school anti-German feeling ran high and Trude and I moved to Vienna and her parents' home. I may have imagined that I was aware of other cultures; I was in reality too young when I lived in Angola with my parents soon after my birth. In Prague, Vienna and Budapest there were prayer scrolls on the door frames in those homes. I was enrolled in a famous school, but the Nazis annexed Austria and came to Vienna at a time when my mother visited me. She refused to raise her arm in the Nazi salute. She was knocked down by enthusiastic bystanders while I stood by powerless, too small to rescue her. A few weeks later Trude and I moved to Budapest, staying with a Jewish family who survived and later moved to Hungary after much suffering, starting early under the regime of Bela Kuhn. Papa met the headmaster of a school in Switzerland who persuaded him that the country was OK for me.

While at school in Budapest I for some time lived with a Jewish family who after the war emigrated to

Israel. They had been persecuted by the communists under Bela Kuhn, then by the Nazis. Still they hated neither Russians nor Germans. Before I moved into a nice villa with a family I had first resided in luxury at a posh hotel which was the abode of the Duke of Windsor (Edward VIII) and Wallis Simpson (both of whom I met briefly). I then moved to the Tausz family near the Vàrosliget Park and also near my school. The German consulate got wind of my stay with a Jewish family and demanded I move to the home of a Nazi sympathiser nearer the town centre. I hated it there. The talk was about wonderful Germany and Hitler. My "disloyal" views were condemned and ridiculed. My youthful socializing with *Untermenschen* was criticized. I was glad to leave the country which I otherwise liked.

One day when about sixteen years old and in Berlin we were worried about some commotion on the stairs. The SS had come to round up our Jewish neighbours in Barbarossastrasse. The men wore stony faces. Many of the women cried. The children were puzzled and were hurried along with blows and shots by the guards. Jews from the house and the area were forced on to open lorries. SS men stood around ordering people about, laughing much of the time. Mama and I were too scared to say even goodbye or leave our flat, watching from our window. We feared for the unfortunates' fate. More than half a century later I still wake up from nightmares. The action was enlightening for my uncle's family had been bombed out. They were allocated a deported Jewish family's flat nearby – fully furnished, the lunch table set out and mouldy food in the dishes!

Later in London, Zoltan Frankl – my dental surgeon and a real professor, told me that he had suffered under Bela Kuhn. When the Nazis dominated Hungary he was deported to Mauthausen (I think) concentration camp. As a qualified medical practitioner it fell to him to treat the camp Kommandant who had fallen seriously ill. He did not use the opportunity to kill that Kommandant and stuck by his Hippocratic Oath and tolerance. He survived and later managed to escape during the Hungarian Revolution in 1956.

The Swiss boarding school was good. I received good unbiased education and even today cope with Latin. In 1943 I was deported from Switzerland at the insistence of the German consulate in St. Gallen. Swiss friends of Mama offered me shelter in Zurich. The cantonal police came to take me to Basle and handed me over at the Badischer Bahnhof to the German authorities. I managed to run away. The friends later joined the French *Maquis* and were deprived of Swiss citizens' rights for some years. They moved to Vienna after the war. Ironically, my father was denounced by a Swiss, aptly name Heinrich Würgler-Hess (a "würgler" is a strangler) to the Gestapo and soon after murdered in Oranienburg-Sachsenhausen concentration camp.

The Swiss, deservedly, suffered an agonizing death. Fireman for some hours could not free him from his car in which he was trapped. Mama kept his death notice from a Berlin newspaper in her purse until she died and searching through her belongings I found it. He got his just desserts!

My school friend in Switzerland, Wolfgang, was safe. a so-called half-Jew (his mother was Aryan), he saved himself from the sadistic Nazi German sports teacher by pretending to be fervently confident all the time that the Nazis would win the war! From him I learnt plausible fibbing. His mother sacrificed her honour throughout the war by sleeping with a black-uniformed SS-officer who protected her.

Ironically, Mama had a job in the Nazi propaganda office under Josef Goebbels. She read English newspapers and secretly took mimeograph copies home for clandestine distribution to trusted friends. She was never found out.

Back in Germany I hid successfully for over a year. During that time my mother Isolde gave shelter to Erika, a young Jewish woman, who gave birth to her baby, a daughter who now lives in Austria. The father was a family friend, manager of a famous art gallery and rescuer of much *enartete Kunst* (so called degenerate art), much of it now housed in a museum in Austria. The parents survived and were married after the war. As a teenager I assisted in the clandestine birth of the little girl Erika – to prevent the mother from screaming – and to protect her and us from neighbours who might have denounced us to the Nazis. I still wake up terrified. The event prematurely launched me into adulthood.

A woman doctor friend of Mama, Hilde Stoltenhoff, told me how to fairly painlessly and deliberately break a bone. Service was deferred for some months. That enabled me to take my matriculation exams. I passed, but failed miserably in biology (what with the nonsense of the Nazis' interpretation of the Mendel's biological rules. Teaching was different in Austria and Switzerland.

My uncle Werner, one of the last writers on the - then banned by the Nazis – *Frankfurter Zeitung* daily also reminded me:"all Russians are not Stalinists, just as not all Germans are Nazis. There are always bad eggs in every country". My uncle Werner among others was granted one of the first licenses to publish after the occupation of Germany. Other relatives were granted publishing licenses in the British, French and US Zones of occupation too. They were recognized as "decent Germans".

A married-on uncle Männe, a former judge dismissed under the Nazis' racial laws, had won the iron cross order in the First World War. Because of his war record, this Jew was spared in Theresienstadt. He was liberated at the end of the war. He never hated

Germans as such. His wife had bravely joined the public protest demonstration of six thousand Aryan wives of Jewish men in Berlin during the war.

Paul Rosbaud later came to play a pivotal role in my life. His contacts with the Secret Service in Britain enabled him to bring me to England, supported by them, with a residence permit, paid ticket and some valuable currency at a time when Germans could not travel, unless the allies wanted their specialist knowledge of rockets – or wire cages. On Guantànamo the wire cage concept was refined. The Nazis had imprisoned my mother's German-born friend – Hedda Carrington-Enders – in a somewhat more primitive and smaller cage. She was released only after pressure from dons at Oxford University. She left Germany, went to Prague and there at the British consulate married Whateley Carrington, a professor of psychic research. At that time the Nazis still cared about foreign opinion and endeavoured to pacify foreign press comment. They also could not offer the "luxury of the tropics" perceived by the US Vice-president – and accompanied by thc slogan "Honour-bound To Defend Freedom". The Nazis proclaimed that "Work Brings Freedom" – *Arbeit Macht Frei.*

Our family friend Will Stehmann was an opportunist, but a "decent" Aryan. When Mama after a devastating air raid could not get through to his house in Bremen or her relatives there, Rosbaud within twenty-four hours established that they were safe.

The greatest boon to my lasting appreciation came, of course, through my marriage to Hella Mandl, whom I had met at my first English job at Butterworth-Springer. Rosbaud then, with the disgraced Robert Maxwell, went to Pergamon Press. I had been proud to introduce Hella's family to Paul Rosbaud, who promptly informed me that they were *Alter Judenadel* or Jewish nobility. The parents reminded me of the great composers and writers and thought my reluctance and shame to speak German was foolish. Hella herself is an Oxford honours graduate, her late brother Franz Mandl, a renowned nuclear physicist and – I believe – once an assistant to Klaus Fuchs. I earned some kudos when I introduced him to Paul Rosbaud as the author of *Quantum Mechanics*. Only quite recently a younger generation physicist relative told me that Franz's textbook was his "bible".

In the light of post-war experience, I came to appreciate my late Jewish optician, Mr Cohen. He delayed the time to wear glasses as long as possible. This in contrast with two later well-known optician shops, who made bifocals which turned out identical to those I had already been given by Mr Cohen. Total cost: £360! They had told me I should have new glasses and – like a fool – I fell for that.

In the 1960s there was still an illogical prejudice

in England – and many other places. Terence Coyne, an Irish friend, found that his walk – to the railway station in south London on his way to work – would be significantly shortened if he could walk across the local golf course. He applied to join the club, but was promptly turned down. His name seemed Jewish. The membership secretary equated it to Cohen.

At home jazz records were being played on the gramophone. Then in neutral Switzerland you could buy records or listen to the radio to hear "degenerate" music banned in Germany. After the invasion of Luxembourg, the Low Countries and France, at school and even after the war I would listen to Hazy Osterwald and his band from Switzerland, where they did not have to follow the crazy rules imposed by the Nazis. Jazz had its funny side: long after the war, travelling home from Hamburg I sat in the first right-hand row on a flight. On the left sat a man I seemed to recognize. One seat apart from him a somewhat landed gentry lady was seemingly absorbed in reading. That man, I realized, was the clarinettist Acker Bilk. Boisterously he ordered two gin and tonics – one for the lady, the other for himself. Bilk ordered another round, animatedly chatting all the while to the rather aloof woman. Gradually they had a lively discussion going. It ended with the by then quite lively lady inviting the musician to her forthcoming garden party.

From Eric Tanzer I learned that to be a successful

businessman did not mean to be fast boy. A wizard salesman, he had come to London long before the war on an intended stay only to learn the business of selling printing equipment. He stayed. Super-salesmen can have cultural brains, too. Once, on a press visit to Frankfurt, when the party was to be lavishly entertained, the evening culminating in a visit to a posh nightclub, he saved me. He excused himself from joining by stressing that he had reserved a seat for a special performance at the opera. He mentioned that he had a ticket to spare by saying that unfortunately his wife was unwell. He offered this ticket to anyone. I jumped at the opportunity to escape the planned forced jocularity. We had a nice dinner and a super evening and managed to get to bed reasonably early. Years later, in Vienna, there was another occasion not to follow the herd in order to enjoy the better things in life. There was no need to go along with social routines.

After all these years and six decades after these terrible times. I still am unable to comprehend the docile manner in which people went to their death, obediently stripping of their clothing. The Warsaw Ghetto fighters fought back. The new Israelis fight – almost excessively in my opinion. My family are fighting back. One of the official reasons given at the time for my father's death in the concentration was that he "attacked a guard when trying to escape". Three reasons were given. We tend to accept this explanation.

So I think I am not a racist. And yet, some Nazi propaganda still has left traces. A Jewish man in Switzerland (and at one time reputed as related to Anne Frank, of the *Diary*) has brought to life some of the obsessive anti-Semitic rantings and perversely distorted views of the *Stürmer* Nazi newspaper. I am ashamed to recall some of these things and hope to have freed myself of these fabricated opinions. I believe in people's right to even the most fanciful views. For instance, I did not cherish the American satirist Lenny Bruce's explicit language (I dislike any foul language). But I hated the efforts of the law to persecute and silence his acts.

Not everyone is perfect, though. This man in Switzerland managed to rob my former wife and me of the substantial inheritance left by Paul Rosbaud's widow Hilde, née Frank. I disdain going to law to win our rights. It is perhaps too late now to fret. Yiddish folklore tells us that "one will never be able to live with the law one goes to live with it". That man broke the trust his aunt had placed in him as a joint executor of the Last Will. He mysteriously claimed to have sort of communicated with the dead, obtained sole Probate of the estate of his aunt and managed to obtain the funds intended for him as a nephew and me as a kind of replacement for her deceased daughter.

Many other aspects of my youth and later life made a great impact on me. Elsewhere I recount my childhood experience of the vicious *Kristallnacht*, which destroyed my faith in too many adults' superiority.

Early on in Nazi-dom's reign I experienced the first general indications of racism while on a visit to Berlin. With shock and horror I witnessed the round-up of Jewish people, herded onto cattle trucks carrying only a small suitcase – if anything. They looked terrified. As yet they did not know of their tragic fate to come. With horror I witnessed small children left behind, guarded by cynical SS troopers overseeing death by starvation.

A decent relative's family was allocated a former Jewish residence after their home had been bombed out. Deportation had come so unexpected that even the table laid for dinner had food rotting on plates on the dining room table of the new home, round the corner from my mother's place. Not all the people the family had helped wanted to remember. After the war those few, perhaps in their just disgust at German deeds, refused to come to my mother's aid. Some survivors after the establishment of the state of Israel adopted almost racial attitudes. Others were very tolerant.

Swiss School

WHEN WORLD War II started, I was happily installed at a boarding school in Switzerland. The boarding school or *Internat* was fairly posh. I have to grant the school that it provided unusually good education, especially in the classics. The atmosphere was too much pro-German. That was because there were many German boys from rich families. Despite the obvious wealth, the weekly bath time in junior school was a disgrace, I think that bath water was changed rarely and we had to line up and dip into scummy water under the supervision of a school nurse. That was quite revolting. When we were older we had individual baths. These days I have reverted to my youth and routinely take a bath or have a shower every day since leaving the military.

I was unable to talk to anyone about Papa's death. Only the heads of the school knew about it and talked to me about the tragedy.

Switzerland was a neutral country. You could buy records or listen to the radio to hear "degenerate" music banned in Germany. After the invasion of

Luxembourg, the Low Countries and France, I listened regularly to Hazy Osterwald and his band. They did not have to obey the restrictions imposed by the Nazis.

To my consternation the neutral country was not the Nazi-free paradise I expected. There were disheartening exceptions. The local chief of police seemed to be a Nazi sympathizer. The sports master, as is recounted elsewhere, was German and leader of the local party activists among us schoolboys were worried children of refugees. So-called “half Jews” tried to show their loyalty to Germany by betting on a German *Endsieg*. Foolishly I bet against them forecasting the allied victory. The Nazi clique and the German consulate learnt of this, of course. In 1943 I was told by the neutral headmaster and the sports master Karl Sommer that I would have to leave Switzerland by agreement. The German consulate occupied a building within the school grounds and had demanded this. I was stunned and refused to believe the demand. Meanwhile Mama in Berlin was allowed by the Swiss consul in Berlin to use his telephone to advise me that I should stay in the school and the country. A reasonable suggestion. The Nazi consulate had stated that because I was German born and almost of military age I should return. Nobody in Switzerland was legally able to speak for me. The school had the addresses of some friends of the parents. The school heads had to keep up reasonable relations with the Germans, as there were many German pupils. Mama was too scared to give me further advice. The cantonal police were called in and I was taken the station on to a train bound for the border. I escaped at the station in Zurich. My guards were having a smoke on the station platform. I used to have meals at that station with Mama in Primus Bon's fine restaurant and also knew the way about Zurich. I made my way to Mama's friend's home and stayed with Charlotte Leuenberger and her partner Hanno Zeiss, an Austrian escapee from the Nazis.

These friends of Mama's (who later fought alongside the French *Maquis*, a "crime" of breaking Swiss neutrality, for which Charlotte was temporarily deprived of her Swiss residency). Nobody had reckoned with the St. Gallen police's thoroughness. They followed me, knocked on the door of the apartment at Utoquai in Zurich (where I first saw an American-style kitchen and where Mama had so often stayed) and put me on a train via Basel to Frankfurt and Grandmother Anna. Once in Germany I went into hiding.

One evening there, in my Donegal tweed jacket and worsted flannels I ambled through Frankfurt station. Police picked me up. They thought me an escaped British POW because of my clothing and English things in my pockets. I tried to impress them with my late paternal grandfather's local standing, which grandmother confirmed. That cut no ice. The police were not local, but from Silesia. In the end, though, they let me go. For a while hiding was no longer feasible. So I travelled to Berlin and to my mother, but went again into hiding. For a while I volunteered to work unpaid for an antiquarian bookseller in the Bayrische Viertel district near home. I believe that was when I discovered my love of books. Earlier and with my pocket money I had already bought Goethe's *Italian Journey* and art books on Gauguin and Goya – I still have them.

This bookseller – a highly educated man – had a treasure trove of books, among them many the Nazis had banned. I was allowed to take some home. I read avidly and tried my hand at somewhat childish writing.

I went into hiding again with a butcher's family in the Harz Mountains. That provided a sort of bonus. I helped out sticking ration coupons onto sheets of papers. I regularly managed to pinch coupons and mail them to Mama.

My mother had paid a futile bribe of three thousand Reichsmark to two Hitler Youth officials who signed the required papers for me to continue schooling in Switzerland. That brought trouble for Mama. Despite my obvious shyness I steeled myself and as a teenager entered a shop for ladies' lingerie to buy stockings for Mama in Berlin. When asked for the size, I looked around with eyes downcast until I spotted a lady of approximately Mama's height. I asked for a size "like that lady over there" would wear. I brought the stockings to Berlin. At one time Mama had roughly a hundred pairs. The little shop taking up runs for her reported her for hoarding. A people's court promptly fined her for subversion of the war effort!

Although we were more aware of the Nazi horror around us, after all – had they not murdered my father? – we did not yet realize what atrocity was being done to millions of their so called enemies and *Untermenschen* (other races).

In Berlin, highly noticeable red posters on Litfass hoarding columns were naming the execution of a Jewess who had slept with an Aryan, and vice versa. Even my mother, friends and I could not believe the unimaginably gruesome stories of soldiers returning from the East. It took another year for the full truth to penetrate to us.

Inge Jaspert had an admirer, Will Stehmann, a wealthy businessman from Bremen, whose luxurious villa there I once visited as a house guest. This man ran a clothes factory in Warsaw in Poland, and was able to save many Jewish German-speaking employees, who he claimed were essential to the running of his factory. He had access to goodies like cloth and butter. And as he had money, to luxuries like dinner invitations to the Hotel Adlon's restaurant, where until late in the war they still served lobster. They charged highly for meals, but luxury meals were not that strictly rationed. Many of the other diners were Nazi bonzes, like those in the West End restaurant of Horcher, which relocated to Madrid after the War and became a favoured meeting place of escaped Nazis and intrigue.

Back in Berlin one night after a fierce air raid and fire storm I was trying to get home, the train service had stopped. In the street a horse lay wounded on the road. Its legs were smashed and the yellow sticky stuff from the firebombs was aflame on its hide. The poor animal was neighing fiercely, writhing in agony. There was no gun anywhere near enough to release it from the agony. The thought "They shoot horses, don't they?" rushed into my mind. I could not help and feeling guilty turned away to find my way home. Our home was aflame, too. It had not been spared.

More than seventy years after the dreadful years I still have sleepless nights and ask myself how could such inhumanities happen? Uniformed Germans, who professed a love for Rainer Maria Rilke's lyrics or Ludwig van Beethoven's music, were shooting to kill human beings, such as that naked woman and baby, to list just one of the nightmare scenarios.

Occasionally I came out of hiding and went to Berlin, where I was on that fateful 20th July 1944. An attempt to assassinate Hitler was made by the army officers – 'good Germans'. Michael Baigent and Richard Leigh recount in *Secret Germany* how the coup intended by the conspirators to restore the good name of Germany, destroyed for generations to come, failed. The two authors commented that "under brutal torture – what the Gestapo, with typical bureaucratic euphemism, called 'sharpened interrogation' – the conspirators displayed extraordinary bravery and tenacity". how dreadful that those interrogation techniques have nowadays been refined by the American 'liberators' at Guantànamo, Abu Ghraib and in Afghanistan or by "rendering" to countries known to employ torture. Deluded military commanders like the American Lt. Colonel Gareth Brand, had no qualms. He declared: "The enemy has a face. We call him Satan. We are going in". Thus America lost its good name.

The Nazi war crimes horrified the world. What is not always being realized is that there were many decent Germans who refused brutal orders. Refusal to carry out some orders, as Daniel J. Goldhagen reminds us in his *Hitler's Willing Executioners*, was possible, if risky. Goldhagen cites actual cases and later promotion of such people. Would that more American and British soldiers in Iraq, acting under orders or recommendations, had had such decency. Perhaps that war will teach the services to scan their volunteers more thoroughly for potential sadists. Sadism was imbued in them at Fort Bragg. Germans under the Nazis also knew what was going on. More than seventy years after the Nazi nightmare I am still puzzled over the very fact that normal-appearing neighbours and even friends of the parents suddenly turned into bigots and all too often into monsters or just looked away when confronted with beastliness.

My maternal grandmother Oma Dora commented on my anti-Nazi rantings and felt that I seemed to have a secret self-destruction wish to end up in a soap factory. Despite their vociferous denials after the war, ordinary German people knew or had some inkling of the Nazi crimes.

Towards the end of the war, living in a Berlin suburb, my mother – who had been bombed out – had moved into her mother's house. One of the neighbours was Reinhardt Gehlen, who later became head of the new German *Bundesnachrichtendienst* or Federal Intelligence Service. He and his family did not like the Nazis and discussed their thoughts and views with me. I got to know a young relative and liked the lively and free discussions, guarded as they often were. We were all in fear of informers.

The military mind is hard to follow. Blind obedience to criminal orders seems to be standard in every country.

I profited from some military thinking: When the German Nazi machine finally caught up with me, the recruiting panel asked me whether I had any relatives in the services. To this I answered truthfully that I was related on my mother's side to a vice-admiral.

Less than a year later the American panel asked the same question. I gave the same answer, albeit even less specific. In both cases I was made an officer's candidate, but never rose beyond basic enlisted rank. Neither panel ever asked me in which country that vice-admiral lived.

I had managed to defer my call up for two months by breaking a collar bone in a deliberate heavy fall against the banisters of the Berlin Theatre to a performance of *Don Carlos* the night before my medical. The panel guessed what I had done but were powerless against the evidence of an X-ray picture.

My mother cried when she saw me in childlike dress uniform with a gold coloured chain holding the jacket together. Soon the quite reasonable naval officers realized that I was not at all a Nazi follower. However, I was still an officer's candidate. First I was trained at the naval base of Flensburg, soon stationed in Esbjerg in occupied Denmark, where food was a bit more plentiful. I was destined initially for service on a fast e-boat, but when we were to be sent to the Eastern (Soviet) Front, Dr Hilde Stoltenhoff, my mother's friend, arranged for me to take Digitalis heart drugs and I was hospitalized. By then the war situation was quite desperate. I was sent in naval blue uniform to Bad Tölz in Bavaria. The Waffen-SS had a training camp there. Drugs made it possible to escape their clutches.

Without much ado transfer was to a Wehrmacht army unit. On my way from the seaside to Bad Toelz in Bavaria I had planned to desert and go home. The sight of summarily executed soldiers hanging from the rafters at a railway station made me change my mind. Placards saying: "he wanted to go home" scared me off when I had almost reached Demker, where one of my uncles' family was evacuated.

Orders came to proceed to the Eastern Front. The fast advance of the Red Army luckily prevented that. We were taken to the train station. One of my fellow cadets was the grandson of a famous naval hero of the First World War. We saw a train, destined west. We ran and jumped on. Staff sergeants trying to herd the confused masses of soldiers were shouting to make us stop and aimed their rifles at us. Soldiers on the slowly moving train pulled us to safety. The train soon pulled away.

We were formed into a shabby *Kampfgruppe Sachs* and were mentioned in false and boisterous despatches. I managed to desert and become an American prisoner of-war. Capture by American soldiers had been terrifying. Half a dozen rifles pointed at me. I was still wearing my steel helmet. GIs shouted something at me – the rifles aimed at me. I was scared mindless. Finally I grasped that the GIs wanted me to ditch the helmet. They feared I was perhaps a fanatic, hiding bombs under the helmet! I obeyed, still scared. The GIs were also scared. Then I was fed and offered a hot shower in a mobile unit. Luxury had arrived. At first we were put into a makeshift camp at Worms (a veritable can of worms). We had to defecate on the ground and could not wash at all.

Then we were moved to Epinal in eastern France. Later the camp's inmates were moved to Nancy. I "escaped" to reach the "better camp" holding prisoners already screened. Eventually I was put to work in the clerical office and then the RTO railway traffic office. We transferred thousands of GIs being redeployed to America from other theatres of war. General George S. Patton came to visit the units stationed there. The stockade was bitterly cold. Notwithstanding that I washed with snow or cold water from a hand pump. My desire to be clean was rewarded. I was hurriedly selected to act as batman to the general and pushed into a GI uniform. When he left, the general gave me a farewell present: a gold-plated Sheaffer pen. It was stolen almost immediately. Later, I donned GI clothes again: on VE – Victory in Europe Day – I marched with proud Americans in the great parade! I was, after all, considered 'safe' and spoke English.

Most of us *Kraut* prisoners-of-war were demoralized, but I and a few others, some German counts among them, like Osvaldo von Breymann, who befriended me, were quite pleased to have left the Nazis behind, and were overjoyed at their defeat. I had longed for this to happen for all those years.

An American soldier gave me two V-mail small letter forms to contact people in allied countries. I reached Rafaello Busoni in New York and Harry Brand in London. They got in touch with people of influence. At roll call my name was called and I had to report to the officer in charge. Asked whether I wanted to serve with the US Forces I instantly assented and was discharged from captivity, but immediately recruited by the Quartermaster Corps. That was probably a subterfuge and not quite kosher. Anyway, I seemed to be with the American forces. The attendant privileges, such as access to the PX Post exchange and a private's GI outfit, laundry privileges, and freedom to move about in Nancy, were suddenly available, although nothing was truly official. I was extremely lucky in this post-war disorganized environment. Amidst the chaotic and expedient postwar conditions and the thriving black market I was advised to make only vague references to my flatteringly mysterious activities with the US Quartermaster Corps.

I learned later that the man who had finally denounced Papa was a Swiss national and follower of the Nazis. Eventually he got his just desserts. After my mother's early death my brother and I, going through her papers, discovered a newspaper clipping. The infamous Würgler-Hess had died a gruesome death impaled over some hours on the rigid steering column of his car. For several hours firemen tried to free him. When he was finally pulled out he was dead.

Mama told me that a small detachment of the victorious Soviet Army and their officer were billeted in her home in Berlin. They seemed to be fairly decent chaps. They liked alcohol and drank the contents of a large bottle of *Joy* perfume and some exceptional wine saved to celebrate the end of the war and the Nazi terror. Mama claimed that the Russian officer in command of these frontline troops was so enraged by one of his soldiers having raped a young German girl he summarily executed him. My mother escaped the horrors inflicted on many of Berlin's women by the second wave of Soviet troops entering the city. Mama, wisely, did not use make-up or wear nice clothes during that time. The soldiers billeted in her home, though, drank her bottles of white burgundy wine which had been saved to celebrate the end of the war. They also bravely drained the large bottle of *Joy* perfume which I had bought in Zurich. When I returned to Berlin after the war I felt shamed by Mama's destruction of antique furniture for firewood during those days of cold misery.

Had the Russians lost all respect for Germans after they had seen the horrors of Auschwitz and other camps? An acquaintance of mine on the British side had seen the emaciated corpses of the concentration camp victims of Birkenau. He behaved strangely from there on. One Soviet veteran I read about saw a shrink even under Stalin, who's NKVD frowned upon such "degenerates". One of my aunts was raped. The daughter of the doctor, who had surreptitiously given me the Digitalis pills that saved me from being sent to the East, married her Soviet rapist. She later divorced him when he was ordered to go return to Russia.

British, French and American soldiers just fraternised in a fairly good-natured way until they were found out by the MPs and posted home or elsewhere, especially when a child was on the way. Fraternization, although a fact of life, was heavily criticized. Some marriages were later allowed.

I had a girl friend, very innocently and proper, while in Eastern France – first as a POW and later in American uniform. We did not wish to discuss politics. The parents invited me to tea and biscuits. In turn I brought some stuff from the PX. I still fail to see why it was so utterly horrible to have a German soldier boyfriend – evil as the Nazis were – to after the liberation have her head shorn of hair and march her through the city and jeering people. German and Italian girls cherished the fraternization. Many later became GI Brides and joined their erstwhile boyfriends in America.

There could be much to carp about. James Joyce commented on carping criticism in *Finnegan's Wake*: "How? c'est mal prononsable, tartagliano, perfrances,

Vous n'avez pas d'o boche provenciale, mousoo. Je m'incline mais mov jay trouvay la clee dang les champs. hay sham nap poddy velour, come on!" I have not yet managed to finish reading the whole book. More to the point: Joyce should have sent that comment to Henri Matisse, when he illustrated an American edition of *Ulysses*, without bothering even to attempt reading the story. That scarce volume is now in one of my sons' library, given to him as a graduation present.

I was then for almost two years attached to the US Third Army, moving jerry cans. In spite of my vague status I even volunteered to fight in the war against Japan. Nothing decisive had to be done. Japan surrendered. When in 1947 the time came to be redeployed, the opportunity came to ship to the US, and things became SNAFU. It was decided the simplest way to deal with my discharge was to make me a prisoner-of-war again and then discharge me. So I returned to Germany and eventually saw my mother again.

Discharge was via the former Nazi concentration camp of Dachau, still having the plain wooden bunks of the old days. I passed through the camp in horror. "How could the harbingers of democracy", I asked, "expose someone like myself to these past horrors? Be that cynical and give such a lesson in history?" The officer-in-charge let me out within a few days.

I was lucky again. I was not a number and had learnt

the lesson that "Democracy is an abuse of statistics" from the Argentine writer Jorge Luis Borges.

Having been – even as an "expediary" – with the Quartermaster corps had definite perks. Food was good, uniforms were fresh. Some of the people around me were on transport duties from the ports. Dealing on the black market they became quite wealthy. They also had to face dangers. Gangs, especially around Marseilles, hijacked the convoys carting supplies. Some soldiers, when the time came to be redeployed to America, had the big worry of how to safely and without arousing suspicion, convert large stashes of occupation money into genuine dollar bills. I also became rich. On discharge I was paid dollars – a fortune in Germany at that time.

After the war the victorious allies became somewhat ignorant, but infamous accomplices in some of the worst Stalinist crimes. The Western allies agreed to repatriate liberated Soviet prisoners. To our disgust and sorrow these unfortunate victims of the war were forced on to trains and shipped home. There they were summarily executed or sent to Gulags! We were appalled. The poor people cried and knelt on the ground imploring us to be allowed to stay. We managed to let some escape, but they were soon recaptured by the "bloodhounds" of the military police. A few unfortunates even received punishment additional to almost certain future death. The ex-prisoners and slave workers plus a few Nazi volunteers, had thought they were free in a democratic society, free again after much suffering. This shameful decision was carried out by British and American forces throughout liberated Europe! Count Nicolai Tolstoy endeavoured to highlight this episode and put the blame on high-ranking people in authority. He failed. Britain's somewhat bizarre libel laws defeated him.

Reading a *Jüdischer Almanach* story about post-war Berlin and how a Jewish woman survived hiding in her house's cellar in the Frohnau district – with her friends meeting near a skylight so that she could hear them speaking about the progress of the war, but her never uttering a word. This reminded me of my aunt's bravery in hiding her Jewish friend throughout the war years.

I urgently had to search for work when currency reform came to Germany. I was penniless by then. My efforts to be admitted to university and study medicine had failed. My mother was worried about my future and enlisted the help of Franz Perneder, an uncle from Austria. He paid a monthly fee to an established Munich publisher and printer to have me trained in the business of F. Bruckmann publishers, who offered the assistant editorship of *Die Kunst & Das Schöne Heim.*

My mother was still worried. I still had not got a place at university. Preference was given to young people with longer military service.

My father's library, which had been sent to Mainau Castle on Lake Constance, was looted by French soldiers. It was lost forever. My father admired the French anthropologist Claude Lévi-Strauss. Perhaps the soldiers were anxious to read these volumes.

While a "fake GI" and as I spoke reasonably good English already, I was put in the office and managed to send letters everywhere. I also managed to be allowed out and visit local people, who did not condemn every German. The occupation had made them understand that some Germans did not like the Nazi system. I even fell mildly in love with a local girl, but this ended soon. I was sent to Metz and then my career in the Quartermaster corps began. I mention elsewhere that consisted mainly in lifting jerry cans off the trains, but also rather vaguely being trained to go to the Far East. The war with Japan had not yet been ended by the atom bombs.

I was put in the RTO (railway) office. American troops from Austria, Italy and Germany as well as eastern France passed through my hands. Eventually my turn came to be redeployed. Complications arose. My American recruitment had not been quite kosher. Officers decided to make me a POW again. I relate elsewhere the outcome of this.

Suddenly I had privileges and was, by the terms of those days, rather affluent and powerful. I was no longer a miserable kraut. I was luxuriously; it seemed, fed and smoked cigarettes – real cigarettes, not stubs. Smoking had been mainly to make myself more accepted by my new comrades. That actually meant smoking perhaps too much. At morning inspection I had fainted, more than once. Elsewhere I relate how I was shocked into giving up smoking.

A friend, the late Robert Bloomfield, had been in the Royal Navy. After the Japanese surrender he and his shipmates visited the bombed city of Hiroshima. He and most of the others on that day became opponents of nuclear weapons. They were horrified by the killing or maiming of thousands of people.

Germany was devastated when I returned from France. The Swiss refused to take me back and I had to try and exist. I was lucky. I had riches, more than valuable US $1,000 in severance pay, plus about a hundred and fifty marks, valueless (but in my case backed by the US occupation forces) in a country in the grip of the black market. I also had the substantial privilege of admission to the American Army's PX shops.

A Significant Encounter

AFTER MY discharge in 1947 I first moved to my uncle Werner Jaspert's home near Frankfurt. At the time I felt I would be a nuisance if I moved back to my home and to my mother in Berlin. Later I lived and worked as a publishing trainee in Munich, a period which ended at the time of the traumatic currency reform, which left me relatively affluent. I had more than US $1,000. Earlier, while living in my mother's house in Berlin, I had applied to General Lucius D. Clay, commander of the US Zone, for a job on *Der Monat*, a magazine edited by Melvin Lasky and Stephen Spender, the poet. Hans Habe wanted me to join. I declined the job. Later I learnt that the magazine was sponsored by the CIA-financed Congress for Cultural Freedom. I realised that by luck I had escaped involvement in nefarious activities. My uncle Werner's friend Egon Kogon, author of *The SS State*, had no such qualms.

One day while I lived in Munich a man was passing in the opposite direction and suddenly turned to me, recognizing and addressing me. Paul Rosbaud had not seen me for six years. He was a voluntary resident spy for Britain in Berlin during the war. I was asked what I was doing in Germany and explained that I had not managed to go to Switzerland when the Second World War ended and I did not want to go to the United States. I told him that I had been discharged to Germany, quite wealthy, with a few thousand dollars, though that money had by then gone. He then asked whether I would like to come to England. I reacted instantly. Yes – that would be wonderful and I would realise my childhood dream. Easy!

The US High Commission in Munich wrote to me and asked me to present myself, just a few weeks later. I went; full of trepidation, but everything was all right. An American officer told me that mysteriously authorized travel documents, and more astonishingly, air tickets and some British currency had arrived to be handed to me. All that was needed were photographs and my signature. Thus I eventually, after some physical delay caused by a severe blizzard in Bavaria, got to England. Andrew (no longer Andreas) Herxheimer and his father collected me from the terminal. I stayed at Andrew's home, and after a few days started a job in a publishing company which had entailed training in Munich and at J. Stürtz of Würzburg. I opened a bank account with the posh Hoare Bank in Fleet Street. I also sold the cabin trunk Mama had given me, as well as an expensive portable radio I had rashly bought at the insistence of that rather rich girl left behind in Munich. They were the only material goods I could then legally take out of occupied Germany.

Paul Rosbaud as a science editor in Berlin during the war had managed to pass to a British Embassy in a neutral country detailed information about the Nazis' Heavy Water project. Apparently no notice was taken of that information until later, when the RAF, after another informants' input, conducted a bombing raid on the plant in Nazi occupied Norway.

Paul Rosbaud, who had for many years been science advisor to the Springer-Verlag, arranged for me to have a publishing internship with their Bergmann Munich branch and the Würzburg printing plant of Stürtz, where I learned more about book production and printing technology. That stood in good stead in London at Butterworth-Springer publishers. Together with an expert from the Monotype Corporation and my then brother-in-law Franz Mandl, printers Acfords of Chichester developed four-line mathematics hot metal typesetting based on German experience.

The infamous crook Robert Maxwell was a director of Butterworth-Springer. His wrongdoings were soon discovered by the co-owners and he was summarily and ignominiously sacked, only to start Pergamon Press with the help of loyal Dr Rosbaud (whose resignation he later shamefully accepted). I am proud to still have the photograph of the Greek coin used for the colophon of the now Dutch-owned publishers.

Paul Rosbaud was the brother of Hans, the conductor and the supreme interpreter of Anton Bruckner's symphonies. He was musical director in the French Zone of occupation. Paul Rosbaud had helped to save Niels Bohr when the Nazis invaded Denmark. The full account of his extraordinary achievements is told in Arnold Kramish's *The Griffin*, published on both sides of the Atlantic and the Pacific – even in China – in some twelve languages. This book is strangely difficult to obtain in Britain, but available over the Internet. Rosbaud's heroic deeds are also referred to in Michael Smith's *Foley*.

Through Rosbaud I met Lotte Meitner, the photographer, in her London studio in Bond Street, and the by then famous atom scientist Lise Meitner in Stockholm, both when a child in Berlin and after the war.

Someone associated with Paul Rosbaud in wartime Berlin was Hilde Benjamin, who later became infamous as a bloodthirsty power in the short-lived German Democratic Republic. Her sister Ruth Lange was Rosbaud's secretary.

Otto Hahn the "father of atom physics" came to London and met me on the stairs of my office in London's Strand. He wanted to see my boss and generous benefactor Paul Rosbaud. It was a real pleasure to meet the gentle man and show him the way.

Dr Franz Mandl and his wife Betty worked at the atomic energy research weapons facility at Harwell and later in America before settling at Manchester University. Franz Mandl and I at one time were visited by Special Branch officers who disapproved of holidays in Eastern Europe and carefully looked at our bookshelves, asking why we had such "communist literature" like Mao's *Little Red Book*. Perhaps they were just deploring the books by Edgar Wallace and Leslie Charteris (*The Saint*) volumes? More plausible perhaps were their misgivings about Franz' holiday plans to perhaps visit some places on the coast of Croatia, (which he was explicitly told to drop for the then communist country). Franz Mandl managed to explain and make me understand some aspects of atomic science, although I know nothing really about the subject. As a child in Berlin I had heard of Max Planck, met adults which appeared highly acclaimed by older people around me. These were in my parents' friend Rosbaud's circle and included Niels Bohr, Otto Hahn or Lise Meitner. Later, as a young man I met some of them again and was aware of the reasons for their fame. I was too young then to realize Bohr's genius and wisdom about the things to come!

Rosbaud was never given proper credit for his brave work. I believe he was flown out of Berlin when the Soviet Army arrived. A special plane was sent to extract him. He signed the Official Secrets Act and was thus barred from discussing his exploits.

I owe Paul Rosbaud an eternal debt of gratitude on behalf of my family and myself. During the worst years of the war he supported my mother and I think we may even owe him our lives. After his early death Hilde Rosbaud, his widow, sold me a picture by Käthe Kollwitz and a book by Fernand Léger. Today these are among my most cherished possessions. These pictures and a Persian rug were not bought for their value, but because of fondness and gratitude. After Angela Rosbaud, the daughter, died young in somewhat mysterious circumstances, I helped Hilde to clear up the deceased's apartment. A packet of personal letters we found was given to me by Hilde, and I gave them unread to her nephew.

In the British Zone Captain Robert Maxwell, a Jewish refugee from Czechoslovakia, oversaw publishing activities. He granted my father's brother, Reinhard Jaspert and his partner one of the first publishing licences in Berlin. Uncle Reinhardt started the Safari-Verlag publishing house. While stationed in occupied Holland he had saved many persecuted people at risk and the Dutch government acknowledged this. Uncle Werner Jaspert, who had during the war worked on the *Frankfurter Zeitung* until it was closed down by the Nazi regime, was given a publishing licence in the US Zone of Germany to become editor of an illustrated weekly. Later Werner was head of the entertainment section of Hesse radio. The US occupation authorities appointed him the first mayor of Oberusel, near Frankfurt. Hermann Goering was briefly a prisoner at Oberusel. Uncle Werner also towards the end of the war had sheltered a French prisoner-of-war in his home despite the danger of execution of himself and his family. His son, Michael, married Colette, the daughter of the Frenchman. They were divorced after many years. The sons from the marriage, Philippe and Stefan, now live in France. My uncle's daughter, Barbara, married Winifred Knorr, son of the owner of *Rhein-Main Zeitung*, the first newspaper the US authorities allowed and licensed at Heidelberg. The son, Achim Knorr, works for the newspaper and for some years was married to Yvonne, daughter of the man who founded the first newspaper licensed at Mannheim. They later separated. Despite the university town's close links with the Heidelberg printing machinery company, the local newspaper bought Swiss-made Wifag printing presses. The spurned pressmakers asked for my help in getting the choice revoked. This was naturally refused.

When I was assistant editor of the German art magazine *Die Kunst* in Munich, I developed an interest in architecture. The Bauhaus and architects like Richard Neutra or Frank Lloyd Wright fascinated me. Concepts of Brasilia and its new buildings and townscape made me feel enthusiastic. My father's older brother Fritz Jaspert and his son Martin about that time published a major volume on the building of cities throughout the world.

Robert Maxwell's activities were nefarious even at that time. He extracted licences from often old-established publishers to whom he had been the provider of publishing licences. Earlier he made himself plausible to the reputable Dr Julius Springer of the scientific publishing house. Elsewhere I mention how he became one of the founders of Pergamon Press together with Dr Paul Rosbaud. Maxwell had been thrown out of Butterworth-Springer for suspected shady dealings. He and Paul Rosbaud soon parted. After Rosbaud's early death I managed to persuade Betty Maxwell to send Hilde Rosbaud £1,000. I had thought the widow was penniless. Maxwell went on to become Britain's biggest swindler, robbing the pension funds of the *Daily Mirror* and the British Printing Corporation. He had apparently been of service to Israel, which sent a special plane to Africa to collect his corpse after his mysterious death. The doors of the first one were apparently too small for his massive body and another aircraft had to be sent.

The painter Georg Grosz, who had known my parents, had migrated to America. He was unhappy with his reputation and work there and returned to Germany, where he met a sudden death. Did he fall or was he pushed down the stairs? He visited me in my office at the Munich art magazine. As an example of his 'worthless work' in exile he displayed *The Painter of the Hole.*

Curzio Malaparte writes in *The Skin* that the fictitious Italian liaison officer to the American Army tells the representative of the liberators that "Fifty years hence Americans will be like followers of the European nightmare". In his later *Mama Marcia* his American driver tells him that he is perhaps a communist and does not care for freedom, but admits that "Fifty years hence America will be like post-war Europe: a land without freedom and justice, ruled by henchmen of bloodthirsty judges and their higher ups".

The Nazis' criminally insane dream of exterminating Jews through the holocaust making the entire race disappear from the face of the earth ironically led to the creation of the Jewish State of Israel – today a world power. The former Stern gang terrorist Menachim Begin and later the one-eyed General Moishe Dayan became highly respected men. America guaranteed the state, and guilt-ridden Germany provided some of the initial finance.

Before the Second World War my mother had contributed text and picture stories to some magazines, including the American weekly *Life.* She resumed some work translating under her maiden name, Isolde Anger and translated books on Persia, South Africa, Thomas Carlyle's *Französische Revolution* and other work for uncle Reinhardt's publishing firm and others. All of Papa's brothers rallied around to help her. Uncle Äd built a small apartment for her on to his house at Bonn.

My mother was trying to get me interested in work. She wrote to friends everywhere. Rafaello Busoni in New York thought that I should be in the movies! He had contacts with Francis Lederer in America, to whom my photograph had been shown. The feeling was that I would get into Hollywood, but that my teeth first needed painful readjustment. That was not for me. So that was the end of a promising career perhaps. One of Mama's friends in Western Australia suggested I should come to his management team and be assistant manager of the brewery in far away Perth.

During my time with F. Bruckmann publishing I also worked with the American authorities and their German artistic expert and advisor, Dr Eberhard Hanfstängel, of the Alte Pinakothek museum trying to recover art looted by the Nazis during the war. I remember – acting on a tip – we visited a Bavarian farmer and admired his floor covering. He claimed it was an heirloom from his grandmother, but Dr Hanfstängel told him it looked remarkably like a famous tapestry from France and that we would have to take it away for examination and study by experts. He was given a receipt and never more. One work of art was restored to France!

At some stage I seemed to be a somewhat mysterious German-speaking GI, enjoying an American soldier's privileges with access to officer facilities. Later I realized that all this was an expedient fake that suited US Army aims, but sometimes scared Germans. Sometimes I met the writer Len Deighton – a bit of a Cockney lad – but amusing and often willing to go on madcap excursions or adventures. We sometimes met with a former friend of mine and quaffed wine at Kettners in London's Soho.

My work at Bruckmann was enjoyable. I designed books. One of them was by an heir of the Beck beer brewery fortune. He had a wonderful collection of art. In his garden stood a sculpture by Aristide Maillol.

On the walls in his house were paintings by German expressionists, such as Franz Marc and August Macke. He had written a monograph on Marc and I had handled it. In gratitude he offered me a Macke painting for a nominal sum. I refused it like the young fool I was then. Later I committed such an error again, when David Hockney, soon after his art school days, offered me one of his pictures for free. I had acted for the then St. Petersburg Press to have it reproduced and printed. This nice gesture I declined shyly.

I recounted earlier that my father had published a book on Max Planck, the German physicist and Nobel prize winner. This was how I came into contact with the world of atomic science. Paul Rosbaud knew many of the men involved.

Rosbaud provided important information on German neglect of atomic science and the rocket project at Peenemünde.

He was shocked and furious at what had gone on behind the scenes and decided to confront Maxwell. Springer astonished me. On his way to Headington Hall in Oxford, where Robert Maxwell had rented at a ridiculously low rent from the council, he asked me to call him a taxi, I imagined, to take the important man to Paddington railway station. The taxi was hailed – and Springer told the driver to take him to Oxford. He did not even haggle about the fare!

Twice I was left substantial sums by deceased friends or relatives. I got only relatively small sums. Relatives laid claim – not having ever cared for the deceased – on the inheritance. I had to accept the nullification of some hopes. In the other case I was in the middle of a divorce and got about one thirtieth of the proposed money. Well, such is life. My brother fared even worse: he thought he would invest his savings – with an embezzler, who later lived in palatial splendour in California. He was sought for many years in central Europe as a major crook.

I had occasionally contributed to the weekly *British & Colonial Printer* (later *Printing World*). James Moran commissioned me to write more regularly. I started with a big bang: disclosing shady secrets of the city company I was the working for. Of course, I was sacked after an intoxicated Christmas staff party.

More important was my meeting Ellic Howe, one-time print genius of wartime black propaganda who also wrote a book on Hitler's belief in the prophesies of Nostradamus. In his wartime trilogy novels Evelyn Waugh suggests that even the spells of an African witch doctor were called in to harm Nazi leaders. We spent many a night in lively discussion. The typographer Elizabeth Friedlander was less socially talkative and did not join our evenings more than once or twice.

My discharge to Germany had included US $1,000 in scrip money, easily changed on the black market at a good rate and at the time a fortune for a young man in Germany. The German currency then was worthless. I changed the dollars I gradually received from my pseudo-GI status (which had been elaborately constructed so as not to break any rules of the Red Cross) into marks, and when the currency was stabilized with the *Währungsreform* (currency reform), my bank account was in reasonably good standing. I wasted it to please my new (married) love and later a girl friend, whom I planned to marry, but then left her behind in Germany and later lost when I went to England. My girlfriend wanted to follow to London, but I dissuaded her. I had already met Hella Mandl who was to become my first wife. The girl I had left behind in Germany was rather stunning looking.

Posters of her face graced advertisements for a beauty soap manufacturer, which were plastered over railway stations and poster hoardings everywhere. Soon she got over my departure She married the son of the heir to the Loden-Frey rain cloth enterprise, whose property adjoined my former home in Munich's Schwabing district by the English Garden park.

Claus Schenk Graf von Stauffenberg, the man who had tried to kill Hitler in the famous generals' plot was a member of a large family. I knew some of those people. Many were reluctant to talk about the Nazi era. Some even called themselves plain Stauffenberg without the aristocratic '*von*'. They just wanted to be ordinary people, like the relatives of Karl Gördeler, whom my mother knew. Sometimes she hinted that he was planning against Hitler.

After the defeat of Germany, Konrad Adenauer, former mayor of the cathedral city of Cologne became the first federal chancellor of the democratized country and its return to the human brotherhood.

Adenauer, when still mayor, so a story went, had a cleaning lady, a long-serving faithful person, working for him at his home in Rhöndorf. She had, unfortunately, no initiative and kept interrupting his work and thoughts by repeatedly asking him what to do next. After disturbing him thus again and again, the mayor was said to have lost his patience and in his irritation told her to "go and hang her behind out of the window". After a lull of perhaps ten minutes the lady returned and again asked her deeply immersed in thought employer what to do next. Somewhat irritated he asked what she had been doing. The lady replied truthfully that she had just followed his bizarre instruction and replied that the passers-by had politely raised their hats or curtsied and respectfully said "Good morning, Mr Adenauer". The humbled mayor had to accept those kind acknowledgements of his public status.

For a while I was assistant editor of a trade magazine *Display* in London. The editor, Arthur Symes, had been with Britain's "black propaganda" and told me at length of his exploits. Some of our regular contributors were quite well known, such as Eric Lucking of the now defunct Simpson's emporium in Piccadilly or the display managers of New York's major department stores.

After the war I travelled from London to Warsaw in Poland to see printing and publishing there. Everybody educated spoke German, but did not want to. Only my (by then) British passport saved me from offending. I learnt quickly to speak only English.

The director of one printing plant in Poland, a nice man, shocked me. He had invited me to have dinner at his home. Suddenly he pointed to the gate leading to the street and said, shaking his head still in disbelief: "This is where at curfew the Nazi soldiers shot my ten-year-old daughter, who was playing – and she wasn't even Jewish". Anti-Semitic feelings ran high in Poland even then. I was too shocked even to commiserate.

My former publishers in Germany commissioned me to write and sometimes to obtain permission to reproduce paintings in some of their books or calendars. Once I had to try for a painting in ducal possession. That duke's wife had achieved some notoriety. The duke angrily replied that he had no intention to let his wife share in his reputation or wealth. They were, not yet, divorced. Later I had more pleasant experiences with Japanese publishers in handling such work. I also covered important exhibitions of paintings and architecture for several magazines.

It seems strange in a somewhat perverse way: many people like to be subjugated, like slaves. I learnt much later, that many people preferred life under the Soviet communists or the – admittedly corrupt – "freedom" under the liberated regimes of the east of Europe. Under the Nazis, life for the ordinary German and later Austrian, too, was well ordered, as long as the "superior" rule of the Nazis was accepted *per se*. It had happened under the ancient Greeks, too, I remembered from my school lessons. My parents, however, did not fit in and were rebellious – or rather – would not be pushed. They instilled independence of mind and also dislike of authority in me. I had hoped to join Cambridge University Press, but Brooke

Crutchley, the university printer, thought my future lay in design, not editing or writing. He introduced me to Herbert Spencer who also thought I was better suited to a writing career. Then Crutchley brought me to the attention of Walter Herdeg in Zurich, the publisher of *Graphis* magazine. I became the assistant editor. The magazine was published in three languages, and I pretended that I also spoke French. My wife also worked, but without permit. One day, in the wee hours of the morning, we were woken up by the local police. They had been informed of my wife's illegal employment and decided to deport her. Her employer, general director of the huge reinsurance corporation, simply telephoned the cantonal police. They made no more fuss. Hella could stay on in the country!

The joint publishers of Amstutz & Herdeg played Uriah Heap games. They often cited their partner's obstinacy when regretfully announcing a tricky decision. When I asked for a better position I was told by Herdeg that he agreed, but that his partner had felt the time was not yet ripe for such a move. I resigned.

On return to London, Gerhard Frankl offered me a job. Once again this was on the design side. I turned that down and the photographer Kurt Hutton then got me a job as assistant editor of the soon to be defunct *Picture Post*. Alas, the day I was to start my job the editor was sacked – and so was I. Nevertheless, I made some interesting contacts, among them Stefan Lorant, and was offered a job on *The Sphere*, which I did not take up.

Princess Margaret had tea sometimes at Douglas Fairbanks, Jr.'s house, neighbouring my home then. She would sit in the neighbours' garden. Around the corner in The Boltons was a new primary school and later Lady Diana Spencer, the future Princess of Wales, taught there. More important to us was our first daughter Elisabeth.

Together with Giorgio Gianoli in Italy, who was soon to become head of the Comprint planning committee, I worked for an international conference for almost forty years. It was a high-powered meeting of printers and publishers, speakers came from all over the world. Heads of state, some of the largest communications firms in the world and the chairmen of major advertising agencies spoke and addressed the delegates. Suppliers provided most of the funds, but the meetings did not allow any mention of their products (the millionaire Robert Maxwell broke the undertaking and blatantly promoted his own and his friends' interests). Giorgio and I together raised two-thirds of the budget which eventually rose to more than million dollars. To do this we travelled the Americas, Europe and the Far East. The Comprint conferences – originally an American event – brought first to Geneva in Europe mainly by my friends Reto Conzett, in Switzerland and James F. Conway from America, as well as a Swedish printer, became important gatherings and also glamorous social occasions in places like Venice and Cannes, Copenhagen and Madrid and many European capitals. I was honoured to write a *State of the Art* report to the delegates for many decades. The conferences endured into this century, but my contribution ended with my stroke just before the final meeting. The events were discontinued. Advertising had crept into the sessions. That was against policy. Only once had Maxwell succeeded in breaking the strict rule years before in Venice. He was severely reprimanded by the chairman of Haughton Miffin, the American publishers.

Maxwell was uncontrollable. In Graham Greene's *The Comedians,* Dr Magiot comments to Martha that "one Hitler is enough experience for a lifetime".

I had arrived in England with no real friends of my age, apart from Andrew Herxheimer, to talk to. I was bored – and rather penniless. Sometimes in the evening I went exploring the London streets. One evening, in elegant Bond Street, as I stood looking at a window display, a quite well-spoken fair-haired young lady asked whether she could help me. Truthfully I told her that I was not lost and knew my way to Hampstead. With hindsight I now know that she was asking me to join her for paid services. I would have been far too shy and naïve to take up her offer. Anyway, I had by then fallen in love with Hella.

Women

THEATRES IN London, so music hall tradition has it, used to have notices on display, telling "ladies should keep seated during the whole of the performance". Perhaps this was just an invention of joke shops but I still have one of these notices hanging up on the bathroom wall.

The war had delayed normal development. People of my generation also were less "liberated" than they are today. My sexual revolution started late.

Before I came to London a married colleague at work was a welcome discussion partner. Her attractive sister was a craft bookbinder and bound some books for me.

I had taken the colleague to one of Munich's art museums. Afterwards, on a fine sunny day we sat on the grass in the English Garden. Suddenly she flung her arms around me and kissed me. I was surprised, but very pleased. Soon we started going out together. I was sometimes a bit embarrassed when I called at her home to take her to the theatre. Usually her husband opened the door. He was friendly. She came to visit me at home by the park in a house described as the tallest in Osterwaldstrasse, next to the Loden-Frey building. In those days it was generally assumed that a gentleman would always pay restaurant or coffee house bills when entertaining a lady. I nowadays as an old man get quite disturbed when a lady going out with me surreptitiously manages to pay. It is usually done by pretending to go to the powder room. We went to bed and naturally I enjoyed it. Thus an affair began.

I met the daughter of a high up director of one of the largest reinsurance companies in the world. We got along fine. One day her friends "arranged" for her to spend the night at my home. We shared the same bed, but I did not intimately touch her, although we did a bit of fooling around. Later, before I left for England, her rich father took me aside and thanked me for being old fashioned. The girl married into the family of my well-known neighbour.

In London I worked for Robert Maxwell. Telephone calls were made through the office operator. I wanted a London number, then prefixed by the first three letters of the name of the exchange. I pronounced the name GULliver in a German-accented way. I used my childhood memory of reading *Gulliver's Travels*. The operator did not understand. Suddenly a multilingual long-admired young dark-haired lady, Hella Mandl, appeared and mouthed the right pronunciation at my flustered and frustrated self. Afterwards we came into much contact, even had some lunchtime red wine from the Algerian Coffee House in Soho on the office building's rooftop in the Strand. I was introduced to her most pleasant parents, refugees, who at first were a bit shocked that their daughter went out with a German. Hella explained that I came of decent background. I went to Berlin and after my return we got married. The marriage ended unexpectedly. I had sinned in mind only and Hella, perhaps confused by the after effects of a serious car accident, divorced me after nineteen years and two much loved daughters.

After Hella had left so suddenly I had started going out with a young lady in my office. She left for the United States and had a good job, but went through some difficult times. I saw her again in Washington DC and was able to lend her the money to sail back to Britain. She visited my bachelor temporary home and we went to bed together. During that first intimate encounter a friend had come to visit, knocked on the door and when we did not respond walked away quite angrily muttering aloud to himself, wanting to be heard. Julia and I had a good marriage with three loving children. Then a good friend died in Los Angeles. I decided to fly to Los Angeles and help the estranged widow Barri Clark, to clear out the home. One evening old man disease struck: we went to bed together. Julia was patient at first, but finally divorced me after about thirty years. I had tried to forestall this by getting a Dominican divorce to be in first. Julia's solicitor accused me before an examining justice of never having been to the Dominican Republic. I was too stunned to reply. Of course I had been to the country. I knew I was behaving wrongly, but felt compelled to persist in my erring way. At the same time I was deeply offended by what I considered truly a breach of trust: Julia had sought consolation by going to meetings sponsored by the Life Training cult. How could anyone close to me do that? My view is – still – that ultimately the Nazi philosophy (if one calls it that) was a cult.

The second divorce was really expensive and gradually began to affect my comfortable lifestyle and curtailed self-indulgent habits.

Separation and divorce seemed to have brought out a new side in Julia's character. She developed an interest in matters of money. Supposedly that is a female mind-set based on securing the future. I am happy to know that both my first two wives have adequate financial resources and love their late mothers.

Barri Clark and I were married. Perhaps I should have been warned: She never changed her surname to mine. I respected that in a modern lady. Then, however, I had the stroke and was flat on my back. Barri quite unexpectedly decided to divorce me in California "by default". I still do not understand the reason for this default adjudication. All papers were meticulously answered by me and I even paid Californian court fees. The divorce had to be again applied for in London. I paid. Barri explained that I was not only "too much work", but also "impossible".

I managed to have a loving long-distance relationship with a sexy and bright lady in Germany. It collapsed when misfortune befell her and she keep sending worrying messages that we had better stop the affair. In the end I gave up. Both of us worried too much.

Looking back, in all I had sexual relations with seven women in my life. Is this a record of philandering? My second wife had indeed made me truly aware of sex. She tried new ways and invented novel play. That was exciting. Today I have calmed down and agree with Sophocles. Two and a half thousand years ago the sage, according to Plato, welcomed old age, which freed him from temptation.

When Anna, my third daughter, was still at primary school she made friends with a girl surnamed Kean whose parents lived around the corner at that time. Her father enjoyed some fame as the painter of oft-reproduced pictures of thin-faced large-eyed waifs' faces. I once visited Walter Kean near San Francisco. He was pretty drunk. I had danced with his wife and he was unreasonably jealous. He called me a lush. I moved out of their place in the middle of the night. The atmosphere became unbearable and moved in with friends in town, where I arrived in the wee hours of the morning. Anna later flew to the girl's home on Vancouver Island, while her mother and I stayed on in Manhattan. She was suddenly famous for 15 minutes for being the only unaccompanied child passenger on the plane from New York crossing into Canada. Other passengers told us proud parents that she had been utterly self-composed all throughout the journey.

In the summer we often rented a house in Spain. It belonged to Gwyneth Johnston, believed to be a daughter of Augustus John, the English painter. She herself was no mean painter. A friend had a wife on the verge of divorce. She came to Spain with her children. When I arrived later from London, two smiling women told me that "I had it made". The two women had decided to share one bed with me. That was an exciting idea. We did go to bed together, but after a bit of horseplay Julia announced that she could not go through with the frolic. The other woman began to cry. I felt guilty. Later, after we all had chatted on the balcony, I made love to the other lady, after all. Later again, she made love to me – again. I was overjoyed and started an affair, which continued in England till she decided to break it off. I had discovered that sex was an adventure. I was almost fifty years old. Julia was aware of all this and seemed to suffer it patiently.

One afternoon, sipping tea and refreshments by the pool side there, the small son of my future mistress at that time had crawled to the edge of the small pool of the house in Spain, unnoticed, and fallen in. He sank to the bottom and did not move. I jumped in, fully clothed, and brought the small body up, laid it on the ground, and then revived the tiny body. It was a dramatic, but largely glossed over, occurrence. All of us were embarrassed by our inattention to the children.

At one time, when I tried to get my then mistress a job, she rewarded me by making love in a copse near the road. It was enjoyable, but to her sorrow she found that she had been lying on nettles, poor thing, and itched for hours. In the evening we went to a party at the nearby castle. Guests were amazed that she unconcernedly hitched up her skirt to scratch herself in public.

The young lady had a friend who at that time thought I looked "dishy". Then I was young and easily flattered. I still, as always, defer to my brother Jürgen and commented modestly that he is more handsome. I still do so today.

I am not made for solitude. I crave companionship and the comfort of friends and women to be loved. I am a loner, though, but gregarious and longing forever for company. The prospect of endless loneliness fills me with trepidation.

My first (Austrian-born) wife was very bright and had a good honours degree from Oxford University. She was and still is also very beautiful and elegant. The marriage ended probably because I fantasized about Catherine Arthur, a journalist and nice Canadian lady, who is dead now. She was not much interested in men. One day I had gone shopping with the two daughters. When I returned home, thinking contentedly that this was the place in which I would end my life I found a note pinned to the hawthorn tree by the front garden gate telling me that Hella had left for an undisclosed place. I eventually heard from her brother and letters that she wanted a separation. I did not and felt innocent, but I was soon divorced and given custody of our two daughters. I had briefed my barrister and given him Law reports which mentioned a case from the 1930s. A father had got custody of his daughters which was unheard of at that time. I was also lucky. The judge himself who heard the case at the Law courts in the Strand had got his divorce just before this case came to court. Reporters attending ostentatiously clapped their notebooks shut and the case was not reported. They, too, were working journalists and felt sympathy for my plight. Much later Hella apparently told our daughters that she regretted the divorce. I have to emphasize that this may be just hearsay.

After thirty years together Julia, my second wife, decided that she wanted a separation after I became besotted by Barri Clark whom I had tried to help, quite innocently at first, after my friend Paul, her divorced husband, suddenly died. Suddenly I thought that salvation and love were by remarrying in America. That left the obvious fault with me. My impetuous decision was greatly influenced by Julia having turned away from me and spiritually been influenced by a cult. There, they had apparently told her that she had never really loved me. Nevertheless, our union had brought forth three children!

Barri married me; perhaps she liked me genuinely at the time. She then saw many places in Europe. We were together and seemed to be a lovely couple, very much in love. She met and was liked by my children and relations and friends. In turn, her family seemed to like me, though her daughter, then still single, may have been doubtful and bemoaned her mother's remarriage.

I encouraged and liked to encourage Barri's wish to paint, draw and study. Through her even more and earlier through Hella and her family I learnt to appreciate classical music. I had since adulthood liked Mahler and Bruckner (though the latter suffered in my mind because his compositions were listened to by Adolf Hitler). I came to listen, and like, Shostakovich, Bach and others. Barri, in turn, seemed to like my jazz records, the piano music of Lecuona and the singing in the American "belting voice" style of Louis Prima. We danced wildly – naked even. I was dotty about Barri, who had real "oomph".

We often drove for a snack and wine to nearby

Venice on Muscle Beach to watch the stunning sunset over the Pacific while sitting in the bar owned by a Swiss citizen. I could have animated discussions with him in my fractured Swiss-German, interspersed with High German.

Barri could discuss any subject and shared a dislike of George W. Bush, the American President at that time, and all around him. Their bellicose statements about Iraq and Saddam Hussein were disliked. They seemed to believe in Wolfgang Koeppen's dictum that Death is Power. Countries seemingly were freed from some horrible dictator only when they had oil and offered opportunities to the President and his cronies. Why bother about Kim in Korea or the Congo in Africa? There is nothing there to attract money for any get-rich society. Send money to those staunch allies like Pakistan, who supplied some of the inmates of Guantànamo, or oil-rich Saudi Arabia and, in the good old days, Indonesia, where they killed two hundred thousand communists just on behalf of the free world. Democracy at work – again and again!

After my stroke I arranged at considerable cost to have Barri's things shipped to America. Packing them was painful and clumsily done. Some of my belongings also were to be shipped back to England from California. There was no space in London. I could not contemplate losing these things or just leaving them in California. They would have to be distributed among my children. It was an expensive business.

I made one last, but doomed effort to save my third marriage at a very late stage. My departed wife had already filed for dissolution of marriage. I wrote to her, telling her I still loved her, and that she should come back to me. Forgiveness for my perhaps eccentric behaviour was begged! It all proved hopeless. Barri's sudden departure and petition for dissolution of the marriage deeply upset me. It upset the rehabilitation from the stroke earlier that year. Prior to that frightening event she had lovingly been caring. Only recently she had assured me verbally, and in letters and faxes after her departure, of her undying love. I loved her, and never before had imagined such an abrupt end to loving aspirations. Only recently she had made love to me. She had written warm letters from America for several weeks after her return there, while I was splendidly recuperating in Spain and with my one of my daughters afterwards in London.

At first Barri wrote she would return later than planned. Then she told me she would decide to come back to me later than I hoped. Then she implied she was not returning at all. Abruptly, without consulting me, she petitioned for dissolution of the marriage. It involved much paperwork and huge unnecessary – as I thought – costs. I flew to California, accompanied by the son then living in Mexico, to collect my books and pictures. Some things were left in Los Angeles, including a good picture I had given Barri as a present before our marriage. Willem did the packing. I could not face the estranged wife alone, but wanted to be civilized, even invited her to dinner, which she declined firmly.

For some years I was not on civilised terms with Julia, but in the first instance and mainly for the sake of the children, softened my attitudes and resumed contact with Julia. So we are on quite good terms again. "Woman is a mysterious, but necessary creature", Ilya Ehrenburg had written.

While men seem important to most women of today, they will probably become almost mere replaceable playthings in future centuries once medical science discovers Immaculate Conception and they can realize true independence. Robert Graves told the legend of the early days of humanity when men were known to be needed for conception. Easily lured by the women of a Balearic Island and ignorant of their impending doom, after serving their biological task they were hurtled to death from the cliffs.

At the present time I still puzzle about women and try to guess where they came from. I am certain that they were extra-terrestrial creatures. Over a hundred years ago Gustave Courbet painted the *Origin of the World.* That painting in the Budapest Museum of Fine Arts still does not explain the mystery of life.

The smell of money corrupts. Women are often

thought of as more rapacious than men. It makes both sexes act erratic. True enough, I am poorer these days than before through my own fault or through misguided generosity.

Some men tell me that they have slept with a hundred or more women in their life. I just listen and do not comment. My life achievement is only seven women – fewer than one for every ten years of youth and mature age, I was married three times and the first two marriages (having children) lasted almost twenty and even thirty years. Only the third marriage did not stand the test of time. Perhaps I will one day come to understand her real feelings.

In a general way women, extraterrestrial creatures perhaps or not, are just nice – whether they want to please or are pleasing themselves. You only have to sit in a restaurant or any lounge; there will be women of all ages and shapes or looks. They all have their attractions, even to the most jaded man – excepting some curious creatures like Zsa Zsa Gabor and her ilk.

I like money and am all too conscious of it. Because I value books and pictures highly I bought my own property back in one divorce settlement. Twice, as mentioned elsewhere, I inherited fairly substantial sums of money. In one case, a 'blood relative' claimed and got the inheritance and I received just a pittance instead of the bequeathed sum. On another occasion when a 'nominal aunt' had died, blood relatives, who had hardly ever cared about her, claimed the money deposited in my name and got most of it.

That reminds me that I have been with the same high street bank for many decades. The service has declined over the years. Then came call centres. I once had asked the lady where she came from. Unaware that India was involved, I asked whether perhaps she was Welsh, judging by her accent. Then I found that an Indian town was her home. Eventually the bank's service got really bad. I set the manager of my branch a cartoon of two humans in hell, with the fire under their boiling cauldron being stoked by two devils. The foreman devil was saying to the novice assistant: "we do not call the damned any more. We call them customers". The branch manager lacked humour or irony he suggested seriously that I should change my bank. After writing to head office a reply came, stating that my custom was valued and I should take no notice of the odd suggestion.

Catherine Deneuve, the French actress, had said it all: "When it comes to falling love, experience does not help you in any way". The main women in my life (three wives and three mistresses) were all very nice, though some had their faults, which did not diminish their appeal to me. Two of them gave me wonderful children. I am very lucky and also proud of them and the ever growing number of lovely grandchildren.

I was introduced to what I took to be adult life,

but after a one-night stand was too embarrassed to continue. Then a young woman and I indulged in fairly heavy petting. Out of respect I felt we should not sleep together, though she was willing. Later and married by then I had a fruitless fancy for a young lady.

I still puzzle about women and try to guess where they came from. I am almost certain that they originally were creatures from outer space or descendants from aliens.

From time to time come dire predictions about the disappearance and irrelevance of the male sex, due to happen within the next one hundred and twenty-five thousand years. Women naturally want children, although they also like the act of procreation, perhaps they want to create life without the crude help and dependence on men. Now cloning has brought this longing forward and there is again talk of a world without men. Not only lesbian couples want to adopt children. Most offspring are wanted and there is little doubt that science is well on the way to make this wish come true. Men will be welcome as companions and a source of pleasure and contentment. I foresee that they will just become enjoyable, though superfluous playthings. In my view time will be found in daily life for women to expand their creativity and not be burdened with having to care for their offspring as their main task.

Just Desserts

JULIA, MY second wife, had been introduced to Life Training – a cult-like organisation – by a close friend of ours, a divorced mother of very handsome children. We had frequently helped the mother in her complicated life. I was truly upset. How could anyone so closely associated embrace the false teachings of a cult? The Nazi philosophy was also a cult, a murderous one. I deeply resented that *schlepping* which ruined a mostly stable marriage.

The head of the British branch of that cult movement seriously offended me when he implied that his father came from Vienna, mine from Berlin, and that we had so much in common! The two cities are very different in atmosphere and character. That signalled to me that my marriage had indeed become a hopeless cause. To be fair, Julia seemed to have used the cult only to break away from me.

As the *Observer* newspaper wrote: "Life Training is just one of several 'therapy cults' that have emerged in America and Europe in the past twenty years. Many stem from EST (Erhard Seminar Training), founded in California in 1971. Life Training uses intense weekend courses of anger-provoking humiliation, sleep deprivation (sixteen hour days) and mass hysteria to break down the inhibitions and fears that prevent people from achieving success. Though course participants are encouraged not to mix socially with the unenlightened, except for recruiting, Life Training (as with all EST spin-offs) considers career and material success to be central to self-realisation. Those who subscribe to Life Training, but cannot afford the price of additional courses, can offset the cost by working for the organisation. Jobs include escorting participants to the toilet, since no one is allowed to spend time alone. Members are encouraged to donate funds.

The *Observer* neatly summed it all up: "reason to join: You'll feel terrific. Reason not to join: You'll feel sick. Bottom line: Nietzsche for salesmen".

This was not funny. I was devastated. Life Training seemed to prey on peoples' disaffection and unhappiness. I knew of at least two others couples whose split was prompted by the cult's gurus.

I did not want a divorce from Barri. I, however, felt powerless to fight this one. Sadly I lost my new West Coast friends. At least, I thought they were friends. They decided, however, to ignore me, unlike most friends on the East Coast. I left most of the furniture and some records and books with Barri. Time and the US Office of Homeland Security granting a visa will tell. Ordinary Britons no longer need visas. I had been a resident alien and am being treated strangely. Regretfully not all my East Coast and Chicago-area friends are still fit enough to travel to places like Canada or Mexico where I am free to travel.

In the pub next door to my previous home my third wife and I met an Arab, a poet and writer, who had a very depressed and, it seemed, somewhat abused girlfriend of Arab North African origin. About a year after my stroke and about the time my unwanted divorce came up, he turned up in The Clifton hotel, probably drunk, and told my astonished unbelieving, but rather depressed self while I was with a visiting friend that Barri had offered herself to him and told him that I was "no longer a man". He insisted on the latter statement. His girlfriend left the table and did not want to be involved in the conversation. I remained unbelieving and remained polite, but the incident left a nagging doubt. Had she really said that? It seemed out of character. Still, the seeds of uncertainty and self-doubt had been sown, even if they stemmed from the drunken ramblings of an intoxicated man. One thing, however, was certain: I had not failed. Our sex life may have strayed from the conventional, but it had been fully lived. Why bother then? But bother I did and told all around me about the incident, worried and disbelieving. I later wrote enquiringly to Barri, but had, of course, no proper reply. That was a case of "ask a silly question, (do not) get a silly reply".

This Arab had some get-rich-quick scams going. At one time he had even tried to rope me in. He praised a quack or patent medicine, a herbal mixture to restore erectile dysfunction, a sort of natural substitute for Viagra and similar and also overpriced products sometimes openly advertised in such publications as *The Oldie* and respectable weeklies sold to the elderly and gullible. He had the charm and confidence of the conman lurking in almost everybody, even and especially so in saints and holy hermits, preachers of religious promises and mirages and so well represented by the captains of industry on whom honours were heaped and who were advising the governments and sitting on quangos, basking in wealth and being much envied. Well, I, too, would not have refused getting rich and recognized, quite liking the idea of really being the conman I sometimes seemed to act. My wish was to stay honest.

I had arranged for life policy benefits for Barri. It needed hefty fees to lawyers to get those well-meant and loving acts revoked to the insurance company's satisfaction.

The worst aspect of the abandonment by Barri was the damage to my vanity, my self-esteem. I was low, but I would cope, as I have always done. Somewhat ridiculously, I queried her ability to cope. Experience should have taught me. Julia had coped admirably and so did Hella. These two were also the mothers of my children. Would any or all three ever miss me?

I sometimes more than suspect that to Barri her ongoing education meant more than her marriage. This may be part of her self-realization and awareness, even unwitting immaturity.

Some of my past life is lost, it seems forever. Some people have turned away from me. Divorce does that to people. Sure enough, I foolishly believe I harmed nobody but my former wives and not those I considered mutual friends. Nevertheless, some have turned away from me and no longer acknowledge my very existence, try as I may. There are also others who have become real friends and support me in my loneliness. They made me come out of myself and go back into society. I appreciate that and have learnt to value such friendships. Saddening is the loss of some friends – mainly in California. They seemed so genuine in their affection and involvement.

Every cloud is followed by sunshine: I am aware and marvel at the sights around me. Children and people smile. Women wear flimsy clothes and short skirts in warm weather, even in some of the more elegant parts of town. They disport themselves with pride and strut their stuff. They take their brood with them and appreciate my smile with pride. Life is Wonderful! They even made a film by that title, rightly so. Music fills the hearts of people, classical music and pop (which I rarely appreciate) though I like good jazz and some singers. This means something to people, all different and beautifully varied.

When Barri was still with me after my stroke and after I was released myself from hospital, the local council sent a companion around to give her a free afternoon once a week. I wanted someone bright and interesting and along came Suzy Slade. She stayed for more than a year after Barri had left and my youngest son became the official part-time carer. Sadly, the local council decided that I no longer deserved Suzy. However, I remained in contact with her. She was related to Sir William Slade, who had founded the Slade School of Art. She was an attractive person with a lively mind. Her successor was Robert Tyerman, with whom I enjoy long discussions ranging over a wide range of topics dealing mostly with our experiences as journalists. Sometimes we would talk about politics and express opposite views while enjoying red wine.

Elizabeth Harvey-Lee sent me a catalogue of original prints. I could no longer really afford to buy such things, but saw a depiction of an engraving of an actual Slade School by the English artist Graham Page of the building where he had studied. I bought the print, had it framed and gave it to Suzy, who was herself a painter in her spare time.

When Julia had decided to separate I was stunned and ran out into the street in desperation and screamed out aloud. London is a big city and people looked away. Then the neighbours took me in, really listened and gave me a big glass of brandy, my first in perhaps fifteen years, for I had given up spirits some ten years before in a bet with Julia to make her stop serving skimmed milk. Julia almost instantly broke her side of the bet. I still stick to it.

The brandy worked. I calmed down and was again able to live among other human people. I was upset, though, unsure of my footing and had to go to the Western Eye Hospital after damaging my cornea in a fall at home. I did not want to go to the eye hospital, but the wife of an Indian newsagent insisted I see a doctor. I went, life went on.

In his message to readers of the German edition of *Kaputt,* the Italian author Curzio Malaparte (the pseudonym of Kurt Erich Suckert), once a dedicated follower of Benito Mussolini and his Blackshirt fascists wrote that a people living under the brutal force of modern and total dictatorship cannot rise up in revolt. Abject slavery controls body, morals and mind. One has only to consider those people, now in the "free world", who have developed some hankering after the oppression of the regimes of the former German Democratic Republic or even the Soviet Union, where their lives had been ordered and controlled.

Today the world is witnessing this same phenomenon in Iraq. There the dictatorship defeated by the West's desire to bring the so-called "benefits of democracy" to the Middle East had abysmally failed. Under the former dictator some three hundred thousand of his Kurdish population were killed. Under the western liberators some six hundred and fifty thousand or more Iraqi civilians, many of them women, children and old people, lost their lives during the first few years of "freedom", thus cruelly experiencing the benefits of democracy.

Saddam Hussein was an evil man, though below the level with other infamous evil men or monsters. The extensive photographic coverage of his sordid vengeful death by hanging on the orders of the Iraqi puppet regime was an uncivilized and shameful act. Britain condoned (and sanctimoniously also condemned) this. The country had abolished the death penalty. Public executions stopped in 1868. Was this gory display the new meaning of bringing democracy to the Middle East? I feel that if the treatment of Saddam yardstick of justice would become universally adopted, some of the free world's leaders would qualify for equally uncivilized treatment.

Like Cassandra of the ancient Greeks, writers often have to carry the burden of seeing the future. Thus H.L. Mencken wrote in the *Baltimore Sun* already in July 1920 that "as democracy is perfected, the office of the president represents more and more closely the inner soul of the people. On some great and glorious day the plain folks of this land will reach their hearts' desire at last and the White House will be adorned by an outright moron". Socrates said over two thousand years ago (to paraphrase the sage) that whoever is too clever to enter politics will be punished by those more foolish than himself.

In Malaparte's *The Skin* it is stated that "The distinction of being the first among all the peoples of Europe to be liberated had fallen to the people of Sicily and then Naples; and in celebration of the winning of so well-deserved a prize my poor beloved Neapolitans, after three years of hunger, epidemics and savage air attacks, had accepted gracefully and patriotically the longed-for and coveted honour of playing the part of a conquered people, of singing, clapping, jumping for joy amid the ruins of their houses, unfurling foreign flags which until the day before had been the emblems of their foes, and throwing flowers from their windows on to the heads of the conquerors."

It had been quite some struggle to find the way back into publishing. I got a job with a trade paper publisher. The directors of the innocuous magazines leant to something cultish known as the Oxford Movement for Moral Rearmament, which even after the war had millions of followers (some British nobility and former ministers) founded before the Second World War with headquarters in Switzerland by Frank Buchman, an American preacher. He had acquired notoriety for his statement which declared “Thank heaven for a man like Adolf Hitler.” Buchman was a friend before the war of Heinrich Himmler and stayed in Germany as his guest. The people I worked for seemed harmless, but Buchman’s antics made me suspicious of all cults.

My former publishers in Munich had once published the work of Heinrich Hoffmann, Adolf Hitler’s photographer. They were now run by a staunch anti-Nazi when they regained a publishing license from the American authorities. I worked there and started designing books.

Dream Job

STARTING TO work in England, my production manager was jealous. I had language skills and earned a good salary for that time. Payment was by urgently needed cheque. I moved my account from the posh bank in Fleet Street which had a uniformed doorman who took my modest cheque to a cashier and spared me from what I perceived to be the sneers which greeted my relatively small salary cheques.

My boss Robert Maxwell had actually been thrown out of his office. On arrival one morning he found his desk removed to the landing. Pinned to it was an envelope containing a handsome amount of cash and a note which everybody could read. It told him that the police would be called if he set foot again in the building. Maxwell then asked me to join him at a high salary. I declined and unwisely resigned. I had no patience with the crook and would not wait to be fired. At the time I had no suspicion that Butterworth-Springer were financed by a government agency.

I was then offered a dream job as assistant editor of *Picture Post* magazine. That was the time when the editor, Frank Dowding, decided, rightly, to print a front cover showing a grinning British *tommy* (soldier) with two buckets containing the decapitated heads of "communist" Malay insurgents. The owner of the magazine was outraged. He sacked Dowding, the man who had interviewed and offered me the job, and later closed the weekly down. For me that spelled disaster. On the day I was to start that new work I climbed up to the offices of the publication in Shoe Lane in London, only to be met by Dowding descending the steps and telling me not to bother to go up any further. There was no longer a job for him or me.

I applied for a position with the BBC (British Broadcasting Corporation) in the German Department at Reading. The job interview went well. On the panel sat Harold Nicholson, who over tea asked why I had deserted from the Nazi navy. He asked me whether I had shot at former comrades. In reply I stated that I had not fired a single shot and would desert again if faced with criminal orders. The job offering was abruptly withdrawn because of implied disloyalty.

Almost the same happened many years later. I was interviewed for a quite important job with Shell International. I again was offered the job. After the formal interview was over the British and Dutch directors chatted to me. We had, I seem to recall, some wine. In the course of a friendly talk I was asked the fatal question – and again I said that I would do the same, over and over again. Result: no job. I had never really wanted it anyway.

One of my first editors in Britain, John Reeve Fowkes, liked to recount his years spent before the war on Majorca. When Britain sent a warship to the island to evacuate foreigners stranded there by the civil war, young John, sun-tanned and black-haired like a local child, was asked by a British rating "Donde es la plaza major" in halting Spanish. To the sailor's amazement he replied in fluent English and led him to the right place. The ship later took him and his mother off the island.

First they were to be landed in Mussolini's Italy, even endangered Jews, "degenerate" artists and writers. Remonstrations made the authorities in London relent. Marseilles in nearby France was to be first port of call.

My mother saw me go to war without my firing a shot in earnest. Anyway, I could not do so. She had brought us up as haters of wars and guns. She did not know the fate of my brother Jürgen, nor me, for some years. Jürgen ended up as a stable boy in Spain and I as a prisoner-of-war in France. Later I was accepted as a volunteer of sorts in the fight against the Nazis and their remaining allies. How can we ever thank our parents fully? Just think for a minute of a mother giving her children away, not because it was inconvenient to have us around, but because she knew that we deserved a better way of growing up. I say "Thank you, Mama and Papa! We are proud of you! We hope we repaid your love and trust."

My Austrian uncle Fritz Wolf had been a student when the Nazis marched into Austria with the *Anschluss*. He was put into a concentration camp. When the war started he had been "freed" and was press-ganged into a so-called punishment battalion and sent with an advance group into suspected minefields. He survived and was captured on the Russian front and soon released as an "ally".

Mama lived after the Second World War in the American Zone of Berlin. Robert Maxwell controlled the media in the British Zone of Berlin. There he began his nefarious career as publishing controller and persuaded the decent Julius Springer to go into an ill-fated partnership: Lange, Maxwell & Springer operated in London. Maxwell acquired Springer's science authors. Many British printers and academic booksellers lost money heavily because of Maxwell's nefarious dealings. One of those cheated was John H. Jarrold, for whose printing company Jarrold & Sons, I later worked. His son Peter was good enough to say a few kind words at a lunch held for me some years back by press colleagues in London.

Working later for Jarrold's, the printers (whose former publishing branch had published one of Papa's books in translation), the work took me to America. I met Bob Guccione, who started *Penthouse*, and obtained the print contract for the European edition, but John refused to contemplate such a magazine. We had good contacts with Harry C. Abrams, and printed best-sellers like Winston Churchill's *History of the English Speaking People* or *The Bible in Pictures*. I was with him when he had secured an option to print the title. That was at the Frankfurt Book Fair. At the time Jarrold had bought one of the largest sheet-fed multicolour offset machines, a Harris. Only Mondadori in Italy had something like it. I liked working for Jarrold's. Only the train journeys early in the day, several times a week, away from the family, made me leave.

My first wife Hella's father, Arthur Mandl, was privately nominated by Paul Rosbaud as a distinguished member of the *Alter Judenadel* (from the rank of extraordinary "noble" Jewish people). He came out of internment on the Isle of Man and Lord Beaverbrook himself congratulated him for his achievements in radar. He was an electrical engineering genius, had designed a traction system for the French railways and such innovations as non-flickering light tubes for the London underground – but in the opinion of Hedwig (his wife) was unable to mend even a humble smoothing iron or a blown fuse. I sympathized with him. When my mother needed a light bulb replacing she would phone up my brother Jürgen in Madrid, but never me! I am still clueless today about things electrical and rather scared of them.

Eva Herman, my first wife's late sister, late in her life converted to Christianity – it was claimed so that she could meet her harbour master son Thomas' wife in heaven.

After arrival England I discovered dancing, became almost obsessed with it and went to the parties given at Harry Brandt's home in Prince Albert Road facing London Zoo and Regent's Park. A few years later I mistakenly thought him a relative of Bill Brandt, the photographer who knew my mother and together with Kurt Hutton got me the dream job with *Picture Post* (which never materialised).

Ella Fitzgerald and Louis Armstrong were in Frankfurt in Germany to entertain the American troops stationed there. My uncle Werner Jaspert was then head of the radio station in Hesse and invited the two to come on to his programme. After broadcasting their jazz music they went to his house at Oberusel and played for him and his wife. I have always regretted that he did not record the unique session.

Werner Jaspert was the first post-war mayor of the town of Oberusel near Frankfurt-am-Main (he resigned as he did not approve of the American detention methods of people like the Nazi criminal Hermann Goering held captive in the valley below his house).

At the Arts & Crafts College of Zurich, I developed

my interest in printing and Johannes Gutenberg's invention of movable type in the spread of knowledge. I had already begun as a teenager in Berlin when I did some work in an antiquarian bookshop and continued in print worked and at publishers in Germany and Switzerland. Returning to England I enrolled in a Linotype typesetting course in London. I qualified and sought a job as a compositor. The trade union, however, would not accept me. No proper apprenticeship had been served. So I eventually had to go into printing management. First I became a clerk in an importer and exporters of printing equipment in the City of London. The owners were engineers – Edward Ruff, a Swiss and an Austrian. The Swiss had been with Rolls-Royce during the war. The bosses had some rather shady dealings with Eastern Europe. My new career as a trade journalist started because I wrote a somewhat outraged story about them for a printing weekly. I started on *Print in Britain* and then *Litho Printer* (now *PrintWeek*). At the same time I had a full-time job with Blandford Press. They became my publishers, too. One of their prestige books was the *Encyclopaedia of Type Faces*, planned by W. Turner Berry of the Printing Library at the St Bride Institute. The other editor was A.F. Johnson, Keeper of Books at the British Museum. I was asked to produce the book and felt that material from overseas was missing. The authors were pleased to accept very substantial additions. Eventually they wrote all royalties over to me and had my name put on the volume as co-author. The book, first published in the 1950s, still sells in new editions and has already been reprinted seven times. I derive a modest income from the sales. I spend it on holidays with children abroad. The publishers have lately been merged into a publisher of illustrated books only.

In London and married, Hella and I had a small place rented furnished from a minor poet (quite frequently published) who astonished us by often telling us that: "one day his ship would come home", meaning one day his mother would die. He showed off because in his sitting room was a rather uncomfortable upholstered bench, presumably intended as a sofa. Francis Bacon, the painter, was said to occasionally sleep there. We were not very impressed.

My first wife and I moved to a rather posh neighbourhood between London's South Kensington and Chelsea. In our street was a dairy depot. Milk floats were still drawn by horses. At night they would be led up a ramp and in the early mornings horses would look down from first floor windows. Horses also looked at you from upstairs at the Kensington Barracks. We used to stare at them when we went to rotten row and a stroll in the park. The future Princess Diana worked at the nearby primary school.

Walter Trier did many of the covers for the by then defunct *Lilliput* sister publication of *Picture Post* and had, while still in Berlin, done the covers and illustrations for two of my childhood favourite books: *The 35th of May* and *Emil & the Detectives*.

Going to school in different countries exposed me to different teaching, especially in biology and history. At the extreme were the Nazi teachings of racial inheritance and biased history. Even the latter subject, however, was tinged with pitfalls. Biology and history teaching differed from twisted Nazi doctrines. I took matriculation in Berlin and obtained poor marks in these subjects.

Erich Kästner was writing quite madcap views into his books. That was alright with me. I just knew that he gave his fantasy full reign when he thought up the fiction that the equator was a flat ribbon of steel, cleaned incessantly by the diamond washerwoman Lehmann and traversed by Negro Caballo, the roller-skating circus horse. I had crossed the equator as a small child and knew that it is simply an imaginary line circling the earth. Reading the book made me doubtful of my acquired knowledge. The book's style made me feel insecure.

Kästner was an interesting writer moreover a visionary. He wrote that in his travel around the world Konrad, the hero of *The 35th of May*, was surprised to see in the Chicago of the 1930s the use of a mobile phone. Today mobile telephones are commonplace and a boring, irritating nuisance in public.

I was anxious to shed my German nationality roots. I still feel ashamed for the country's atrocities under the Nazis. For some years I avoided speaking German, my mother tongue. When explaining my ethnic background I embellish that with allusions to Belgium, Russia and South Africa. I felt flattered when somebody commented that I had an Irish lilt to my speech. When the first daughter Elisabeth was about to be born. I wanted her to be true-born English and applied for naturalization. This came shortly after her birth. No matter, she was British-born anyway. Before my papers came through the Special Branch police came to check me out. We offered them a cup of tea and had an amiable chat, while they quite admired the library.

World Traveller

DURING THE Hungarian Revolution of 1956 I was in Budapest, still with the smattering of Hungarian learnt at school, I arranged to get a train leaving for Vienna. I rushed to my hotel and told the stranded foreigners there about this means of escape from the bloody uprising. We gathered our belongings and ran, like a detachment of recruits on a forced march to the station up the road. Indeed, there was the train and we bought tickets first-class and were able to board the train to the West.

En route to Austria we saw many Soviet tanks going to the border. I took good note of this and in Vienna I phoned the military attachés at the British and American embassies. The British Embassy was not at all interested, but at the American Legation they listened attentively.

Scandinavia's newspapers were ahead in pioneering new printing technology in Europe. It was time to report on this. In the late 1950s I was visiting the newsroom of the Swedish daily *Dagens Nyheter* while in Stockholm to ponder an offer from the Swedish publisher Albert Bonnier, Jr. to work for him in the Americas. There were television screens installed and suddenly the journalists went quiet and awe-struck. The Soviets had launched Sputnik – the "fellow traveller" satellite – and the Americans were beaten in that space race by Yuri Gagarin. Their response spacecraft crashed ignominiously while millions watched on TV. Communism seemed to lead. A by-product of my visit was the offer to join the Bonnier Group, but was not taken up.

The war was over by then. In London my primary school friend from the Berlin days and I decided to have a grand night out at the Royal Festival Hall. He was then a junior medical doctor. Today he is internationally famous. Our ages are almost the same. So that night we first had a – for us then – a rather sumptuous meal in the concert hall's restaurant, accompanied by a wine we thought would be something special. It turned out to be that indeed. We each had a glass and quite liked that. The sommelier poured more wine into the rather small glasses and what appeared to be the decomposed body of a dead mouse plonked out. The wine was hastily withdrawn and another bottle of a similar wine substituted. We enjoyed the extra drink and the meal. When it came to paying the bill, we were astonished to find that we were being charged for one and a half bottles of wine. That was, the waiter explained, because we had indeed drunk that much wine. We remonstrated, but our protests were unrewarded. So we paid up and went to the concert.

We had our revenge, though. My friend knew the medical officer of health for that part of London. The restaurant was duly inspected for hygiene and ordered to be closed down for four weeks. At the end of that period we returned there for a modest dinner. We chatted up the head waiter who told us of the sad loss of income over the last few weeks. My friend then asked him whether he remembered us. "No" was the reply. So my friend reminded him of that dead mouse in our wine, just mentioning that he was a doctor and had alerted the medical officer of health after that incident. We had, I seem to recall, that rather cheaper meal "on the house".

After the earlier incident we attended the concert, conducted by a famous German maestro who was somewhat arrogant, autocratic and though outstanding, somewhat cold and dictatorial in the Nazi style. Herbert von Karajan was known for his liking for spectacularly stunning young ladies. We had good seats in the auditorium. Irritation came from a fair-haired lady in the row in front of us. During the performance she would from time to time rise from her seat and clap her hands, shouting "Bravo" whenever the music had been quite dramatic. The conductor acknowledged the disturbing applause with a deep bow and smiling, looking at that annoying lady. She was, we gathered, his wife. She was indeed, as the wagging tongues indicated, more than good-looking. She was fairly glamorous in a show-off sort of way. She wore a strapless gown. Her shoulders were bare. A wraparound shawl lay on her knees. Whenever she stood up to applaud – and annoy the audience – she had to first move the big item of warming cloth out of the way.

When the interval came, my junior doctor friend said in a very audible whisper in German, (which both of us speaks): "that lady should have the large pimple on her shoulder urgently seen to". As the lady went to meet her husband we followed for a few paces. She seemed worried and had placed her shawl firmly over her bare unblemished white shoulders.

During the second half of the performance she no longer felt it necessary to ostentatiously applaud.

A maternal cousin departed from his parents' home in Madrid and reached New York. There Klaus Anger was severely beaten up by people who mistook him for a German Nazi. He was hospitalized for the better part of a year and never fully recovered. Today, after living with post-war Germany and Franco's Spain, he looks back on a life for many years in Brazil (for six month with Amazonian Indians (*National Geographic* did his story) and later as a photographer for the Vatican.

Some airlines awarded me Gold Cards with

access to their airport lounges all over the world. A large British airline would not admit children to these lounges. Had the principals of those companies not also once been children? They did not even heed Queen Victoria's admonition that "children should be seen, but not heard". My second wife and friends had a brainwave. They started the "We Welcome Small Children" campaign, approved by the local council, and published the names and locations of child-friendly places. Some restaurants were awarded plaques for their welcoming facilities. A major daily paper supported the idea.

Some highlights, travelling with the family, before the boredom of bothersome security checks, were the scenic train rides on the *Glacier Express* in Switzerland and the travel between the country and Italy via the Gotthard route, passing the same church again and again, while sitting in the dining car, drinking coffee, sometimes a glass of wine or eating. The *Blue Train* in France had a fashion boutique and my wife Julia had her hair done on the journey. After dinner on the *Talgo* from snowy Geneva to Barcelona one woke up on the sunny Costa Brava. Spectacular train rides in Mexico were through the Copper Canyon or to the Grand Canyon in the States. The trip down California's coastline went part right by the sea. Impressive were the autumn colours of the forests of the American North East and to Canada. Travelling by bus through

Corrientes in Argentina and on foot to Igazu and the great falls to Brazil was a wild experience. On the other side of the world a small seaplane flew from the southernmost tip of New Zealand to the small Stewart Island and its lush vegetation. I spent a weekend on a farm relaxing on the West coast of Japan, remote and separated by mountains from the temples of Kyoto. I learnt about chicken sexing, and the way the thousands of birds were kept made me stop eating chicken.

In the 1960s I published a series of profiles of the innovators who changed the face of printing at the time. Europe, America and Japan were covered. Among these people were John F. Crosfield in England and Dr Rudolf Hell from Germany. In the Second World War they were on opposite sides, but thought alike. The ingenious and threatening sea mines thought of by the German, who was the father of the teletype and later of a picture scanning system, were quickly immobilized by the British genius who disliked discussing his wartime exploits – no doubt obeying the notorious Official Secrets Act.

The journalists' union had organized a trip from London. The flight was long and boring on a propeller-driven contraption. As at the last moment I could not travel. The first daughter went with her mother, who rightly complained about the boredom of the journey. Soon after I then travelled to Manhattan with Roy Brewer. We were strolling through Central Park, where a friend had a marvellous balcony flat near the Essex House hotel. We were startled to see a man being coshed violently by the police. Roy remonstrated and told them that he was a British officer, etcetera. He never was. They turned round and told him to watch out or to face deportation!

Better luck came soon afterwards in Colombia. Beatrice was with me and we were warned about armed kidnappers. I worked in Cali for a few days whilst she basked in the sun, in a heavily bodyguarded affluent home of the Carvajal family, and then we had a few days' break on a small island in the Pacific frequented by young surfers from America. Beatrice was only twelve years old. A young American took a particular liking to her. That was lucky. It was carnival time and in the nearby town of Tumaco everything was shut. The airline bookings made in London were worthless. The young man's father was captain of a commercial shrimp boat and invited us to dinner and managed to arrange a new flight for later. We were invited for dinner on board ship and informed that we could eat shellfish by all means, but he would eat *Spam*. When we finally arrived at the airport, staff were still in a carnival mood. They poured a bucket of water over us in an exuberant display of "fun". Clothes were soaking and only slowly dried on the flight to New York via Miami and home.

Anna once flew to New York and Chicago with me

and was much impressed with the harpist performing in the tea room of the Drake Hotel in Chicago who talked to her caringly. Later, on a visit to Manila, she (being reddish blonde) was much admired by the locals while her parents sipped cocktails served on floating trays in the Manila Hotel's swimming pool. She accompanied us on other trips to Hong Kong or Delhi and Mumbai (as it is now called). One day in Rome – Anna was by then a rather stunning-looking teenager – we stayed in a small hotel overlooking the famed Fontana di Trevi. While we sat sipping white wine on the rooftop Anna was by the fountain, hemmed in by an admiring cluster of young soldiers on leave. In vain we tried to attract her attention to free herself from that crowd. In the end we had to leave our rooftop piano bar and go down to release her from the admiring military force and have a cosy dinner in a trattoria up the road.

I flew to Boston. Willem, my eldest son, came along. The hotel had lost the reservation. Instead we were put up in the suite once occupied by Charles Dickens. There was the desk he had used whilst writing in America. Willem wrote a letter home from there. Later we travelled to Key West and at first stayed in an older "Hemingway-type" hotel. On the second day there the manager took me aside and suggested we move because other hotel guests seemed to be rather keen on my young son. So we moved to a beach place and fabulous sunset cruises.

Later, Augustus' turn to come along came. We holidayed in India, Singapore, Mexico and Tokyo. In Malaysia – he was still under twelve years old – his size was considered adult. Stewardesses and customs inspectors were affectionate and he wrote his first little booklet which he entitled *Stewardesses Who Loved Me.*

When I was into my first year of my happy (I thought) third marriage, my grandson Matthew telephoned unexpectedly to tell me that he had found his mother, Elisabeth, dead at the door of her home. I rushed over. Policemen stood in front of her home in London and would not allow me to see the body. I did not believe the death for some days, but saw the other grandson, Nicholas and my son-in-law Alleyn Comben, who confirmed that my beloved eldest daughter was dead at the young age of forty-two years.

I began to travel frequently to Japan and later even lived there in a sort of way. I made friends, among them Kenichi Sawamura – who came to Switzerland and brought with him the Toppan TH-gravure offset conversion process – and then came Takaharu (Roy) Ariga of Toppan Printing, one of the two major printing groups in Japan. I even brought the great rivals – the Dainippon and Toppan Printing Groups – onto speaking terms. The president of DNP, Yoshitoshi Kitajima and Toppan's Kazuo Suzuki met socially after I had brought them together. I made friends with

Makoto Isshiki of DNP and – since the early 1950s – have had a good friendship with Ken Terada, whose open mind astonished me already when I first came to Japan through the Process Shizai company, and earlier through Seikichi Wada of Press Arto Kai and his family who told me of Japanese art and culture. I began to write about that.

The Yarakasukan Printing Company in Japan, who did some design printing for Kanebo and others, wanted me to recruit English designers. Some stayed in the country for many years. My frequent travels to the far away country gave me a liking for Japan and things Japanese. At that time anti-Japanese feelings ran high (and understandably so) in Britain and some other countries. In the course of my work as a journalist I was often at parties with other journalists invited by manufacturers big and small. I eagerly went on these trips and got to know many interesting people. I even found old mates from school, such as Paolo de Lucca from Varese in Italy. His German wife seemed unusually suspicious. She was firmly of the opinion that on his many overseas trips he explored the local talent. I had just been to Hong Kong at the same time as he. A friend there had lent Sophia Loren his stunning flat on Bowen Hill, overlooking the harbour. A film, *The Countess of Hong Kong*, was partially shot there. Paolo's wife asked me point blank about his imaginary exploits. He looked on and his patience broke. He demanded his say and told of arriving after the long flight from Europe. He wanted to sleep, but first ordered some snack and half a bottle of wine to his room, where he took a quick shower. Then, so he told his fantasizing story, he came out of the bathroom, wanted to lie down but, lo and behold, in the bad was a smiling Sophia Loren. Shrugging his shoulders he simply said "what could I do then?" His wife was stunned, but somehow did not doubt his bizarre and fabricated tale.

Evenings on welcome press trips were often a problem. I did not cherish the idea of spending boring hours in equally boring nightclubs or other such sordid establishments. The 1960s and '70s were especially difficult. Business practice seemed to include female entertainment.

Once, in Belgium, the hosts had organised a swarm of ladies-of-the-night to join us. Some of my colleagues were delighted to take the free fun offered up. One even went so far to demand a better "bridal room". Some of us however, walked out in disgust.

Another time in Italy I succumbed to a nightclub and strip show invitation. My host's man cried when I turned down the offer of a lady. He was meant to accompany me. He explained his crying. He was grateful for my excuse of being tired. He went on to say that the next day he would get married.

On a press trip to Germany the almost obligatory

nightclub visit was offered again. I was able to turn it down because Eric Tanzer, the British representative of the manufacturer, had booked seats at the opera and invited me to dinner and to join him. He found me only too glad to take up the offer.

After a lively and quite lavish dinner in Tokyo a cavalcade of black limousines took us back, not to our hotel, but a big hotel in the area of Asakusa. Grinning men coated in black business suits informed us that we all were invited to have female company. I insisted that I was too tired for anything else and just needed sleep. So the cavalcade of black limousines drove off to my hotel. Our hosts and guests, once there, saw me get my room key and then left for the other hotel.

The absolute nadir of such occurrences was reached in Bangkok when the Vietnam War was going on. The place was swarming with American soldiers on short-term leave and very much "on the town". The obligatory entertainment was offered. I made the usual excuse of tiredness. So my host was unabashed and simply asked "You prefer boys then?" I just walked away.

In the old days there was fairly heavy drinking in New York. Many people lived in the suburbs and went home after some drinks in a city bar, then more drinks in the Pullman cars back home. Then they sat slumped in their armchairs and disdained the dinner the wife had prepared.

In Düsseldorf, where I had to spend sometimes a week or more, I occasionally rented a penthouse apartment. I shared this with friends from Sweden or Britain, I stocked the refrigerator with food and some drink. When after a hard day's work I returned to the flat and wanted to pour myself schnapps, it was gone. Swedes and Finns, I learnt quickly, drank copious amounts of hard liquor, which I always replaced, only to find the cabinet empty next evening again.

In Holland one night, my secretary, who to my amazement drove an X-type Jaguar, and I were taken to some nightclub. There she confronted the barman and when asked what drink she would like, replied (as it seemed to sound) "have you got blue balls?" To this the barman reasonably said that he had not looked today. She was then served a Blue Bols cocktail.

Soon our host's man left assuring the party that everything, including the ladies who had meanwhile turned up, was taken care of. I was lucky to escape with him, a true-born Englishman, for a quiet drink nearby.

In the late 1960, so I was told, the Norse god Thor paid another one of his visits to London and went to Hyde Park, listened to the speakers at Hyde Park Corner and then – as was his wont – sought an encounter with a young lady. He met a lass from Yorkshire and after some frolicking in the grass, but behind bushes and hidden from view he recalled his godly good manners and told the young lady that he was Thor. To this she replied, in her lisp, that she was "thore, too, but thatisfied".

Through my work as a reporter and journalist I made notable friends. A Dane, Niels Christian Nielsen, brought me into contact and good understanding with the Swedish tycoon Albert Bonnier, Jr. Nielsen had been tortured by the Nazi occupiers of his home country. He fled and settled in Sweden. When he became a bit emotional he talked about his sufferings. He died suddenly while his wife Gunilla was visiting his parents in Copenhagen. We had many lively times together. He drank too heavily. One night in Finland he woke me up at 2 a.m. to ask whether I had any drink in my hotel room. As it happened I had a bottle of duty-free whisky which was intended for him once we got to Sweden, where at that time spirit drinks were available only in state shops or with meals in restaurants. He woke about four or five unenthusiastic colleagues, asked them to come to my room and bring their tooth mugs with them. He then proceeded to fill our glasses until the bottle was empty. Amazingly, he never seemed to have a hangover in the morning. He was always fit and ready to start the day's programme.

Uwe-Jens Philipp in Germany had lived for some years in England, but was basically resident in Germany. Sarah, his elder daughter was born in London and later lived for some time with us in London. We keep in fairly close contact. Like me, he and his wife Heidi like to travel to new places.

When one wants to believe an illusion, one does. My family and my brother's tribe holidayed in the Basque country. We went on an adventure walk in stifling heat and unexpectedly came upon a tall rock and a welcome waterfall. We all stripped to our underpants and had cool water splashing over us. Two days later we sought that refreshing waterfall. It had disappeared. Locals from Frias told us that there had been a pipe burst. There was no waterfall.

Who remembers (old enough) the day in November 1963 when America's President, John F. Kennedy was shot dead by Lee Harvey Oswald – who in turn was murdered a few days later while in custody?

I distinctly remember that day. While shopping near Piccadilly Circus in the heart of London's West End, suddenly the big news screen flashed and read "America's President Shot" or something like that. I did not admire Kennedy, but would never have wished a violent death for him – or anybody at that (Nazis excepted). Londoners stared in disbelief. Was this true? Had the nuclear war begun? The world was stunned. Even Moscow radio played funeral music.

I rushed home. The news was unbelievable. Gradually confirmation arrived. Over here people asked why guns could be bought that easily in the US.

One publication I wrote for extensively was the

British Printer, then the bible of the industry throughout the British Empire. It was then edited by the late Roy Brewer, who became a frequent companion and friend. He and his wife Ingrid went to live in Bristol. Among his editorial colleagues was Brian Innes, of Temperance Seven band fame. Under Roy Brewer the magazine maintained its role as the leading printing journal of the former British Empire. Roy himself was steeped in music. His father, I believe, was first violin before the war in Düsseldorf and he himself was active writing and playing until he suffered from failing eyesight.

My wife Julia travelled with me to a big trade fair in Düsseldorf. She caused a sensation: news photographers photographed her boarding a tram in her mini-skirt. The garment had not yet really arrived in Germany.

The *British Printer* had some eccentric editors, like Roger Hutchings, who wrote books on type and bred rabbits, or Frank Colley, who later edited *Printing World.* He was said to travel to foreign meetings and return to his home office, fling a bunch of handout literature on the desk and declare to his dejected staff that "here was everything needed to file an eye witness report". Later the once proud *British Printer*, now defunct, was incorporated into *Printing World* and edited by Roy Coxhead, then by Rod Hayes, Terry Ulrick and Gareth Ward. The first three had worked for the British Printing Corporation which later was taken over by the flamboyant crook Robert Maxwell.

I went to the Leipzig Fair almost every year when there was still a German Democratic Republic (GDR). Bernhard Temme, though a convinced communist, assisted me in getting travel permits to visit much of East Germany and I met some interesting people, among them Miroslav Rostropovitch, the cellist, later a conductor, who was then relatively unknown in the West. I also made friends with Erwin Ludwig, lawyer and a journalist on one of the permitted liberal dailies to which I contributed the weekend motor page. As a non-driver I saw cars from the angle of the passengers and commented on their suitability for drivers and mothers with their children. I also met Günther Wadewitz, now a bookseller in Zwenkau, and his wife Ilse and daughter. He was then in a privileged position. Because of his excellent English he could travel abroad and came to London several times.

His wife, though, was never allowed to accompany him. At one time, I think, he was offered a diplomatic post in Helsinki, but turned it down because the GDR authorities would not allow his family to accompany him. Soviet East Germany's future and last Prime Minister, Egon Krenz, who was later imprisoned for some years, accompanied me on a trip to Sweden to see some printing plant. While we were in the DDR and on the ferry to the north, he was full of the glories of his country's politics but once we were in Sweden he talked freely and sensibly just like most anybody would have in the West.

I also often met Rudi Sternberg, who was British, and very friendly. It was said he was a businessman doing some spying for the Soviets. Harold Wilson, the British Prime Minister, may have believed that he was a spy and double agent.

Ken Terada in Tokyo, who most unusually for a Japanese of the old school, speaks German and English, was a lawyer by training. He invented a colour fidelity reproduction process, called Densitograph, which his son Masami improved through his computer skills, but Efi Arazi and John Crosfield and their colleagues made computers ever more versatile and revolutionized colour fidelity reproduction. Ken founded the Tokyo-based Kohan Research & Development Institute specialising in graphic arts. I was privileged to be one of the opening speakers at the centre.

Kurt Schlössing Paul, a German immigrant, had his own broadcasting programme on the BBC's German service. Like the late Gerhard Frankl he assembled around him outstanding graphic arts technicians, some madcap inventors of machines.

On one of the first trips to America I reached Raleigh in North Carolina. The alcohol rules were confusing. Drinks seemed to be served only with meals. A restaurant served me to my intense astonishment with a pitcher of beer. My neighbours in London, a professor from Raleigh with family, from, had not told me of these absurd regulations. I continued to Alabama and felt embarrassed when an elderly black man sitting on the verandas of the small houses got up to lift his hats when I – a rather young man – was passing the house. Those were the days of segregation.

One of my old schoolmates in Switzerland came from Prague, and settled after the war in Australia. He wanted to help his parents stuck in the old country. He wrote to me and sent money I was to take to his family. Arriving at Prague I was shunted by the then communist authorities to a large Stalinist architecture hotel halfway between the airport and the city.

It was not easy to leave that hotel unobserved. Finally, I located a service exit and ran to the nearby tram stop, boarded the first tram going and arrived in the city.

There I got a taxi and in the dark of night arriving at the parents' doorstep, was invited in. I handed the money over and had tea and biscuits. Then I took my leave and went back the way I had come. Back in the hotel my disappearance had been noticed. I managed to explain to the doubting "guardian" that I had innocently gone for a walk and knew that nobody had observed me leaving. My passport was then held by the hotel and I pretended that I thought that was normal when staying in a hotel.

A disturbing thought was spurred by the *Guardian* newspaper: the German Legation in London had a counsellor who went by the name of (in German) Rat Fink von Finkenstein. Other papers also commented sarcastically on this. In my old age I met socially a distant relative of his. She was an Egyptologist and I silently admired her shapely legs, but more significantly her intellect.

Terence Coyne lived in south London near a golf course. He applied to join as the way to the railway station would have been much shortened. The club refused him membership as they "did not accept Jews!" Terence was annoyed and pointed out that a respected local transport firm was called Jews' Transport!

There was a time when I enjoyed special treatment when travelling to America. Edward McSweeney III had made me a sort of member of the Sky Club located on top of the skyscraper PanAm (now Metropolitan Life) Building. The helicopter rooftop landing stage was then used for services between Kennedy airport and Manhattan. Juan Trippe, then head of Pan-American Airways and the Inter-Continental Hotel chain, was often there. For a while – that was in the days when people and not faceless giant corporations counted – mention of his name got me upgraded on flights and in hotels.

On my trips I encountered Paul Sargent Clark, who was editor of one of the American magazines I wrote for. We first met at The Press Box in Manhattan. He later married my future third wife. He had moved back to California. I was happily married, but that didn't stop me from fantasizing about his wife Barri coming into my bed. Both my daughter Beatrice and I stayed with them. After Paul's sudden death I finally fell into bed with Barri. I liked the daughter Jennifer and continue to like her. She had a birthday party given once in the luxurious, but strangely sterile, home of two homosexual friends. It was an astonishing surprise for her and she was stunned by it. I was pleased for her. Her then boyfriend, thought of as her fiancé, was there. She had had bad luck in her love life. Perhaps this time it would work? Sadly, it failed – again. The young man from San Francisco seemed pleasant enough, but he lusted after things outside his reach and outside her tolerance. The daughter is married now in California.

The whole world used to think the Rockefellers were running America (and Standard Oil). Once they owned New York's Rockefeller Center. One of the "poor" of the family was John W. Rockefeller, Jr. with whom I had dinners at the Red Lobster, a quite cheap chain of eateries in American cities. He and his beautiful wife, looking like Rockefellers indeed, had enough money with which to indulge their fancies, but behaved like good and real people.

I started collecting miniature perfume bottles. Their shape and sparkling variety (and the colour of their contents) intrigued me. The collection has grown to well over a thousand small bottles, displayed in mirror-backed cases and safeguarded by my daughter Beatrice in Spain, where I also have a sizeable collection of wine corks (from wines I have drunk), beer mats, crown corks – and at one time had one of Europe's major collection of beer cans. I was then a member of Beer Can Collectors of America. For some years I was an ardent collector of empty beer cans from all over the world. The craze had started in America. I travelled worldwide and had at one time what was believed to be the largest collection of beer cans in Europe. I was able through another collector to stay with the American commander of the Panama Canal Zone and even self-importantly passed ships going through the canal. Always the ship's captain would salute me from the bridge!

Once, in Hong Kong a Japanese trade mission group was there. I knew its leader, and after dinner one evening saw him stop in Kowloon extracting beer cans from dustbins. He was a collector too, and a millionaire in his own country. His villa in Tokyo boasted of some one hundred and fifty decorative carps. A special canal had been built to give the fish access to the living rooms.

Some people claim that my passion for collecting almost anything is a sign of obsession. I collect sensible things like artists' books and fine prints, but also beer mats, match covers, and other things. I also collect assiduously for friends: hotel stationery and guest soaps or sugar cubes and sachets from restaurants and bars.

Sweden had donated to the incoming Cuban government, headed by Fidel Castro, a Solna press and plenty of paper to print *Granma*, the newspaper. The young Cuban consul in London had given me a visa. On arrival at Havana the friendly immigration officer would not recognise the document. The wrong stamp had been put in my passport. I was nevertheless allowed into the country, took a taxi to the Hotel Naçional (the former Havana Hilton) and the next day set about regularizing my sojourn to the country. My visit to cover the story of how a revolutionary newspaper managed to cope with aid, however, proved a total failure. Outside *Granma's* plant a hillock of newsprint was slowly rotting into a hard rock mass. The paper reels had been unloaded and left in the open to be attacked by tropical rain. I felt I could not write a sensational story of failed, though well-intentioned aid and thus lend support to the irrational hate of all things linked to Castro in America So I left again after visiting Old Havana and its fine, but dilapidated buildings. The charm of the country and its people impressed me. I stared, too, at the incongruous, but often beautiful policewomen wearing hideous frumpish dull grey Soviet-style uniforms. The shops were empty. As a foreigner I was able to invite a few good-looking foreign office ladies to dinner at the Hotel Naçional, where food was lavish and paid for in cash. A few years later my visit had worthwhile after effects when I went to the then East Germany. During that visit the Cubans gave a party during the Leipzig Fair. I was invited, not by a dignitary, but by Castro's bodyguards, who remembered me from the time I had called on their Maximum Leader in Havana. The men slipped me in by a side entrance.

At the party I met Vyacheslav Molotov (he of the infamous Molotov cocktail). We chatted meaninglessly. A few years later I met him by chance again at a prestige lunch at the Soviet Embassy in Brazil as it happened, we both were guests at another party that night. There Molotov very obviously was very bored. He recognized me. Then he asked whether I was willing to join him in leading the conga dance. His minders looked unhappy. Impetuously and in a sovereign gesture, before I could answer, he got up, had grabbed a mulatta's hips and beckoned me to do the same. We led the long snake dance. The other guests joined in.

Thus I came to dance the conga with Molotov. Elsewhere I also recount how I also danced the conga following Kazuo Suzuki, a Japanese business leader, in Rio de Janeiro. Such are the foolish things of one's youth!

Molotov was always skirting around questions

about Soviet atrocities and misdeeds. In personal life he was a lively and quite humorous man, so it was said. Sir Winston Churchill called him "a perfect example of a human robot". I disagree with that.

Time was when Barri and I danced wildly to such tunes as the drum virtuosos of Baby Dodds, Eric Burden's *Tales of Drunkenness & Splendour* or Errol Garner's *Meatless Payday*, which latter music had been privately recorded by the Danish Count Rosenquist. The pianist did not approve of this recording. While later living in Los Angeles, Louis Prima and his *I'm Just A Gigolo* were enjoyed with passionate abandon. The bellowed-out songs were danced to by Barri and me. Marlene Dietrich had imparted sadness to her rendering of the song. Louis Prima lent the song wild fury.

The systems of colour reproduction were changing dramatically. Some of the most dramatic innovations came from Germany, so it was obvious that the trade press had to report. Some press colleagues and myself were invited by a leading manufacturer. With us went the rather elegant Frank Colley, editor of a weekly trade paper. He often wore a monocle and wore a "British" warm overcoat in winter times. It was cold when we arrived in the other country. We had little luggage. We passed customs and as a routine check one of us had to open his bag. The task fell upon the dignified editor. He opened his bag rather shyly. To the officers' amazement it contained mainly rather explicit colourful girlie magazines. To my embarrassment the editor insisted on trying to explain – and asked me to translate – that Germany had a high reputation for her colour reproductions and he had brought these magazines along for technical reasons!

A favourite "aunt" – not a real relative – came from Vienna. She was Jewish and literally showered me with affection. In Prague, Vienna and also for some time in Budapest she looked after my needs in the absence of my parents. Her family welcomed and accepted me. She suffered much for her Jewishness. She had managed to reach England, worked in London as a cipher clerk for some time during the war, and then joined her parent and brother in Argentina. After the war I visited her, of course. I invited her to London and then after she had left anti-Semitic Argentina for tolerant Canada, she was my guest again in Washington DC and California. I keep in touch with her daughter Elena and her new family, now in Canada.

Inflation was ripe in Argentina at one time. My hard currency was welcome. I stayed at the posh Plaza hotel where some remaining tolerant and liberal people sometimes met with the then rulers of the country. Conversation was secretly taped, one suspected.

During the early days of the junta there was still a free press. Newspapers like *La Opinion* or the English language *Buenos Aires Herald* and their liberal voices could still be read.

In French-speaking Geneva, a Swiss professor with a German-sounding name has started the post-modern theory explaining the powerless or impotent role of today's citizen. I understood his thesis. The theme was taken up by two writers, Theodor Leuenberger and Rudolf Schilling in *Die Ohnmacht des Bürgers*.

On one of my all-too-frequent long haul flights I went to Port-au-Prince in Haiti. I did not know my way around in the poverty stricken country, then still rules by Papa Doc Duvalier and his Ton-Ton Macous bullies. I found a taxi driver and asked for advice, not wishing to spend too much money. He promised me a "super place". So I agreed and he took me to the outskirts of the city to the Hotel Oloffson. It was like being transported back into the 19th Century. Out of the jungle rose the wooded structure of the Charles Adams-like building. I had just stepped out of the taxi – and before I could even pay – was handed a Cuba Libre to cheer the weary traveller. On the veranda and in the bar there were wicker armchairs like those of the South Sea chieftains of lore. All was like a dream! Towards the end of my life I found a limited edition colour print, bought it and added it to the hundred or so pictures on the walls at home. Perhaps my older son and his bride will go there for a few days on their honeymoon, provided the hotel still stands there after the earthquake in 2010.

The press officer of a huge industrial group, which also made printing machinery, was a nephew of Paraguay's dictator General Ferdinand Strössner. Eventually he migrated to the country, confident of a comfortable future. However, his uncle was toppled and found refuge in Brazil just while I was there, but I did not find out about his eventual fate.

Dr Aurelio Pecci, of the Club of Rome, agreed with Giorgio Gianoli and me to present one of the club's pacesetting studies looking into the future at a Comprint International gathering.

Private life was happy. One time we holidayed in Cadavedo in northern Spain. My brother and I in the evening went for a drink and chat – in German. The place was unusually lively. Suddenly a tall man from the table next to us got up and approached. He told us that he was a major in the Guardia Civil, a feared force in Franco's Spain. Jürgen and I had just discussed it in hushed terms. He told us that he had the power to have us deported, but as we were honoured guests in his country he did not wish to make life difficult. Would we therefore, please, stop denigrating the Franco government and have a drink of cider with him? Naturally we agreed.

Years before we had a holiday in the north of Spain at Tobalanilla, not that far from Bilbao, where my mother and brother had lived for some years. A great holiday and I had my daughter Elisabeth Jaspert on my back when I swam across the artificial lake through the former road tunnels. That was fun and love, not competitive sport.

During one of my several visits to Brazil I stayed as a guest of Adolfo Bloch, the Ukrainian-born printer-publisher and art patron. The penthouse apartment on the bay facing Sugarloaf Mountain was like a museum. I was alone. During the night I thought I was imagining strange shuffling noises. It turned out that a guard was checking the paintings and sculptures. Nobody has bothered to tell him about me.

Jarrold's, the printers of Norwich, were no longer book publishers. Through John H. Jarrold they had an active interest in Thames & Hudson, though. The publisher there, Walter Neurath, discussed offering me a good job, but I swiftly declined. I did not really want to return to art books and magazines. I had earlier tried to work for Phaidon Press, but there was no hope. The publisher believed that his photographic library kept safe by one of my uncles in Berlin had been surreptitiously made use of.

I developed good contacts with the Mondadori publishing house through Giorgio Gianoli. I interviewed Giorgio Mondadori, later the founder of the *La Repubblica* daily newspaper. One quite hot evening at a Comprint conference reception held in a rialto-side old palace in Venice I danced with his wife, who seemed to enjoy "free style" movements.

Giorgio's wife, though, thought our dancing "dirty".

At Strega on Lago Maggiore I encountered Silvio Berlusconi, who amazingly was later elected Prime Minister of Italy. Even in those days he struck me as a somewhat slimy Uriah Heap character.

When I wrote to one of the major American news weeklies magazines – and long before 9/11 – that the Western world should beware of the rise of fundamental Muslim strength, the magazine rubbished my thoughts and declined to publish. Habib Bourguiba in Algeria knew better and thought the Muslim birth rate alone would bring about world domination by sheer numbers.

Two notable April Fool hoaxes intrigued me. *The Guardian* newspaper's Geoffrey Taylor, a friend of my first wife, ran an April Fool's story about the new imaginary island state of San Serriffe in the Indian Ocean. The story was picked up by other editors and publishers. People tried to book holidays and travel agents looked at their tourist maps and guidebooks in vain. The story was based on Henry Morris' Bird & Bull Press's book, authored under the pseudonym of Dr Theodore Bachaus. Silver and copper coinage, even a hundred corona paper banknote, were produced.

Another imaginative and inspired spoof was launched by the British Broadcasting Corporation and made serious by the ponderous commentary of Richard Dimbleby, a trusted commentator on major events. It claimed that spaghetti pasta grew on trees in places like Italy and was harvested by peasants. A supermarket chain ran advertisements publishing the alleged photo. The story was widely accepted by an amazed public. It even reached Japan. I have a framed colour picture of this in my kitchen. A print of this I took to Japan where I convinced some people of its truth!

Tony Underhill, an Australian friend and a war artist in the Second World War, sold me some paintings. I cherish these. They are in my home and with some of my children and a granddaughter, I feel at home with them wherever they are now. One of my children has a painting by John Duguit and there are Jack Yates' paintings all over the places. I also cherish a picture by Heinz Trökes – and many others. Tony went for a few years to America to be artist-in-residence at some Midwestern university. We met for long talking sessions with the writer Kurt Vonnegut. Sometimes we met in New York City when I was working there on an on-and-off basis. I stayed in a conventional hotel, preferably The Waldorf (where they at one time treated me as an 'old patron' because my mother had stayed there before the war) or often with Hanna Busoni, the widow of the painter Rafaello Busoni, son of the Italian composer Feruccio. She lived near Carnegie Hall and Central Park. Rafaello, my parents' friend, managed to escape the Nazis because he could claim he was Swedish through his mother. His son Mario, with whom I played as a child in Berlin, now lives in Manhattan and before my virtual banishment from America. I used to always, when in the city, go and see him and his wife.

My Australian painter friend stayed at the then rather seedy Chelsea Hotel when in New York City. There at a time, shortly before his sudden death in London, I met the punk musician Sid Vicious, bass-player with the notorious Sex Pistols, and together we went to spend late nights at Max's Kansas City, then a punk Bohemian hangout near the Bowery and SoHo. In the Midwest, Tony fell on hard times and the university took some of his paintings as security for a loan. I rescued them one night by breaking into the store and reaching them out through the window. Then I took them to Cedar Rapids airport in the middle of the night in the morning I got a bag for skis and rolled them up for the flight home. The airport at night had been deserted and closed. There was only a night watchman. I attracted his attention. He let me in and offered a cup of coffee from his thermos bottle.

Max's Kansas City restaurant in Manhattan had been convenient for me. I could stagger "home" to Lorna Murphy and John Kelly's loft in Green Street, where around the corner was a pleasant small bar run by an ex-flyweight boxer of Italian descent. The couple later divorced.

Lorna Kelly became almost famous as Sotheby's (New York) first major woman auctioneer – and if rumours are to be believed, a part-time lesbian and later a member of Alcoholics Anonymous. She did well independently, and started by taking me to posh restaurants instructing me to tip heavily at twenty or more per cent of the bill. I complied, reluctantly. John continued working with – amongst others – Kiss, a rock band known by the runic lettering used for the spelling of its name on record covers, T-shirts and the like. John remarried in a posh Long Island setting. I was a guest and we all had to wade in our finery into the sea for the ceremony performed by a priest in a soaking cassock. My trousers were ruined, but we feasted on fresh oysters which had arrived in a large barrel, not quite a man's height and much bigger than the baskets they often come in. Champagne flowed.

Lorna distinguished herself at one St. Patrick's Day Parade in New York City. Standing outside the Plaza Hotel she was badly embarrassed when a group a women carrying a banner proclaiming "Lesbians for Kennedy" broke ranks to embrace her in front of all the onlookers.

Public life seems unchanged. Charles Bukowski said many years ago that "the difference between a democracy and a dictatorship is that in a democracy you vote first and take orders later. In a dictatorship you do not have to waste your vote". Michael Moore expresses similar sentiments.

Lorna Kelly's father, after a rather silly charge of resisting arrest against me had been dismissed on appeal, was a police superintendent in a well-heeled community near London. After the appeal was won, he told me I could early one night take my revenge and spring a leak through the local police office's letterbox. I did not take up that otherwise helpful advice. The police sergeant, whose daughter attended one of my sons' primary school, and who had tried to arrest me with half a dozen officers to assist him arriving in a Black Maria police van, was reduced to the ranks for a while. He was even made to walk the local beat!

For many years summer holidays were spent in the Welsh hills and mountains. A friend, the painter Jack Yates, had a cottage there near Aberystwyth. Several of his pictures are well liked in my various homes. His paintings are now in Germany, Spain and Switzerland, and of course, in England and in the States.

In 2005 the Italian journalist and writer Oriana Fallaci elaborated on the dumbing-down and expounded views on this threat in a volume which discusses the decline of European thinking, the impact of dogma and heretics and stipulating that the decline and fall of Europe are inevitable.

I am suspicious of psychiatry. It seems that Graham Greene was right when he tried to explain that "I still don't know myself, for I have no wish to know myself.

I am somewhat in the situation of Rainer Maria Rilke, who was afraid of psychoanalysis. He said that he was frightened that it might clear up everything to the detriment of his unconscious mind – the part that nourishes creativity.

"I think it is unhealthy to dwell on the negative side of one's character, as analysis and auto-analysis inevitably do; they reinforce the Christian idea of guilt. It is never one's positive side that comes to light." But although I find it difficult to agree, Greene also thought that he "lived like a lord at (my) analyst's. I met all sorts of people – writers for the most part … this was what helped me rather than the analysis itself, which came nowhere near to sorting me out".

During a trip from California to London I went to see my doctor for a routine check-up. Prostate cancer was suspected and confirmed by the local hospital. The surgeon wanted to operate immediately. I consulted a second opinion. And was advised to just keep a careful watch. That was at the time of writing this down some eighteen years ago. Anyway, I am scared of surgery. A small hernia surgery had disastrous consequences and sent me back to hospital three times. Occasionally a desperate need to pass water overcomes me. One morning, most places still shut, I found myself in a major business district. No restaurant or accessible washrooms were open. I rushed into a luxury hotel and stumbled in agony to the gentlemen's room. I managed to relieve myself. A uniformed man was standing there, brushed my shoulder and handed me a guest towel. Obviously a tip was needed. Fumbling through my pockets I could find only a £2 (about $3) coin which was handed over in embarrassment. Returning a few years ago from the airport in London, pressure became so urgent I had to get off the transport and relieve myself against a building wall in a deserted city street. Unfortunately a policeman went by and gave me a serious ticking off. Both my brother and I, though earning reasonable well, have no luck with investments. I put some money into a widely acclaimed merchant bank's scheme. The "trust" soon went bankrupt. I bought shares in the doomed Scottish newspaper venture of Robert Maxwell. They collapsed. My brother invested in Bernie Cornfeldt's Investors Overseas Services, he lost his shirt.

Britain may have learned from the Argentine Junta: how do you define a terrorist? General Jorge Videla, the Junta's military ruler of Argentina for some years in the 1980s said: "a terrorist is not just someone with a gun or a bomb, but also someone who spreads ideas that are contrary to Western and Christian civilization". Well, by that definition almost everybody qualifies as a potential terrorist. Britain's high court thought otherwise and set free four such Guantànamo men who presumably had spread wrong ideas. General Leopoldo Galtieri of the notorious Falklands or

Malvinas War faithfully copied Videla's thoughts – and Margaret Thatcher gave orders to sink the *Belgrano* cruiser after disregarding her advisors' views and thus by a single stroke negated the armistice mediated by Peru and caused some four hundred young men to die in a watery grave. Peace loving combined with national pride is a truly lethal combination!

I thought of this one night at a party in Buenos Aires in the house of late cousin Peter Anger's wife Renate, who has remarried. She lived opposite the Argentine Navy's headquarters and knew many officers. Some of them got lively and told me that Argentina would take control of the Falklands very soon. The party was on my last day in the city. In the morning I telephoned the British Embassy. They brushed me off by saying that the Argentines were always boasting. Next day I was in London and rang up the admiralty. Nobody was interested. So I spoke to the American Embassy. There somebody actually took some notice of my report. The same thing had happened when I managed to leave Budapest during the Hungarian Revolution. On the way to Vienna I had counted about a hundred and fifty Soviet tanks. I had a friend at the British Embassy. Even he brushed me off. What I told him was not interesting. Again, I rang the American Legation. Notice was taken. Twenty-five years later I complained about past neglect to the Foreign office. They assured me this would not ever happen again!

One night in Kettner's, London's Soho restaurant, we gave a party to Len Deighton, who was writing bestselling spy stories then. I was impressed by his cockney character and his personal bravery in driving a mini on a rally into the then communist and exotic Yugoslavia.

During my visit to Cuba I had met some rather friendly bodyguards of the "Maximum Leader". Later, on one of my periodic visits to the Leipzig Fair and on the occasion of Fidel Castro's state visit these self-same bodyguards invited me to a VIP party to the consternation of the East German officials. I was taken into the area where the reception was held via the back entrance.

One of my children, then in India, got into some currency trouble I had inadvertently caused. I managed to get her home. First the British representative in Madras drove his car almost a thousand miles to assist her. I had phoned the British office at night in Singapore after my wife had telephoned to alert me. Singapore informed the High Commission in India. My daughter is now again a full member of society, married and was for some year a lecturer at a London college.

I was in Cairo for a printers' meeting arranged by Ted Eckhardt, addressed by speakers from America and Europe. We had dinner in one of the hotels facing the pyramids. The setting was brilliant … but we were distracted. The international financier Adnan Kasshoghi, a modern age version of the infamous Basil Zaharoff, gave the wedding reception for his daughters. A special ramp had to be erected to enable bejewelled elephants and a bevy of sequined belly dancers to ascend to the banqueting room. The fabulously wealthy Saudi saw us and invited everyone to join the festivities. We were awed. Everything seemed to make the *1,001 Nights* come to new life.

A major London event of the decade was an exhibition of Mexican art and anthropology. Alongside exhibits from the museum of anthropology in Mexico City were artefacts on loan from Britain and other places. I contributed a special section to *Die Kunst* as London correspondent for which I drew on additional information from the Mexican organisers staying at the Rembrandt Hotel near Buckingham Palace.

A splendid occasion went wrong in Germany. A famous paper maker celebrated the family company's centenary. I was invited as a guest speaker, flown in style there, put up in luxury in a large hotel and also paid a princely fee. Guests had been invited from all over the globe. The chairman was to say a few words before I was to comment on. His speech, however, went on and on. The timetable for the event was upset and I was asked to cut my words to just a few laudatory notes. That I did. We sat down to a festive meal, chatted and dispersed again. I went home with my pocket filled with banknotes. I had been paid in cash for just a few minutes' words!

For some time I had played with the idea of turning to freelance writing. Tom Margerison invited me to join him and the *Sunday Times* (then a Thomson newspaper). I did, wrote a bit, and with him and a technician started up the *Reading Evening Post*, now defunct, but then a pioneer in new technology. The job was interesting but beset by office politics and rivalries. We introduced Lumitype-Photon filmsetting and web offset after visiting American pioneers of the new technology. I resigned my post in frustration and never again earned that much money. Lord Thomson of Fleet had warned me that I was giving up the good life. Money though, is not all!

Walter Partridge suggested I join him at the Westminster Press and the *Financial Times*. I liked the job and socially met some of the owners, including the Duke of Atholl, who alone in Britain was allowed to have his own army. More important, the newspaper also owned Château Lafitte and the famous vineyard. I bet His Grace a bottle of my vintage port against his case of vintage wine that there would not be identity cards in Britain by the turn of the century. I won, but the Duke died. Now the government is planning to introduce identity cards after all. Rudimentary such cards were used for a short time during and after the Second World War but people and the police disliked them and threw them away. In the German-occupied Channel Islands British police rounded up Jews on Nazi orders. They used data from the identify card files of those days. At some stage they must have realized what fate waited these unfortunate people. They nevertheless obeyed those racist orders. Who is going to prevent any future evil misuse of the intrusive system? In the 1950s identity cards, disliked by police and the populace, were abolished. People congregated in Trafalgar Square to joyfully burn their cards on a huge bonfire. The police, arms folded, smilingly attended the occasion near Parliament. The public and police were of one mind.

When I left the *Financial Times* I worked for a time for the Swiss printers Conzett & Huber and their promotion of the Japanese Toppan TH-gravure process. I was based in London, but money was paid into my Swiss account which had been opened for my use in my youth.

I was working for the *Financial Times*. The printing department's St. Clement's Press was overstaffed and was losing money. It was decided to close it down. I was conned into giving an "expert opinion", thus sealing its demise. It still shames me that I was instrumental in making over-confident and pampered people lose their jobs. Once my job was done, I was on the plane to New York and sat next to a man who nonchalantly unfolded confidential papers outlining plans to print an edition of a subsidiary weekly in America. He was lucky I was not from a rival paper and kept quiet. How could that man have been so careless as to unfold and spread these confidential papers for anyone sitting near him to see?

I had been equally gullible and was induced to write an article about a seemingly praiseworthy company. What I did not know was the chairman used this text in a puff when the company was floated on the stock exchange.

The Hungarian composer Zoltan Kodaly said that "what we do not know we do not pine for". The Guinness brewery reflected this in an oversize poster for Harp lager featuring a bedtime-eyed blonde stating about the brewer's lager beer "I do not like it, I do not know it".

When I lived and worked in Switzerland just after the war, I was assistant editor of *Graphis*, an international design magazine published in three languages. The printing of the publication was at Lucerne at the famed Bucher printing plant. My publishers felt I should learn more about printing itself. I thought I knew most of it already. I was made a *Volontär* – a sort of intern. Years later I met Lars Janneryd, a Swede, who had shared his Swiss training at the same company, though later of course. Today he has strong associations with Switzerland.

I became obsessed by two irritations. They were

'doggie decorations' on local pavements and the widespread practice of pavement parking in London's Hampstead residential area. I campaigned against these annoying practices and joined The Pedestrian Association. I even acquired a sort of criminal record by intentionally breaking the aerial off a pavement-parked vehicle. The offending aerial had grazed my eye. I reported what I had done to the Police, and was convicted and fined.

This self-reported offence came back to haunt me. In America, the Office of Homeland Security decided I was a criminal, though this offence is no longer on record in Britain.

Afterthoughts

SITTING IN the pub next to my then home I listened in unashamedly to a lively conversation at the next table. I learnt that eavesdropping sometimes pays. I introduced myself and thus came to make friends with Steve Brown, who has taken charge of the important production aspects of this book. Drinking red wine makes me reminisce.

How attitudes change! In the mid-twentieth century in the southern states of America segregation was almost universal. Visiting Alabama in the early 1960s I was acutely embarrassed (then still fairly young), while walking along in small towns by respectable looking and well-dressed black people sitting outside their homes getting up to greet me – the unknown white stranger. Nearer home things were not that different: When the vessel *Irpinia*, coming from the Caribbean and bringing many black immigrants to Britain the ship stopped in northern Spain and picked up my mother together with others as new passengers. My wife and I were waiting for the boat train at Waterloo station. Around us was a sea of black faces. The (white) uniformed stationmaster saw us and invited just us whites to his office for a cup of tea. Things changed quickly. In the English film *A Taste of Honey* we saw Rita Tushingham standing on a ship canal bridge and calling to a young black man on a boat passing underneath "where are you from?" he shouts back: "from Liverpool"! Once, on holiday with the family in remote Wales we were walking in the hills and saw a young man sitting on a stone wall. I asked where he was from. His answer: "I am the local shepherd"!

I was travelling home from Frankfurt to arrive somewhat late to our annual pre-Christmas party which brought relatives and many friends together. I got off the PanAm plane in London, where the flight was changed to a larger Boeing bound for New York. A friend came very late to our party and told the terrible news of a plane crash. That was Lockerbie where my continued flight exploded. On the feeder flight from Frankfurt there was much speculation about a First Class passenger, said to be the CIA's top man in the Middle East. Surely that could not have been so the CIA would ensure top security! I did not take this in at the time.

Next morning I set out to collect some presents made for my wife. Suddenly I noticed the headlines of the newspapers. I bought a paper and read of the disaster. I felt dizzy. I had heard on the plane that an American bigwig in the Middle East was travelling on the flight. That was not important to me. In the first row in front of me in the rear cabin had sat a nice couple flying on their honeymoon to the Big Apple. We, the passengers, knew that because the loudspeaker told to us that the captain sent the young couple a bottle of champagne to celebrate their union. They were to be dead a few hours later. Next to the empty seat by me sat a young student from Beirut University. We chatted animatedly. He was looking forward excitedly to the holidays. He, too, and all the passengers lost their lives. I was shaken and unsure of my surroundings and hailed a taxi in Bond Street. The driver asked where I wanted to go. To that I simply said "take me home". He shook his head at my words and asked "where is that?" I managed to tell him.

Facing Hampstead Heath and Primrose Hill was my mother's house. In the cellar were my electric trains and track, as well as some four hundred or more good wines. After Mama died so early, my brother agreed that the house should be let rent-free to a friend's student daughter. Her friends drank all the wine and re-corked the empty bottles. We decided to ask the girl to leave with her friends and sell the nice house, part of a protected terrace. Today I wish we had not done that. The place has risen phenomenally in value and would be ideal for a single person like me now. Nearby was the Soviet, now Russian, embassy residential compound. Some of the diplomats' children went to the nearby William Ellis school. One of those boys was a classmate of Willem. They remain in contact.

Worldly goods are not my success story. On my travels I bought some Mayan pearls and had them set into a gold necklace by Paul Preston. That necklace was stolen. With the proceeds from the insurance money I had chunky gold nuggets from five continents set and framed by Roger Theiler, a Zurich jeweller. I bought that necklace back from my second wife, and gave it to one of my daughters. She has never worn it. That upset and saddened me. All ends well: now my granddaughter Poppy has the valuable jewellery.

My second wife still has a silver chain necklace and bracelet with roman coins of the various empresses Julia. One daughter occasionally still wears my mother's genuine Egyptian scarab ring which my father had had set for Mama.

After my appeal to Chancellor Konrad Adenauer my mother finally got some compensation and a lifetime pension following our father's sudden death. We children only received a piffling sum in the hundreds for each of us as a token for lost education. More than half a century later we each received a lump sum of $1,000 from an international restitution commission.

One boon of widely travelling was the opportunity to see and hear new performers, hear concerts and opera, see famous and less famous museums or go to the Bolshoi in Moscow.

My travels in Eastern Europe always depressed me. Foreigners did not have to queue. I was able to get admission to palaces of culture or famous stages and could take friends to posh restaurants without having to queue. Some of it was reflected in Scandinavia, too, where buying a drink was sometimes difficult, but easier for a visitor. Occasionally locals would therefore ask me to buy them a drink and offer to pay.

The old and pleasant word "gay" acquired, unbeknownst to me, and regrettably, a new meaning. This was brought home on a visit to the research laboratories of Radio Corporation of America. It coincided with a courtesy visit by a Royal Navy frigate. I sported a full beard then. After my rather strenuous visit to the electronics company I felt like a quick drink and went to a bar near my hotel. It was a pleasant and fairly quiet place. Two men stared at me with curiosity. We talked and they suggested dinner. Out we drove. Waiting to be seated and standing at the bar one of the two men asked whether I was gay? I replied that I was not only that, but also obviously drunk. Thereupon he started to cry and moan that this always happened to him. People just did not want him. Well, it certainly and suddenly dawned on me what this was all about. So I asked the barman to call a taxi back to town. He refused, commenting that he did not have to do this sort of thing for perverts. I started walking. It poured with rain. There was a railway crossing: one of the few in that single-track area. I spied a cab with the light on. In vain I tried to hail it. Finally I managed to knock on the window. It was rolled down and the driver told me that he did not take passengers like me! I remonstrated and explained. He finally agreed to take me back to the hotel – but it would cost me. He demanded $20 – quite a hefty amount at that time. I agreed and was safe at last.

There had been many nationalities at the school in Switzerland. At a private party for old Rosenbergerianers some Hungarians recognized me as "the boy who spoke some Hungarian". A former Swiss classmate had come specially to meet me again. I was flattered. I had somehow envied one Jewish boy I liked at the school. In 1942 his family got a permit to come to (what I thought was exciting) Cuba.

I had, of course, heard through my parents of, and even read some books by, the Spanish philosopher José Ortega y Gasset. His years at Oxford had made him fluent in English. Before Generalissimo Francisco Franco died – and when a liberalization of the press was generally expected – the philosopher planned for a new daily for Spain. *El Pais*, now almost four thousand issues old and also published in the Americas, began its premature life with a Harris press from America without a paper to print as yet. I went to see him and his ambitious project and have followed the paper's fortunes ever since. I was pleased to see it spread to places like Mexico or in association with some pages in Britain's *Guardian* and *Le Monde* in France. I was able to present a photo of those former days to the editors in Madrid.

Neil Armstrong, the first man on the moon, was the keynote speaker at a prize-giving at Monte Carlo and hosted by DuPont, the American chemical giant. I was honoured by linking a technical support speech to his address. Later I danced with his wife (and Julia danced with him) after I had jumped from the speakers' platform. On another occasion, hosted by Tom van Breen, there was a festive party – again in Monaco. I pleaded in vain with the women journalists at my table to dance with me. Rejection seemed total until a female voice from another table in the café rang out to alert me to the fact that there would be an American lady partner for me after all. The place was jumping from then on and the band leader came specially to thank me for getting the other guests to dance.

I went on Concorde – the supersonic plane – from New York to London after visiting a printing exhibition in Chicago and then seeing friends, and some second-hand booksellers in New York City. The flight disappointed. The plane was indeed fast, but seating was cramped. Two things struck me: Six of my co-passengers, who were printing industry managers, were soon drunk on too much champagne and snored in their seats. Before we landed in London I had asked for orange juice. The stewardess wanted to give me champagne to avoid having to open another carton. I had managed to get a free "upgrade" by arranging later on to fly first class to South Africa, then still ruled under 'apartheid', and needed a special visa as a journalist to that country. The visa interview was conducted by an arrogant colonel, but I passed the interrogation. I was going to see printers and my grandfather's house. I disliked the policies of the country at that time, and instead of going on to America via Brazil, got a seat home without seeing my grandfather's house in Port St. Johns in the Transkei. I managed that some years later.

The French inventors René Higgonet and Louis Moyroud of Lumitype-Photon fame made phototypesetting a real success. Moyroud was later invited to Switzerland by the principal owner of J. Bobst, of Lausanne and worked for Bobst Graphic. Nothing much came of the bold venture, but the company achieved some acclaim for its Registron press register system.

In America the RCA company had developed a colour scanner and in London John Lyons promoted the *Time-Life* colour scanner with some good results. Many of the so-called coffee table books were reproduced on these machines. Today scanning as such is near-dead and has been replaced by enhanced computer technology.

The *Encyclopaedia of Type Faces*, published since 1951, with my name as chief editor, had made me well-respected in the circle of cognoscenti. I was invited to give talks all over the world. I was very pleased when a professional association, and I have several such memberships, made me a Fellow of the Institute of Printing (now of Paper, Printing & Publishing). I also have similar memberships of American equivalent institutions. In 2009, a fifty-fifth anniversary edition of the book was published.

The Internet and e-mail have changed information gathering and communications. Facts – but are they always facts? – can be accessed almost instantly. There is now too much unchecked and outright biased information available.

Books and libraries still provide a better source of information, though all too often they require the serious information seeker to physically go and seek out and compare or check what he or she are looking for.

Printers, and especially compositors and the now almost extinct race of proofreaders, have the reputation of being well read and literate – perhaps occasionally undeserved.

It has all been said before! The gurus who keep telling us that the world of Gutenberg is passé are at risk of talking to a small blinkered circle of so-called experts who think that just because electronic information services on the Internet are convenient they must be embraced by everybody everywhere.

There is no need for the lazy person to press buttons to look up information when it is easily available in written form, preserved intact and not mutilated or even outright misleading. Of course, it is true that the Internet gives much useful information and is widely accessible. It does not beat the written word which has been recorded and filed for hundreds of years.

These thoughts I expressed in an address to a Wynkin de Worde printing society meeting entitled *Will It Last?* in 1986. The reading of books in Sweden is reported to have risen by an impressive percentage. Worldwide that increase is today at an average of a lower, nevertheless gratifying, and six per cent. People may say that Sweden's remarkable readership figures are due to the dark and cold winters which force Scandinavians to spend more time, like the Canadians and Scots, in their homes. Not all of them feel more content with drink or endless sex than with reading a good book.

They say that people up north are often better educated. Perhaps that is so. Today's illiteracy and those "functional illiterates" are bemoaned by the headmasters of our schools who tell of children of twelve years and more needing remedial classes or by level-headed businessmen, who complain that their often well paid personal secretaries cannot spell.

The urge to read is a foundation of freedom. In Argentina, I believe, the law at one time stipulated that there had to be a school within every square mile of the country! In that country and in Canada reading skills are also much better than in the US If we are going to pay more than lip service only to the idea of a free society, then the spread of literacy and the inherent freedom to disagree with authority must become a prime concern again. That happened when the education acts in various countries were formulated and made education a cornerstone of social advance. On the minus side it must be granted that literacy does not necessarily make people civilized.

Most of the litter louts thoughtlessly discarding empty beverage cans on pavements and front lawns of residential streets or in parks can read. Some of *Hitler's Willing Executioners* were proud to recite Goethe. Monsters like Josef Goebbels quoted Rilke and other German classics. Reinhard Heydrich played the piano and Adolf Eichmann, supervising mass murder, was said to have loved children.

Joseph Heller in his *Closing Time* asks whether anybody has ever set out in his dreams in a career in public relations. It may have some relationship to journalism. I had different ambitions!

Milestones should be celebrated: my then wife Julia Jaspert had arranged a magnificent party to celebrate my sixtieth birthday. Most of my family and friends came, including those from Argentina, continental Europe, and America. We went to see Berthold Brecht's *Threepenny Opera* and to a concert at the Royal Festival Hall. During the interval we sipped champagne standing on the balcony overlooking the Thames – and suddenly a magnificent fireworks display erupted. The demise of the Greater London Council, decreed by Margaret Thatcher's government, was being commemorated. My guests thought I had arranged the great spectacle. Not so! The next day my party was on a riverboat, with Caribbean food and a band making people dance. The children joined in. Soon after another riverboat party ended tragically when the *Marchioness* sank in the Thames.

Continuing the party at my home started on a bad note. The coach driver taking us there mistakenly assumed that the German-speaking guests would appreciate their host being addressed as *Gruppenführer* (group leader). I was furious, turned away from the coach and took a taxi home. All was calm again and some of us drank a small glass of Chateau d'Yquem 1945 and other good wine.

In some way the theatre visit reminded me of seeing the Berlin ensemble and Brecht's *Mother Courage* some years before in London with Helene Weigel and Ernst Busch from the Schiffbauer Damm theatre – from what was then communist East Germany – a memorable performance.

Twenty years later a surprise party was given. Some forty relatives and close friends were there. I had expected only a handful. Imagine my surprise when I arrived at the restaurant venue and people – again from all over Europe – sang "Happy Birthday". The event was organized in secret over a period of six months by the children and Julia. A few friends who had not been able to come or whose invitations were overlooked gave me separate celebrations later. Those were memorable events.

Becoming eighty years old brought the facts of old age home. Living alone I know that eventually I shall become perhaps incompetent to cope with everyday life. It is no good to shelve decisions about where and how to live.

The neighbourhood where I lived for more than a score of years, interspersed with my simultaneous fortnightly commuting to the residence in California, was much liked by me. So is the kindness of my friends who granted the use of the flat I occupied. The time had come to move into sheltered accommodation. Luck would have it that a truly splendid waterside flat in a house with a warden turned up. I took it. The children and friends urged this. Regret had to be overruled by common sense. Much of my independence will be lost, though, but personal safety is enhanced. So I assumed, but I had to find out by bitter experience that there is much crime hereabouts.

In 1989 I was in Portugal to attend the opening of new premises for the agents of the Heidelberg printing machinery company, invited as a guest of the company's Dr Wolfgang Zimmermann. The festivities followed a staging of *The Lusiad*, the Portuguese epic celebrating the history and pioneering discoveries of the country's people. This was followed by a gala dinner. The foreign guests were somewhat curious why all attention of the waiters seemed to be given to the radio and TV broadcasts. I was one of the few people who had a smattering of Portuguese from my infancy in Angola. I was asked to find out and did.

There was momentous news: the Berlin Wall had been opened and thousands flocked through the suddenly open gaps. Our host ordered champagne to flow. I phoned home and begged my son eldest Willem to fly to Berlin, where he stayed with a cousin of mine and danced with thousands of others on the Wall: a totally unexpected earthshaking event. I joined Willem a few days later.

Friends from East Germany came to see me in the glittering West. I ordered some exotic gourmet food, but the daughters were dubious and rejected the sumptuous dishes. That depressed me and the girls' parents.

On a visit to Switzerland I obviously visited my daughter there. During the night I telephoned

California. My daughter overheard my besotted mumblings. She sent a loving letter to London telling me to think carefully. Unfortunately I saw that letter only much later when I rummaged through her mother's papers, worried about the impending separation. Would I have thought more calmly at that early stage of my infatuation and tried to endeavour to save a good marriage?

New brooms sweep cleanly. The new editor of the German magazine I had worked for some thirty-five years invited me to dinner (which he then cancelled) and proposed a forty per cent cut in my monthly fee. Naturally I resigned in pique although this action cost me a substantial part of my income. Perhaps I should have followed my colleague Kurt K. Wolf. He remained with the magazine and is today uncontested guru of digital and reproduction technology.

Blithely and self-indulgently, riding roughshod over the feelings of others, I had started an affair with Barri. Circumstances made it lead to marriage, which soon failed after my stroke (I am of the marrying kind). Had I but known it: my actions condemned me to loneliness in old age. It is always difficult to know in advance what kind of mortgage our acts put on the future. I am on good terms with two of my former wives. After all, we have children together. I occasionally have some contact with my third wife. We had good times together. I managed to show her much of the Europe I love. She remains, however, a stranger with unexpected almost immature reactions. Nobody can foretell the future. Cassandra of ancient lore seems to have known only of the bleak things ahead.

My mother had gone to school with Marlene Dietrich, and knew her at that time as Magdalena von Losch. The two of them lost contact, but later I established indirect contact when I lived in California. I met a friend and confidante of hers and learnt much about her person. Signa Scott's late husband, Jerome Thor, had for some years been a post-war radio commentator based in Europe. He was much like Ed Murrow, whom I had met several times with my benefactor McSweeney. Together we went to New York's Chinatown and favoured splendid meals accompanied by lively gossiping.

Marlene Dietrich, whose father was the Royal Prussian policeman Louis Erich Otto Dietrich, was born in 1901 and attended Auguste Victoria gymnasium, Berlin, where Mama was two years her junior at the school. She seems to have somewhat neglected her daughter Maria, born 1924.

In 1994 my plane to Sao Paulo landed early in the morning. That was just some time after the aircraft bringing the body of the racing driver idol Ayrton Senna's home. Along the main road from the airport to the city throngs of people watched the cortege. I still think there were more people there than for a royal funeral in London.

Sometimes I ask myself whether my infatuation with Barri while I also thought that I was in love with my then wife Julia was just what in German is called *Torschlusspanik* or 'fear of the gate about to close'. I was unable to listen to reason and behaved illogically and in a self-centred way. I believed myself in the right and in love with Barri, too. And thus lost my normal sense of loyalty and responsible care. That was an aberration and at variance with my Calvinist emotions. Religion was not involved, though. Remorse came too late. However, what propelled me towards divorce and remarriage was the belief that a cult had taken possession of my wife Julia's mind and actions after thirty-odd years of being together. The cult was Life Training. I exacted some faint revenge. I fought their tax-free charity status through Glenda Jackson, my then Member of Parliament, through the charity commissioners, newspaper letters and *Inform*, the cult information centre. I broke my marriage vows, though. Nevertheless, this cult business seemed to me worse than money-grabbing and equal to a breach of faith by my wife whom I thought never to give in to outside persuasion.

Friends offered me accommodation in a vacant flat owned by their mother in elegant St. John's Wood, who was getting older and needed their help. I got to like the area after almost forty-five years in my previous home.

In later years I was able to revise local records by pointing out that, for instance, more artists than those previously listed made their residence in the area. The call girl Christine Keeler operated her liaisons there. Her intimate knowledge of a cabinet minister in Harold Macmillan's government caused a national crisis and the downfall of the government.

Though I had nothing to do with all that I, through work, innocently knew one of her 'friends' who later ran a nightclub in Israel with Mandy Rice-Davies. Of the cabinet minister, who at first denied the accusation of misbehaviour, Mandy coined the memorable "Well, he would, wouldn't he" phrase.

The wages of sin is death. Even the innocent know this for a fact. Justice knows something, too. Bernie Cornfeldt, who persuaded so many (including my trusting brother) to invest their savings, was released from Swiss jail to return to California to lead a sybaritic life there. The mammoth fraudster Robert Maxwell was given the honour of solemn burial on Israel's Mount of Olives. In a generous parting gesture at the end of his presidency, Bill Clinton allowed the embargo-busting financier Marc Rich return to his country. No wonder that the "honour-bound" slogan graces that infamous camp at Guantànamo.

In Switzerland Vincent Frank-Steiner, whom I also mention elsewhere, seemed to have achieved a unique paranormal breakthrough. This nephew of the late Hilde Rosbaud – but not a blood relative of Paul Rosbaud – appears to have established contact with his late aunt. In his grief he probably forgot about her intentions. This enabled him to read the mind of the deceased and change her Last Will, drawn up by solicitors Black Graf in London's Hampstead. Both he and I, as well as some others, had a verified copy. He did not mention this to probate court. He thus got all the inheritance. I was the loser. The humbug attitude of social benevolence ill becomes that man. Money is not my forte. Sadly this manipulation of a deceased person's intentions by this modern age reincarnated flesh-and-blood Uriah Heap seemed to confirm the stereotype view of some groups. He by no means represents the image of all Jewry. In the same way that all Germans are never all Nazis, nor are all Russians to blame for Soviet atrocities. The frenetic murder of ethnic Chinese is not the crime of the American people or the Indonesians. Politics and religious teachings all too frequently play an evil role.

The smell of money corrupts. It affects even the nicest people. At the time I had arrived in England I had acquaintance with a sensitive and respected poet. Almost every time we encountered each other, he would mention that "one day my ship will come home". In practice that meant that he was waiting, perhaps even hoping, for his mother's death. Was that a demonstration of filial love?

Bare Midriffs & Never Give Up

DO THEY think they are sexy? Some of us, perhaps because we are no longer adolescents, do not find the sight of an exposed and protruding navel button – although we benevolently approve pregnancy of expectant mothers or even young women as often very attractive.

Careful research has shown that these are not one-man views. Others – many of them husbands and fathers – think such exposure boring or even ugly.

In some countries, where young people dress even outrageously in extreme fashions one never, ever sees a bare midriff. In places like India, where saris are worn, the midriff is bare but never flaunted.

Where is becoming modesty? Do young women really feel so sexually insecure that they have to expose even the top line of the pubic hair? Is it to prove that they are female? "Builder's Bum" is a sometimes ridiculed affliction, though confined to the rear and not the pubic region. Even the majority of pop idols do not flaunt all their physical assets or what they believe to be assets.

Someone, probably Tom Lehrer, the American satirist, used to ask his nightclub audience this simple question: "You have heard of Christopher Columbus!" Lehrer would explain: "he never gave up". Next question from Lehrer: "You know about George Washington?" Lehrer provided the quick answer: "Well, you know, he never gave up". Then he proceeded to the next stage: "Who recalls Oliver Twiddledee?" After an impressive pause he would solve the riddle accompanied by a loud drum rumble and proclaim: "So – you see – he gave up!"

I, too, never gave up, though this did not make me famous. Social workers and doctors told me after my stroke that I was too stubborn and took too many risks. Probably true, but infinitely preferable to just bemoaning fate and staring at the ceiling. Anyhow, most illnesses and afflictions (except breakages and such) are – a personal view this – self-inflicted. The stroke was predictable. I had not taken care and took no precautions or care. *Mea culpa.*

Günter von Hagen's macabre show of human plasticized cadavers came to London. I was shocked when Barri Clark, my wife, went to see it. Rumour had it the Chinese and the Soviets had sold bodies of executed prisoners for the exhibits. Cannot the dead be shown some respect? *De mortis non nisi bonum.* Almost ten years later the horror show was returning to London, sponsored by one of those mobile telephone companies.

The US, and seemingly Japan, are the West's leaders in the application of the death penalty. It seemed barbaric to execute in the state of Georgia a man kept imprisoned for thirty years and after many stays of execution kill him legally. Surely the time in prison should be taken into account. George W. Bush, when governor of the state of Texas, held the ignominious free world's record for state-sanctioned executions.

Lillian Helman, in the third volume of her memoirs, observed that for some reason the liberal United States of America has its own version of notorious illiberalism, which makes the world distrust the traditionally much admired country.

Most of my adult life I had been a paid-up member of the Labour Party of Britain. The Iraq war depressed me and I resigned. Allied forces had killed about a million civilians there in their efforts to bring democracy to the country. By no means did I support the murderous Saddam Hussein.

Stroke!

ON A trip to London one morning I went to a press conference and felt squeamish. Barri was asked to accompany me to the nearest bus stop. Half an hour at the meeting feeling really unwell I asked Roy Coxhead to get me a taxi. Once the taxi set off, I felt myself going rigid. I could not move my limbs and, arrived outside my home, the taxi driver (I had lost any power of speech) told me he had called for an ambulance. The taxi all that time waited. I signalled to the driver to search my back pocket for his fare. He did that – and would not take a tip! Months later I made every effort to trace the driver and reward him. I failed.

After almost nine weeks in intensive care I discharged myself to crawl home against doctors' advice. Physiotherapists patiently taught me to use my legs and hands again. After a wheelchair and then two crutches, movement and speech returned. One day I picked up enough courage to have a morning cappuccino – now one of many.

Stretching myself to a top bookshelf to get some heavy tome down, a muscle snapped: hernia! That was successfully operated on next year, but the dreaded hospital infection came. My scrotum swelled up to almost football size. Three stays in hospital (each a week long) were needed. After-effects are disheartening. Serves me right!

The need to take Warfarin rat poison lifelong and the risk of blood clotting – and another stroke – made the thought of having the knocked out two front teeth replaced by implants vetoed by the doctors. Shame of shames: I acquired a denture.

As I mentioned earlier, most of my adult life I had been a paid up member of Britain's Labour Party. Allied forces had killed nearly a million civilians there in the pretence to bring democracy to the country. Saddam Hussein was a bloodthirsty tyrant. George W. Bush could easily have arranged for an Israeli hit squad team to assassinate him. Tony Blair, the British Prime Minister then, has effectively destroyed the Labour Party and some of the principles upon which it is based. Arabs will hardly trust his efforts as a UN Peace envoy for the Near East.

Years ago life was simpler. Front doors – even in London – were not always shut firmly. My mother left her keys 'under the flower pot' by the front door and had a note on the door telling people so. On Fridays fresh fish was delivered and actually put in the fridge. The local fishmonger over the weekend caught wild salmon in Scotland. His son would deliver it.

Disaster strikes unexpectedly. After having been out shopping and when home again I often feel unusually tired. So I lay down for literally only six minutes. I soon get out again to do some local shopping. When I returned I realized to my horror that the front door keys had dropped from the pocket of my trousers while I had lain down. I stood outside the home, looking forlorn. A policeman walked past – a rare sight these days on residential streets – and asked whether I was all right. I so obviously looked distressed. Of course I was OK, just dejected, and I told him so. "Leave it to me" he said and set off down the road only to return a few minutes later carrying a builder's ladder which he had requisitioned. He then put is against the wall of the house, told me that I was too old to climb up, but asked me to steady the ladder while he climbed up and pushed the first floor window open to worm himself into a room. A few minutes later he opened the front door and handed me my keys. They had been lying on the bed. I thanked him. The constable never even asked my name.

Life sometimes seems strange. I have good friends. Among them a witty husband and an attractive, bright wife. I found out that they after many years together and with pleasant children have not slept together for years nor shared the same bed. I think they have separate bedrooms. During the day they appear to – mostly – tolerate each other. To me all this appears quite bizarre. One lives and learns – and remains puzzled. Grandson Alexander, the son of Anna and Mario Cocca-Jaspert, who was born prematurely, was doing alright at his school in Switzerland. He was beginning to learn sign language and loved his school. Sadly, a psychiatrist consulted by social services said that he did not fit into his school surroundings and he wanted to send him to a school for handicapped children with serious problems of behaviour. His distressed parents were reluctant to appeal for fear of irritating the experts. Alexander is quite intelligent and is learning to speak, albeit belatedly. Today it is rather difficult to ever stop him from talking in Swiss German.

Oscar Nicholas Werner Jaspert, so far the youngest grandson, talks classical Greek or whatever his proud father Augustus and I imagine. He talks the dead language perhaps. Neither of us can understand what he means to tell us so cheerfully. His mother Millie always listens attentively. Now he talks clearly. He is just over two years old.

I am very lonely. The fault is all my own – and perhaps I deserve this. A friend of mine in a very similar position hired himself a tart for a night – just for company and, of course, gratification. I cannot and would not do that. I do not want to buy affection, however pleasant and deserving the girl may be or even genuinely giving. Some people deliberately want to be lonely or be hermits.

There are compensations. A complete stranger in the pub next door stopped me one night and said: "You are what a gentleman is supposed to be". That really was flattering. A young lady flattered me by telling me that she thought my mind sharp. One day a middle aged lady stopped me in the street and told me that I looked like Spike Milligan of *Adolf Hitler: My Part In His Downfall.* The author had reached fame as Bluebottle in the Goon Show which had fans abroad too – even in Austria. Some years back Eric Harben pleased me by saying that I was "truly getting to be a real Englishman", because of thinking about cricket. if the truth be told, I like the game only because – weather allowing – it enables oneself to enjoy a day in the open, resting lazily with a glass of red wine in the hand and, in olden times, a copy of *The Times* shielding the face from the sun. That makes for a perfect day out in the open!

Tante Ensel (Elisabeth Jaspert), my favourite aunt and mother of three cousins (one of whom considers me almost a brother) knew me from my boyhood days. She had her one-hundredth birthday. I was privileged to join her centenary celebrations. On that occasion she sang. She always loved song. That time we all fell silent in admiration and loving joy. She was then in a home in Berlin run by catholic nuns, mainly from Italy. They cared for her and almost jokingly served her sometimes a glass of bubbly or eggnog, calling her a "frivolous girl". She rightly replied that she was not a girl, but the mother of three sons. I combined visits to Berlin visits with seeing her and also family and friends.

Religious catholic ladies seem very benign. My first wife had gone to a religious school where the nuns, came teenage to her, mentioned the "division between the legs". That was sex education of a sort.

I am by nature garrulous. Even real strangers open up to me. I listen and then opine. Some people tell me of intimate things I would rather not hear. I really do not want to know of their conquests or needs of the sexual kind.

Life Goes On

I ENJOYED writing and publishing a little book,among them *Popo* (the German word for a nice bottom). I got many kind compliments, but sales were sluggish. I had made the mistake of publishing in England. There are simply not many German-speaking readers here.

Suddenly I was considered “racist”. A son-in-law argued that my insistence that immigrants – in this case Indians and black people – should adapt when living in other countries and “when in Rome, do as the Romans do”. He objected and said the colonial powers had for so long oppressed other countries’ cultures, that it was only right to demonstrate ethnic background now in the new home countries. I myself am an – albeit white – immigrant. I try to blend in. I do not agree to the Nazis policy of imposing their Teutonic habits, like they did after the invasion of Czechoslovakia. Street signs suddenly proclaimed that, forthwith, driving in Prague would be on the right and no longer on the accustomed left.

Then there are those to whom by some actions of others harm was done. They were probably too weak to stop it. They – like myself for instance – might really rather be gregarious and, like some Dostoevsky character, find being alone at times difficult to bear. At the same time I think I am rather lucky because I have loving children and attentive friends around me. Good friends after my stroke made me enjoy life again.

Roy Coxhead had rekindled my interest in the theatre. Michael Freer came to visit for two days. We had a great time together. At one such occasion we saw the film of *Lost Weekend.* When I was 'flat on my back'. Michael unconditionally offered his savings – and I was grateful but did, of course – not accept. However I accepted his help for some months when he travelled from Norwich in East Anglia and then by bus and underground train to take my bag of laundry to the launderette's service wash. I was too weak at the time to carry heavy loads. Now I can walk and only carry the stick when I go out-of-doors for security. His help I no longer needed. If need be, I can even make the bed these days. Muriel and Philip Burton rallied round and made me come out of my shell by suggesting I take a renewed interest in art. They take me with them to the large exhibitions at the Royal Academy or the Victoria & Albert and other major museums. Most times we then have a meal eating out.

Of course, I realize that it needs an element of pigheadedness to do things normally. Physiotherapists, social workers and my doctor originally described these as “dangerous risk taking”. I wanted to be able to do everyday things, but am grateful for all the help I have had and am getting. There are many aspects to being independent (or trying to be). Realistically thinking, my situation is not bad at all. People like to talk to me – and I am (I believe) – a fairly good listener.

I spend a lot of time writing at the computer. Some of this time is spent noting down jokes everybody around me has heard before. In the *Financial Times* I ran such anecdotes regularly. Sometimes I become preoccupied by reminiscences, often painful.

Mostly I write in English, but looking back I find that there are well over a thousand of my articles in German, as well as some notes for a new book following in my father’s footsteps.

The Swiss author Roger Graf was right when he stipulated that computers were invented for peculiar people – people who cannot cope with other people.

How the world has changed. Today we take running hot water for granted. When I was a child baths were an ‘occasion’, especially when visiting relatives away from the glitzy city of Berlin. A zinc basin would be filled with hot water and one was scrubbed down. Later we had hot water everywhere – but when I went on holiday with the family the farm cottages in Wales lacked such amenities. Ablutions required a dip into the icy waters of the waterfall in front of the house. Washing ourselves was what was important.

I never studied the *Talmud*, but once read a detective story by Lawrence Block about some New York petty criminal and it quoted the book of ancient wisdom: "Therefore was a single man only first created to teach thee that whosoever destroyeth a single soul from the children of man, scripture charges him as though he had destroyed the whole world." Yet, even today some barbaric countries (even so-called civilized nations/states like the USA's Georgia) retain capital punishment. Before his presidency and as Governor of Texas, George W. Bush held the free world's record in upholding death sentences.

The hero of Michael Dibdin's *Comisario Aurelio Zen* series of detective stories set in Italy, in one of the tales describes an epidemic of modern society: apparently rational people are seen walking about and agitatedly talking to themselves. They walk or drive oblivious of others. They sometimes frighten others by sudden maniacal laughter or shouting. Closer inspection often reveals that they seem to talk into mobile phones and to an invisible person.

The comisario (since promoted) also notices a strange mating rite among modern couples. Both have a mobile telephone. They walk along, holding hands – and even talk to each other through their hand-held phones!

British newspapers reported early that American government sources indicated that the anti-torture legislation, passed by the Senate, would be vetoed. Surely this was slander. The United States stands for the rights of mankind. It would, I think, never allow itself to be likened to criminals like Hitler or Stalin. In my life I have seen many terrible things in war and peace. Three or four times some aspects touched me personally. I was badly upset by a lady pop idol called Madonna likening an American presidential candidate to Hitler. She knows nothing of history and slanders people for their ideas. The candidate is not a murderous and genocidal monster. That lady, a poor imitation of Marlene Dietrich, infuriated me. Bad memories came back of the time my father was murdered in the concentration camp. Then only my hatred of the barbaric Nazis and that despicable crowd's notorious capability for horrors protected me. I feel fortunate because I do not have to watch Madonna's antics and noiseful shrieking and gyrations.

My first divorce left me speechless in a way. I was fantasizing about another woman, but not unfaithful. The second divorce was devastating, but I knew I had blundered into it eyes wide open. The third literally stunned me. I thought that I was blameless, was recovering from a stroke, four months of hospital and after having lost ten kilograms in weight. I needed help and was recovering – and then the unexpected blow came. I was thought to be "impossible and too much work". Another ten kilograms in body weight were lost. I was to be alone for the rest of my life. Perhaps I was to blame and would have another stroke?

I write few articles these days. Some of my former magazines stopped publication; others are impecunious or went bankrupt. In any case, I prefer newspaper contributions and have published a copious assembly of *Letters to the Editor*, mostly about Iraq and the plan to introduce identity cards to our country. George W. Bush and his henchmen as well as Tony Blair want documentation of people. Liberty is being eroded in the "free world". These days, superior, "Big Brother Is Watching You" societies may eventually result in dictatorship in the name of upholding democracy. The new identity cards pry into too many private spheres. The Nazi occupied channel islanders of Jewish race were rounded up dutifully by British police obeying criminal orders unwittingly.

My children are a joy. Elisabeth and Reginald had a modest honeymoon in Britain's Cotswolds. Beatrice and Shane went to Sicily. Anna and Mario were given a honeymoon in the Far East and even met orang-utans. The youngest son Augustus, and Millie went to Brazil. Willem remained single. Now he plans to get married to Stania. Where will they want to go for their honeymoon?

Physical progress amazes me – touch wood. I feel fit, move about and accept that my former agility is restricted by normal old age afflictions more than the effect of my stroke of several years ago. The doctors seem to think that recovery has been remarkable. That is not to say that things are perfect. I walk sometimes a bit hesitatingly and still have difficulties making the bed, cleaning the bath or vacuum-cleaning and window washing.

A poster at bus stops in London intrigued me and seemed to justify my dislike of sport. It proclaimed that "this drink will restore your energy after exhausting sport". Why drive yourself to exhaustion? The German saying of *Sport ist Mord* (sport is murder) has truth in it. A former friend, quite a successful international athlete in former times, limps along these days. Proof of the risks of driving yourself too hard.

I resumed my travelling. My cousin Martin celebrated seventy years of life. We gathered in a famous eleventh century former monastery. He had a vernissage of his paintings in Wiesbaden the day before – and it was great. So many family were there from all over Europe. Earlier I had visited my daughters in Spain and Switzerland, and a friend of mine specially travelled from Milan to Zurich to meet for lunch. I also spend nice weeks with friends in Scotland. Relatives from Berlin came to visit me, too. All very nice and cheering.

An otherwise minor event, a hernia operation, proved scary. It was a bit like Russian roulette. The reason being that I must take rat poison to thin my blood. Doctors had to wean me off for a few days and then – after the operation – wean me back on to it. An unwelcome side effect of the operation was a common hospital infection with after-effects even now. Unreasonable fear prevented me from having a tooth (recommended by my dentist) pulled. Silly me: the operation went well, though I had to live with some irritating complications for probably three months. I did not have to lie in hospital. Obviously I did not want to be laid up. After the hernia event I pleaded for my discharge on a Friday from the surgical ward (very nice and kind doctors and nurses, and an annoyingly aggressive alcoholic patient who physically attacked staff) and lied by pretending my son Augustus was getting married the next day! He got married years later. As for myself, the infection persisted and required repeat stays in the hospital.

After the earlier stroke a competent physiotherapist bullied me into trying to stand on one leg (usually the left one). As I an infant child I had been admiring my African (Bantu) houseboy. He and his people stood on one leg to relax the other one! I copied that practice and could stand for half an hour in that position. After my stroke I had seemed to lose that skill. Physiotherapists patiently taught me how to get up, walk upright with the aid of walking sticks and count small change.

In other respects I am becoming very much aware of old age creeping up. My bloated physical appearance (when naked) must send a shudder though the mind of any woman not a nurse.

Among the people I met during the course of my fairly eventful life are some very rich and influential men and women. Has their wealth and power made for better lives? Material comforts they may enjoy, but some of them experienced personal tragedies. One lost his wife although money tried everything, including a liver transplant or two. She died suddenly and fairly young. Another scion of industry was struck first by the suicide of his wife and then again by his son's self-immolation. Another good man rose phenomenally in this world only to be shamed by one of wives publicizing their divorce quarrels through the newspapers and losing the affection of his children.

Occasionally when taking morning coffee there is TV. On *Sky News* after the disastrous hurricane Katrina hit the New Orleans region of North America, the headline read: "Bush: one of the worst disasters to hit the US". Comment enough, I thought.

At last the American Embassy in London confirmed that I could now apply for a visa at $100. Why should I pay when other Britons can travel unrestricted? There was no longer any real bar to going to the United States. I have good friends there. I would have resented being stopped from seeing them, but am still wary of risking imprisonment, especially in America. Since then I have been found out for having been to Cuba, Iraq,

Iran, Libya and other suspect countries.

The erstwhile US Vice-president Richard (Dick) Cheney spoke in June 2005 to defend the treatment of almost exclusively Muslim prisoners at the American detention camp Justice (!) at Guantànamo Bay on Cuba's soil: "They got a brand new facility down at Guantànamo. We spent a lot of money to build it. They are well treated down there. They are living in the tropics. They are well fed. They have got everything they could possibly want."

The *New York Times* reported at the time that while some military doctors treated the medical needs of prisoners, others were deeply involved in efforts to extract actionable intelligence by conducting and refining coercive interrogations including advice on how to increase stress levels and exploit fears to break prisoners' spirits. Earlier Arturo Gonzales, a former White House counsel brief, told President George W. Bush that in his judgement, this new paradigm (the war on terror) renders obsolete the (Red Cross) Geneva's strict limitations on questioning of enemy prisoners and renders quaint some of those provisions. Thomas Jefferson would have reminded them that "he who trades liberty for security deserves neither and will lose both". Helmut von Moltke worried the Nazi High Command about the human rights of enemy prisoners in vain.

Honour-bound has real meaning: Dr Zoltan Frankl,

who looked after the family's teeth, had fled from communist Hungary. From Austria he had reached London. He had been an inmate of Mauthausen concentration camp. The camp commandant fell seriously ill. Dr Frankl was called in – and saved his life. It would have been easy to let the horror figure quietly pass away. Dr Frankl stuck by the Hippocratic Oath. Being Jewish, that non-action also probably saved his life, beset by persecution: first in Hungary under Bela Kuhn, then the Nazis and finally escaping during the Hungarian Revolution to the West and freedom.

I had met the American biochemist Paul Greengard in London. When I was in America I spent some time with him in New York. One Sunday we went with his family to Einstein College's recreation park. It was a very hot day and the children joined him and me in a rowing boat and jumped again and again into the water. Suddenly on of the boys did not return and was lying at the bottom of the lake. We both jumped in – fully clothed. Then we rowed back to the picnic place. Paul's wife looked puzzled at our wet clothes. We said nothing, only Paul said he wanted to drive home. So we did in our dripping suits. Paul's Hungarian-born wife repeatedly asked us why we insisted driving in sodden suits. We assured her that was very comfortable in the hot weather. The boys kept mum. We were all terrified of the bad tempered lady!

When over a dozen years ago I was diagnosed with

prostate cancer and the consultant who brought the news wanted to operate almost immediately, I fobbed him off, got a second opinion and am under observation every six month at a leading London teaching hospital. I have had no treatment except Tamsulosin and the seemingly benign over-the-counter homeopathic Saw Palmetto. I am on Warfarin, the rat poison, but have dropped Statins against my NHS doctor's strong advice, but with blessings of the prostate consultant. I fear surgery.

The family trend of stubbornness and a tendency not to accept authority may have helped. It seems cranky. Many of my family oppose what we think is wrong and unreasonable. The paternal family have a perhaps silly reputation of being *spökenkiekers* (ghost or spook seers). Whateley Carrington some decades back investigated that in his experimental psychic research, but did not arrive at any conclusions. Physiotherapists and doctors have repeatedly told me not to take risks. My reply is that is prefer risks to just sitting around vegetating. At one time I needed two helpers to help me walk stumblingly. I told them that I wanted to invite them for a cup of coffee in the Italian cafe round the corner. They smiled condescendingly. So one day I sneaked out and supported myself against the garden walls and managed to get down the road and round the corner to the cafe, where I was welcomed back with open arms. I telephoned my physiotherapist helpers and invited them to join me. They arrived shaking their heads and wondering how I had got to the coffee bar. We had cappuccino, though. Afterwards I hardly made it back to my home despite help. I was really tired, but soon went exploring the streets again.

In France Dr Emilie Coue many years ago held that many illnesses (not things like fractures, etcetera) are often imaginary. I hold to that belief my mother also held.

Meanwhile Barri has flatteringly told me that I taught her not to have credit card debts. In California one day I had paid her card debts off and implored her not to run up any further bills. Barri assured me that she now pays up.

I tend to think that increasing age gives me greater insights. I write new books. Last year yet another reprint from 1953 was published.

So my layman's conclusions are: it pays to be bloody-minded! And never give up! Or, as Ambrose Bierce defined it in the *Devil's Dictionary*: "Self – the most important person in the universe".

I find the Internet not that comfortable to use. People like to read. Deucadion Rediadic in a letter to *The Economist* wrote that "no amount of tinkering with *economist.com* can match the pleasure of reading the pages on a Sunday morning on a beach (near Athens), "Reading Endangers Stupidity", proclaims a German publisher.

Eternal life came a step nearer in 2008: at the Museum of Modern Art in New York. Two Australian artists, Oron Catto and Ionat Zur, showed living leather. Mouse skins had been kept pulsating in a fluid broth, agitated by electricity, some newspaper reported. Those stories may have been fancifully extended sheer fantasy, but seemed plausible. Is immortality just around the corner? In Curt Siodmak's science fiction *Donovan's Brain* he forecast a nightmarish sort of immortality depending on a steady supply of cryogenic fluid.

Will the science of life find ways of lending man eternal life by replication of emotions and speech? Could such a replica have real physical sensations, even an orgasm? Nightmare or "oh death – where is thy sting?"

The Gadarene rush to privatize the Post Office in Britain and nullify the pioneering achievements of Heinrich von Stephan and Rowland Hill in the eighteenth century appal me. Sure enough, these days the services are not perfect, but they remain superior in concept. Time was when in England the mail was delivered to the door on Christmas morning. In the old days the postman even got a small gift.

The UK *Press Gazette* newspaper (for journalists and publishers) had died – and was resurrected. Some thirty or more years ago I wrote regularly for this paper when David North was editor. He later lived in

Hungary. At the time of working for him I had been able to arrange for him to travel to Sweden. As it will happen, a change of editor made my contributions unwanted. The weekly was sold and repeatedly taken over by newcomers, last by a suddenly rich-by-perhaps-ill-gotten-gains editor who had it closed down after a few months of losing money. Serves him right, too! It had changed character and the closure was no great loss perhaps. Some people thought otherwise. When all seemed doomed a rescuer was found and the magazine reappeared again.

Winter is cruel. My favourite aunt, Tante Ensel, died at the age of almost one-hundred-and-three years. She and her husband, my father's elder brother Fritz, were wonderful after my father was killed and ever after. They protected my mother and built a small flat for her in their home when Mama was penniless. The family truly rallied around her.

The film actress Cate Blanchett, according to the *Metro* newspaper feels that "the best way to get to know people is by having sex with them … or by working with them". This should eventually perhaps give comfort to all those bosses accused of sexual harassment. All they sincerely wanted probably was to get to know their more attractive female staff as a prelude to promotion, while at the same time sleeping with them. Will the lawmakers think about this statement coming from a woman?

Throughout my life I clung to respect for authors and their writings. While I often just glanced at newspapers or magazines, I almost inevitably finished the reading of books. Towards the end of my life I have suddenly acquired the freedom to disregard the reading of a boring or simply trashy book. Such go to charity. Let others be bored and provide a modest income to a good cause.

An outgoing British Home Secretary wanted to scrap the European Convention on Human Rights the better to fight terrorism. Are we then considered terrorists? All of us?

Stewart Valdar fought by the pen (and paste) against this onslaught on civil liberties and the warmongering terrorism of our elected rulers. Right up to his death this journalist and editor published a newsletter documenting evil deeds. I am proud of having known and worked with such a man.

At my ripe old age thoughts and afterthoughts come. Take my three divorces. Well, the first was not wanted. I still think my first wife Hella is beautiful and so intelligent. A pity we split up. I had been fantasizing about an admittedly attractive lesbian. That was too much for the mother of my first two daughters. Nevertheless, I was awarded (for, I believe the second time then in modern English law history) custody of two little girls). Almost my age, Hella fell into depressing moods. The past had too many sadnesses to account for.

I met Julia. After some years we finally married. We had three children. A German journalist commented nastily that we were adding too many people to the world. Then after many years I misbehaved, admittedly. I had approached a dangerous age and desired last chances. I did not want a divorce, but felt that Julia was tired of me. I had misbehaved before, but foolishly believed that had been sanctioned by Julia. Stupid me! I still like both like both Hella and Julia more than very much. Then – in a sort of *Torschlusspanik* (German for Last Fling) I married again – and was, perhaps rightly, divorced quite soon by Barri. Serves me right, probably?

The secret services know about my past life and contact with Paul Rosbaud.

During the War in Berlin, Rosbaud seems to have had unusually good sources of information not only within science circles, but also perhaps in the police. When my late father Willem, was kidnapped by the Gestapo, he told Mama that the case seemed hopeless and scoffed at the idea of buying his freedom. True enough, all efforts failed. We collected his ashes and gold pocket watch, which was later stolen.

When a truly devastating air raid was done on Bremen, my mother could not contact relatives and friends there. Mama telephoned Rosbaud. Within days he ascertained that they were safe and sound.

Elsewhere other of his information is discussed.

In 1943 and at the request of the German consulate located within my school grounds I had to leave Switzerland to eventually do military service. Friends offered me shelter in Zurich, but the cantonal Police found me and took me to the German (Nazi) border at Basel. For a year I managed to hide. One day Rosbaud phoned my mother and warned her that I had been located. He suggested I give myself up, pretending I could not understand why I had not been called up. I dutifully reported and was enlisted immediately – bizarrely as an officer's candidate because of family relatives. That night and on a friendly doctor's advice I deliberately broke my left collar bone and thus gained a three months' reprieve. Later I deserted together with the descendant of an illustrious German First World War war hero to the US Third Army.

Rosbaud died young. Hilde, his widow, died much later. She had left Julia and me each substantial sums of money and also appointed Julia a joint executrix. Although the co-executor had a signed and witnessed copy of the will, he managed to declare it lost and we got just a courtesy payment. Neither of us thanked him for that conscience money. While Hilde was in the care of a nursing home he somehow appears to have bullied the old lady into giving him power-of-attorney. She did not want to do this and managed to get the head of the home to witness the withdrawal of this document. Such are the rewards of looking after for many years the lonely widow of my great benefactor Paul Rosbaud, who had treated me almost like an own son. Respect and morals made me decide no longer to pursue my rightful inheritance claim. Money is not everything. The man in Switzerland is perhaps religious and might be headed for the special cauldrons with hot and spicy old whore's oil they keep there for people like him.

A child of mine was heavily into drugs and had joined a colony of addicts, who all seemed to come from respectable homes in Europe. In India this child became dependent. Everybody seemed to give up except me – the father. On a visit to India I met a young German, who told me that he wished his father was coming to see him and would rescue him. There was a child, a blonde and beautiful granddaughter. Local villagers in Goa gave her breakfast while her parents slept, seemingly endlessly. Viren Chhabra phoned from Delhi and told me to do something to save my child. The High Commission in Delhi, which I called upon, would not help in any way. Probably they were fed up with hippies' problems.

I paid for tickets home and was warned that it seemed a waste of money. I was the only one not to believe that. Finally the parents and child came home. It had been touch and go. Viren Chhabra, the friend in Delhi, had put on his reserve officer's uniform and literally taken her to the plane. Up to the last minute there was a real risk that the tickets home would be sold again, like the first ones I had sent. On arrival in London, my child collapsed and cut a leg so badly on a glass-topped table that an ambulance had to be called to take her to hospital to stitch the bleeding wound.

Back home this child started selling small quantities of drugs and was eventually busted and sentenced and only set free on condition Julia and I looked after the daughter while my child went to a rehabilitation home under strict supervision. The anti-drug regime was strict, but worked. My beloved child is now drug-free, became a lecturer and lives today in southern Spain in a very nice home – happily married and rarely looking back on the past.

While the granddaughter lived with us in Hampstead, police were watching the house, but fortunately botched the job. Julia and I asked the child to leave and not endanger the whole family. My second wife took the distressed grandchild, Poppy Jaspert, in and we brought my granddaughter up for some years. She was wild at first. Though a toddler, she washed her own clothes in the bath by stomping on them. Today she is a beautiful much admired young woman. My own children loved her but resented the attention sometimes paid to her moods. Initially she cried a lot and had to be taken into our bed and be comforted. My children were jealous, but also good friends and "siblings". I had custody of the two daughters from the first marriage. I sometimes felt sorry for their mother's loss of the children. In practice, my second wife took charge and looked after them. True enough, I read stories to them and especially made my oldest daughter, Elisabeth, love the real classics, such as the *Iliad* and the incomparable *Odyssey*. It was my love for the latter that later caused me to give the name of the hero of the classical story (not James Joyce's Irish book mistaken for the old story by Matisse's illustrations) to my youngest son. (The illustrated book was my son's graduation present.)

After the divorce from my first wife, caring for two girls, I did something terrible, and realized the error of judgment which my oldest daughter never forgot. The children were having a bath and the older girl was behaving terribly. I could no longer stand it and gave her a very strong whack on the bottom. I instantly regretted this and apologized profusely – too late. All my life I had argued against physical punishment – and then I had actually carried it out and would carry guilt, forever. My daughter remembered that cruelty all through her short life.

The sad outcome of that regrettable awful smack was that the girls went to live with their mother. I was speechless when they packed up and left the home. I asked myself whether to be left and abandoned was to become a pattern governing my life.

Sometimes, after my eldest daughter Elisabeth's death and burial, I would go to Highgate Cemetery in London, sitting in solitude and quiet contemplation on a stone bench near the grave. I found peace there in the gardens. I hope to have my final resting place close to the site.

While still schoolboys my two sons had found a splendid way when around ten years of age, to do something worthwhile. They started a nature reserve in town. It was really only a piece of wasteland behind a day clinic opposite our home. The boys were allowed to cultivate it. The local paper published a story about them and their effort at saving the environment and some wildlife. Alas, all their enthusiastic endeavours came to an end. The space was needed for a parking lot and was paved over.

On his first visit to the theatre, my then six year old son, Willem, watched a Shakespeare play. An actor was "killed" and fell to the floor. The audience was asked, what had befallen the prostrate man. My son exclaimed: "he's alive … he is not really dead". The actors were dumbfounded. The play stopped for a few minutes, with the actors on the stage helplessly laughing and falling all over themselves.

I was married three times, and was ditched by every one of the three wives. I was guilty, in the legal sense, only in the case of my second marriage which lasted almost thirty years, though my rather stunningly beautiful and elegant second wife, who kept her slim figure and good looks, had apparently had qualms about my moods for the last ten years or so. These moods were unconnected to my adultery, which was committed with the apparent connivance of my second wife.

My second wife cleaned me out financially, sadly. She refused to share the cost of university for the two sons, who were doing well and thriving at the time of writing. The children lent me much valued moral support. I was strangely surprised by their support, but valued the children's love, care and interest (to name but a few aspects) of their kindness.

I bought back my books and pictures, even those I had inherited. My second wife wanted only a few books actually for herself. She steadfastly refused to contribute to any costs incurred in cleaning the former matrimonial home or other incidental costs of losing the much loved home.

Travelling with the family on the *Settebello* train on the way to Rome, the sons, Willem and Augustus, were practising their violins. In the adjacent compartment sat a Spanish (catholic, of course) priest, who did not speak English. The boys talked in Latin instead. Augustus did so brokenly. The cardinal invited him to see him in Madrid, where the boys went quite often to visit my brother, their uncle. The youngest son called on the man and had tea and cake at the palace.

Family

THE FAMILY worldwide on both paternal and maternal sides is small. Perhaps there are only around fifteen-hundred Jaspert or Anger families around. The youngest of my cousins, born in Berlin and living in Spain is soon to get married to a doctor from Cuba. We look forward to a second family member in the beautiful Caribbean. Perhaps the wedding will be there. Some of us would love to be there.

Willem Jaspert studied in Leeds, Barcelona, Lisbon and Mexico City. He is more literate in Spanish than most Mexicans. His bosses in Mexico at a well-known magazine commented: "he writes better Spanish than the locals". Small wonder, he succeeds in whatever he tries his hand at. The youngest son, Augustus, has a First Class honours degree from Edinburgh and also studied for a year in Vienna. He has other degrees too. Now he is a civil servant somewhere in the more exalted regions of the government. He is married. Both sons wrote their final papers on the Turkish invasion in the East and on the Moorish rule of much of Spain in the West.

My eldest daughter, Elisabeth, who died young, was a librarian after graduation. She gave her husband, Alleyn, two sons (one adopted from her first marriage). The boys, Nicolas and Matthew, are very different in makeup, but both have generosity in common.

Beatrice Jaspert-Cormican in Spain leads a life of wide-ranging interests with her husband. She has managed to get some meaning out of life.

Anna Jaspert always wanted to live in Switzerland. She had gone there to finishing school and stayed. She married. Now she has studied more, acquired a Master's degree, and has a good position in a world-wide company.

My grandchildren began to arrive. The first two came in a race against time or a contest between my two oldest daughters.

The third grandchild, Poppy, who as a teenager turned into a beauty, was the first grandchild to be born abroad: in Ireland. Her parents did not marry and soon split up. The next two, grandsons, arrived at about the same time. Their mother, Elisabeth, died early. One day her younger son, Matthew, coming home with a friend – they were just doing their final pre-exams before leaving school – found her dead at home.

These two boys turned out bright, though at first not very promising. They went to university and did well. Poppy studied design and learned some Spanish.

For a while she moved to Spain and then Belgium and the Netherlands. Now she is in England again. At first she worked as a petrol station attendant, then as a waitress. She earned good tips, looking attractive. Male drivers queued up for her attention. She will get married soon.

Then there was a long gap before the family grew again. A little boy, Alexander Cocca, was born prematurely in Switzerland to my daughter there from the second marriage. A lovely boy, who turned out not to speak when growing up, but now rattles on endlessly in Swiss German. Another grandson came: Oscar. More grandchildren are sure to follow. One of my sons will soon get married to a beautiful Czech girl. He asked her father in Czech to give him his daughter.

"In the spring, a young man's fancy…" but there was nothing light about it. Back in Munich the woman who introduced me to adult and real lovemaking was married. It did not interfere with my actions. I greatly enjoyed the new activity and the intellectual pastime of taking her to the theatre, buying extravagant clothing on shopping sprees, but my puritanical upbringing caused worries. The lady's husband was polite and courteous. Surely he had an inkling of the ongoing affair? It caused me nail-biting worry and sleeplessness, but then I enjoyed the new-found activity of sex.

Voltaire had written that "divorce is probably of nearly the same date as marriage. I believe however, that marriage is some weeks more ancient".

Dave Brubeck, the pianist and his sons gave a concert on his seventy-fifth birthday. Stéphane Grapelli accompanied the group, playing his famous fiddle. In the interval he came to talk to Willem and Augustus, who proudly mentioned to him that they, too, played the fiddle, though they were only beginners. They talked amicably, the proud mother Julia and father listening in.

There are nice couples, they like each other and have children, but they sleep apart from each other – sometimes in separate bedrooms. They did at some time along the route of their marriage have partnership. I find that changed relation impossible to comprehend.

Looking back, I see how the view of life changes with growing up. The fate of my marriages troubled me. Hella, my first wife, left me on a sudden impulse after seventeen years. She gave me the children, two girls, Elisabeth and Beatrice.

I was very perturbed, but delighted to care for the girls. I liked being the father, but could not care for them alas, like their natural mother. I engaged a nanny. This lady from Assam was the widow of a Gurkha soldier. She was pretty successful. Occasionally she would cook a curry for me, but that was rare. Normally she refused to cook for me, but looked beautifully after the children and prepared their meals.

Julia, my second wife and partner for thirty years,

did not leave, but we divorced. She had loved me and bore me three children, Anna, Willem John and Augustus James Ulysses (so named after my favourite book, by Homer.) Later, this son was given my collection of *Odysseus* translations and versions.

Print Start

PRINT PRODUCTION was going to be revolutionized. It began slowly and undramatically. I was still a child and unaware of it. My father and his brother Reinhardt had an inkling of the things to come. The 'nominal' uncle Franz Perneder, a director of the famous Albert Frisch printing house in Berlin (some directors emigrated and founded the Ganymede collotype businesses abroad) felt there was something developing, though no one fully realized the force of the developments of scanning (the Belin and *Time-Life* scanners in France and America) and phototypesetting (the Uhertype in Germany) followed by computer assisted typesetting. Arthur Phillips in Britain became a forceful proponent of computers in typesetting and was one of the leading lights at a university conference at Newcastle-upon-Tyne. I was selected to edit the proceedings.

In Britain and under Kurt Schlössing Paul, Peter Purdy and Ronald Macintosh developed the K.S. Paul machine, which was later incorporated into the Linotype and competed with the German Digiset.

Companies sprung up to improve computer-assisted systems and programmes. The first to embrace the new technology were newspapers in America and Scandinavia. Eventually agreement was reached with such bodies as the Society of Compositors in Britain and other trade unions to accept the new technology. The first books produced by the new technology in Britain were Penguin's *Private Angelo* by Eric Linklater and Margaret Drabble's *The Millstone*.

The more than five hundred years old letterpress printing process was quickly replaced by offset lithography, based on grease or ink accepting surfaces. Gravure – printing from recessed image surfaces – was in the hands of only a few producers of mass circulation publications and only some picture specialists, continued with flexography from raised images used primarily in packaging and some newspapers. Screen process retained some application areas. The vast office computer business brought digital printing, still a marginal business, but promising new short run printing economies.

My background made for an affinity with printing and publishing. Both my grandfathers had tried their hands at writing – in German and (in South Africa) in English. My father was an author and a publisher. One of his brothers, Reinhard Jaspert was also a book publisher. My father's brother, Werner Jaspert, was editor of a daily newspaper closed down by the Nazis.

Elsewhere I recount how he started up again after the war and one of his daughters marrying the son of the publisher of a regional daily paper. Fritz, father's elder brother, was an architect but also wrote books (together with his son Martin Jaspert). My cousin Michael Jaspert and his two sons Stéphane and Philippe Jaspert co-authored a travel book on the former French West Africa. No doubt more writers will emerge. I also have more distant relatives in America who are writers or broadcasters.

So I had a liking for print and books. When in 1950 I came to Britain, with a full labour permit, I worked for the (late) Robert Maxwell and his Pergamon Press. I left Maxwell's employ, and started my writing career with John E. Reeve Fowkes, as associate editor of his *Print in Britain* and founder co-editor of *Litho Printer*, now *PrintWeek* magazine, and a manager at Cox & Sharland (printers), later a part of the British Printing Corporation.

For some years I worked for Jarrold & Sons, the Norwich printers, and also for St. Clement's Press, the *Financial Times* subsidiary, now closed.

Later I started writing for the late Kurt Kohlhammer and his *Deutscher Drucker* (forty-two times a year). In America I contributed regularly to *Gravure* and *Printing Magazine*, and in Europe to *World-Wide Printer* and *El Arte Tipografico*. These two magazines were bought and came under the editorship of Theodor

J. Anton, who renamed the Spanish-language title to *Graficas Mundiales*, and added *Euro-Printer*. I acted as consulting editor, wrote most of the contents of these magazines, (sometimes under a pseudonym).

The magazines I edited are now published in Brazil, India and the Far East, and still survive, though for how much longer I do not know. I enjoyed working on them and many of my travels were reflected in the pages of the various editions. The editor-in-chief, Theo Anton, retired some years ago with honour and his successor is not free to do as he may like. I myself write for magazines all over the place but am naturally slowing down, though I still travel extensively.

Efi Arazi invented Fiery – a colour management system which revolutionized colour reproduction. Canon in Japan adopted it for their copiers. Arazi had caused a sensation at the Milan GEC printing show. He was a founder of Scitex. His inventions, like digital printing (later promoted with a boisterous fanfare by Benny Landa) and computer-to-plate technology and so many others in the change to electronics in the graphic arts, were the application of mapmaking and facsimile technology gained through Israel's wartime experience.

Does anyone out there still remember *Ovonics*, a no-impact space-age printing system invented by some scientist with a Russian-sounding name to allow the printing on even extra-soft egg yolk – or rather more practically – any fruit (soft or not)? Its day has not yet come.

I had published, mainly sub-edited texts, but also some own stories, as an invited contributor. Needing employment (also referred to elsewhere) I also worked in the City of London in a basement for a trading company. The owners, a Swiss and an Austrian, of an export-import agency doing many print related deals. James Moran, who was then editor of a printing weekly, heard some tales about the somewhat nefarious activities of my principals and invited me to write about them. I did so, wrote two or three stories which were published and proved constructive to my eventual sacking, although I really misbehaved at the firm's Christmas party and incautiously told the owners, who had plied me with drink, what I really thought of them. I woke after that party with a hangover and was sacked. But then I found a new job. Work in those days was fairly easy to find and I got a job as a production editor of Blandford Press, a small publisher in the centre of London and ruled by bosses adhering to moral rearmament, the high-minded semi-religion of Frank Buchman.

Blandford were planning the publication of the *Encyclopaedia of Type Faces*. The original book had two co-authors, W. Turner Berry of the St Bride Printing Library and A.F. Johnson, Keeper of Books at the British Museum. I was to look after the production of the book. I looked through the manuscript and found it historically interesting but lacking an international approach. Many typefaces could be traced to Continental type founders and their counterparts in North America. I asked my bosses' permission to add these, annotated at that, and also requested the authors' permission to do so. It was readily given and more so, the authors generously invited me – a mere stripling then – to join them as third author. I was pleased and today receive a modest income from the royalties, all made over to me these days, of the always reprinted book, now described in some catalogues as "the standard reference". At some time I felt revision of the book was needed. An acquaintance offered to swap flats in London and Paris. There the smell of slaughtered animals from the old abattoirs was sometimes overpowering. On return to London there was a large telephone bill. The flat exchange proved costly: daily telephone calls had been made to Australia.

Australia alone bought several thousand copies of the book. Even of the recent unrevised paperback edition, some sixteen hundred copies of the book were sold. Now a fifty-fifth anniversary edition has been published.

I am proud of my first book, which was more a labour of love than an achievement. My royalties, as an employee at the time of the publishers, were rather modest. They still are so today, but I am now the sole recipient of any royalties.

At Blandford Press, repeatedly taken over by larger publishers, Arthur Symes, my chief editor was not convinced that I, the newcomer and sub-editor, could write good English. Another editor, Percy Pearce Sales, doubted my ability to write in an acquired language. I told him that my learnt English was superior to naturally acquired English and was able to prove that. This editor wrote rubbish which I refused to have printed. In those days, journalists and editors had their writings carefully checked and scrutinized by proofreaders or people like production managers, even lawyers. Those times, alas, have gone today!

Until a short while ago I wrote for over thirty-six trade magazines worldwide, contribute on art and general subjects (and also wrote *Letters to the Editor*). I am phasing out my trade magazine writing. So many publishers have gone out of business or are unable to pay. There is no point in working for nothing, though I volunteered for many years writing the international stuff for an American weekly newsletter as unpaid correspondent. I still write without much pay for some publishers because I like their magazines.

Now much writing has stopped – in the main – though I continue contributing to some magazines and newspapers just because I enjoy being busy. There is no plan to sit all day at home and stare at the ceiling.

So I write books.

Years ago I felt it was time to move on and left Blandford Press to join a small publishing firm, Newman Neame, whose *Take Home* booklet series, financed as part of a "be happy at work" scheme, was funded by Aims of Industry. I started work there and was embarrassed by a gushing telegram from a former colleague, Eddie Armstrong, a moral rearmament disciple, wishing me luck. I became the laughing stock of the new company. One of the owners of the firm had a flashy car and spectacular girlfriends. He and one of the women were killed in dreadful car crash. I was preoccupied at the time: my first daughter, Elisabeth, was due to be born. The morning after she arrived I went to tell one of the partners in the publishing firm and was told, not listened to, that the firm had gone into bankruptcy and that I had lost my job … and pay. Nevertheless, I decided that the small family should go on holiday to Wales. There in the hills the postmistress ran up to me when we returned from a long walk to inform me that there was a long distance phone call for me. John H. Jarrold, owner of one of Britain's largest and old-established printers, offered me a job, a good part-time salary and demanded I break my holiday and join his company in the cathedral town of Norwich the following Monday. I complied and at the crack of dawn boarded the early train from Liverpool Station. I worked very successfully and was happy in my work, but the frequent "commuter journeys" exhausted me.

My new employer took me along to the Book Fair in Frankfurt and bought options on what he believed were future best-sellers – and printing profits. I managed to sell some of these ideas in New York. I also learnt that it was cheaper to phone than to fly every time to America. Soon I went to America where, at first, there were big problems. As I had been with the US Army, but declined to go to America on my discharge, I had difficulty in obtaining a visitor's visa. I since had to waive my later acquired Green Card rights.

Unbeknown at first were tenuous links between Jarrold's, the company and my family. The now defunct publishing branch had published my father Willem Jaspert's *Through Unknown Africa* in 1930. The printing house also had an interest in the Thames & Hudson publishing house of Walter Neurath, who in turn was interested in my uncle Reinhard Jaspert's stock in pre-war photos of the art publishers Phaidon, who also fled Germany. Nothing came of this, though my uncle complained bitterly of misunderstanding with Phaidon.

Reto Conzett in Zurich befriended me and for some time paid me a retainer, which I tried to honour by finding customers for a gravure system he had acquired from Japan. Kenichi Sawamura had told him of this system developed by his company while he was gaining expertise with Reto's printing business. Reto later sold the business. He had started *Du* magazine, still much admired and sought after by collectors. It often ran issues devoted to a single subject or a complete profile of writers like Dürrenmatt or Max Frisch. Reto fell ill, limped about and then died. I often met his widow, the late Mia, whenever I could because my daughter Anna lived nearby with her husband Mario Cocca and Alexander, my fourth grandchild, a handful of trouble. I had some retainers from large organisations and gradually turned to full-time freelance writing, mainly for the international trade press. Jürgen in Madrid turned my English or German into impeccable Spanish.

Anna was resolved since the age of seven to live and work in Switzerland. Reto arranged for her to go to finishing school there for a year and she stayed on. She also trained in America, England, Germany and France.

For most of my life I had stayed at luxury hotels, latterly mainly paid for by myself, but in earlier days by generous hosts in the printing field in the hope that I would write good things about them.

These are some of the people who over my many years as a freelance made an impact. Martin Lange, who I met more than forty-five years ago and in all sorts of places, is a disciple of the legendary Dr Boris Orentschuk, who in Argentina had the idea of founding

Ferrostaal, the international engineering and turnkey service. They built railways, sold textile machines and buses, and founded the Intergrafica and Printpack printing machinery sales and planning group. Today many of the "graphics" people of his group are leading industrialists and entrepreneurs. Peter Farer and his wife Gisela worked with me in Singapore; they later moved to America where they lived for some years.

Then there was Eric Tanzer, a super-salesman, who had come from Hungary and lived in England. It was said of him that his loyalty to customers extended to his taking "dud" machines back and clients in turn trusted him fully. He brought four-colour printing on Roland machines to Britain when almost everybody disliked German machinery after the war. At a Vickers subsidiary, one of its directors, Paul Scheffel, an ex-German director, tried to persuade the Vickers management board in Britain to build machines for which he had the pre-war plans. He failed and returned to his old employers, Roland Offset, now MAN-Roland, in Germany to lead it to success. Thus a British company missed the chance to become one of the world leaders in colour printing machinery.

The German company for many decades kept in close contact with me through Hans Schniedewind (who had fled the then German Democratic Republic), Bruno Stochay and Uwe-Jens Philipp who for some time lived with his wife Heidi in England. They had two daughters. The older girl, Sarah, was born in England. She later lived with my family for many months. There was also Gerd Finkbeiner, a director of Man-Roland, the new owners of Roland Offset.

Roland's main competitor was Heidelberg. After the death of Dr Hubert Sternberg, who had secured the continued existence of the company through a deal conducted with the "enemy" via neutral Sweden, Heidelberg's international activities were conducted by Dr Wolfgang Zimmermann and promoted by Fritz Niepert, who had earlier worked for the occupation forces and the British Army of the Rhine. After Dr Zimmermann's death – caused by the bite of a tick which had embedded itself in his body – the company underwent many and frequent changes. He was succeeded by Ulrich Mauser, who resigned and was replaced by Hartmut Mehdorn, who soon left to head Deutsche Bahn, the German railways, and the less flamboyant Bernhard Schreyer. The company rapidly grew to be first in its field for a time, but this led to some arrogance and a sudden fall from being the star in the controlling RWE Group's activities. Many top executives were sacked, and then many left of their own accord.

In offset printing machinery Italian factories at one time were competitors, nay even technical pioneers. Omsca pioneered electronic drives – "shaftless systems", but Dr Guido Jarach came too early on the market and met with serious problems.

George H. Wood brought the Nebiolo products and also German typefaces to Britain. Later he moved to Switzerland, but soon returned with his wife Edith to England.

Nebiolo stayed more traditional and became internationally known under sales director Paolo de Lucca, who incidentally had gone to my school in Switzerland. He left to join the textile machinery industry. Paolo was a brave man. He was in the Italian Air Force during the Second World War. He flew in northern Italy. Once he had shot down a plane, he landed near where the enemy's parachute had floated and with great courage rescued the airman or airmen from capture. He took them over secret border paths which he knew from his childhood into safe Switzerland, where they gave themselves up to be interned. After the war he often came to RAF Hatfield and was accorded a hero's reception there. I have seen him carried on the shoulder of wartime crews. The company's sales went down and today, little more than remnants of the enterprise remain. Dr Grazia Schenone, the public relations expert, left to run her own business.

Among the big three German printing machine makers KBA is noteworthy. At first led by Dr Albrecht Bolza, it was then guided by his adopted son, Hans Bolza-Schünemann, who brought many innovations to printing. His son succeeded him.

There were seemingly frantic inventors, like Peter Purdy and Ronald Macintosh, whose joint company – and also Harris Intertype – revolutionized phototypesetting. Their invention was taken up by Kurt Schlössing Paul, who was of German origin and broadcast a popular weekly BBC programme to that country. He surrounded himself by lively and eccentric people like Peter Pollock and Sergio Lamberti; the latter later moved back to Italy and formed his own business. Peter Pollock died suddenly and early. There was also Otto M. Lilien, who had come from the Berlin newspapers and was an expert on gravure. He worked for a time at the Springer newspaper empire in Germany and later, as technical manager of the *Daily Telegraph*, produced a Sunday colour magazine which was printed to the highest quality in Germany to tight schedules. He was also an author and an expert on the history of the gravure printing process.

Like Dr Hell, his German counterpart, the team led by John F. Crosfield revolutionized picture reproduction and printing with the help of a brilliant team of technicians and salesmen, among them Dennis Bent and a Swede, Lars Janneryd, whose training included a period at Lucerne where I too had learnt much. Denis Havard worked on exhibitions and as a press officer for Crosfield. He was sacked and stayed in the printing equipment field till he joined a public relations outfit. He and his attractive wife Kate became my friends. I also did work for him, as I did for Lars, who also still keeps in close touch. Together we also talked successfully to sponsors of the international conference we supported.

Reeve Fowkes and I, with a friend went sailing on Southampton Water. We took the precaution of buying from the duty-free ships' stores a case of gin, intended for weekend drinking and claiming we were sailing for France. We never travelled there, however, and got thoroughly drunk drifting around the Isle of Wight, almost drowning on the first night as we tried to take the dinghy to our boat in the dark. When we were returning to our mooring next morning we had a terrible shock. A hovercraft going to the Isle of Wight port loomed over us and the captain of the craft threatened through a megaphone that we would be banned from our club. True enough, we were told to find a sailing club that was stupid enough to take people as incompetent as we were. It was no good trying to explain that weeks before there had been no hovercraft and we were caught out by a British invention triumph.

Real print skills found their uses in the war. The Nazis tried to sink the British pound, forcing skilled concentration camp inmates – who were quite well treated during their working time on the project – to forge £5 banknotes (the large airmail-type white paper ones) The British, so it is claimed, managed to encode escape messages to allied POWs hidden in the Waddington company's innocent *Monopoly* games sent to prisoners via the Red Cross.

In *I Am a Camera* Christopher Isherwood wrote about the ominous changes that were coming to Berlin with the dawn of the Nazi era. In a different context, I was a camera observing the transformation of the printing and publishing worlds. First came the change from letterpress to offset. Metal type slowly started to replace lead and type alloys. Phototypesetting arrived. The share of printing by different processes changed and is still changing. The most profound revolution, however, was the disappearance of the old-type compositor and the proofreader. When I was young there was a proofreader to check spelling and facts, politely (usually) drawing one's attention to possible errors. That safeguard hardly exists today. Authors and journalists are expected to provide clean copy. The arrival of digital printing, simple to use as it may be, seems only to make life more complex. Authors are expected to provide their work on disks, formatted to the needs of the printer and, by implication, the publisher eager to save money. Writers had to become experts at handling technical matters. The results are those stream-of-consciousness or verbose books and quite horrible misprints in newspapers, the sort of embarrassing errors the magazine *Private Eye* loves to quote from the *Grauniad* (sic).

Andrew Bluhm, a friend and editor of a magazine, lost a job. I managed to get him on the payroll of some magazines with offices near the German city of Stuttgart. Andrew already had knowledge of German. He became quite versed in it. He also spoke French and some Italian, and was pretty good at Latin. He wrote beautiful English, was a stickler for facts and corrected and improved my writing. He also invented a pen name, the anagram which I often use.

Sadly Andrew could not resist topping up his beer or wine with schnapps or brandy. He also smoked heavily he had diabetes and finally both his feet were amputated. Nevertheless, he seemed on the mend until one day his French-born wife Sylvie telephoned to say that she was afraid "he was going to snuff it" (her idea of colloquial English). Andrew died suddenly. I gave the funeral oration. Sadly. Another good man of many over the years!

Philip Windsor, who also died too early, was brilliant and had a remarkable breadth of reading based on imagination, intuition and his interest in big issues. He advised governments across the Atlantic, and as a scholar at the London School of Economics and the Institute of Strategic Studies. He was said to have written a serious book in one night, fortified by strong coffee and Scotch. I secretly admired him for his tumultuous relationship with Kim, a lawyer whom he forgave most things.

Another friend, Julyan Watts, has an uncanny knack for speaking foreign languages. He spoke Icelandic, Arabic and Russian and was able to pick up local foreign accents, for instance those different dialects of Zurich or Berne in Switzerland. At one time Olga Haigh, a Russian who had worked at the British Embassy in Moscow, and he were in Prague during the "Spring" when the Soviets entered the country. He managed to talk to the Russian guarding the border to Austria and a route to Vienna was found for him which he and Olga used to escape.

Later, between my second and third marriage I took Olga out to expensive places. She was blonde and good-looking, but to my eyes top heavy, myself being a legs and bottom man. Olga liked being taken out. A friend and lover of hers said she never offered to pay for anything. Julyan, by the way, was later in Tashkent, Uzbekistan, advising governments. Is he a spy, we kept wondering? We knew that he had signed the Official Secrets Act when he was naval attaché in Europe's Baltic area.

John Reeve Fowkes in Southampton made me his assistant on *Print in Britain* magazine and later the editor of *Litho Printer*. It was there that I began publishing interviews with the pioneers of modern print technology.

John Crosfield for a time during the Second World

War worked on sea mines. Both he and his German opponent, Dr Hell thought somewhat alike. Dr Hell would design a sea mining device, John Crosfield would think of a mine tracking and premature exploding device. Both men were friendly rivals and friends. They lived to a ripe old age. Rudolf Hell and I occasionally each had a glass of Pouilly Fusée in the lobby of the Baur au Lac in Zurich. Dr Hell reached his hundredth year before his death.

I became deeply involved with the affairs of an international conference of people concerned with the fate of printed communications worldwide. Comprint International lasted for almost half a century until it was merged into a more commercial enterprise. During its heyday it attracted notable speakers, ministers and Dr Aurelio Pecci, the founder of the Club of Rome, mapping out the future, and international bankers and advertising people of world fame as well as the chairmen and presidents of the world's largest printing, publishing and newspaper organisations. My friend Giorgio Gianoli headed the efforts in planning the events of the conference, conceived in America, but becoming a major European event when another friend of mine, Dr Reto Conzett and a Swedish colleague brought the event first to Geneva and then to the capitals of Europe. Among the speakers was Simone Weil, who had fought with the anarchists in Spain and later was in the French government.

For over thirty years I wrote a general *State of the Art* commentary for the delegates to these meetings, which was translated into Spanish by the late Dr Boris Orentschuk's Intergrafica consultancy and also formed the basis for many sub-conferences. My main function, however, was as a fund raiser. I am proud of my achievements there. Through my contacts, in Japan especially, but also in Germany and elsewhere, I raised some US $350,000–400,000 or more each time for the meetings during the conference's life, even in my old age.

I had formed strong links with Japan. My friend Ken Terada gave me the use of an apartment in Tokyo's Bunkyo-ku, the metropolis' publishing and printing district. Kazuo Suzuki, the president of Toppan Printing and a great supporter of the Comprint conference was a driving force to the formation of a museum of printing in Tokyo. I was invited with a handful of European guests to the opening in Tokyo. I met William Sheehan, Keeper of the Library at the Vatican. The Canadian, a kind and erudite man, forgave me my Protestant, but atheistic views. He reminded me of the late Father Gatterer at the Vatican observatory, a friend of Dr Paul Rosbaud.

I was pleased at having been invited for another reason. The invitation seemed to confirm that my feeble support for London's St Bride Printing Library and my book on printed type were worthwhile. For years I had been donating all the many printing magazines from all over the world to the library. I felt vindicated. The new librarian, Nigel Roche, told me that his library would eventually be rebuilt and become a showpiece of the specialized library world. Welcome news indeed, though perhaps a bit premature.

I contributed to London's *Financial Times* "Observer" column. It was easy money. Some jokes are universal, just slightly different when rehashed in various languages. When I travelled, I therefore retold the same jokes, but adapted to a different mood. Sometimes they became novel variations, which I could then publish in England. A benefit was that, as the paper's main owners also owned a French château famed for its red wine I was sent a complimentary case of that come Christmas.

For a time I was editor of the *Journal of the English Speaking Union* – a society with many American members. The mayor of Cologne had come to London and was Guest of Honour at a Mayfair dinner. Also present and at the top table was "Bomber" Harris, the man in command of the RAF air armada which had destroyed so much of many German cities.

The German mayor gave a speech lauding peace and reconciliation said that such terrible things as the bombing of his city should never happen again. Ronald Fredenburgh, who had been Canada's John Diefenbaker's PPS, was secretary of the union at the time. I also sat at the top table between the two men because it had been ascertained that I could translate German into English. I did this, but softened the accusatory sentiments about the bombing. Harris, who spoke German, angrily seized the microphone from me and – explaining that I had mistranslated – gave an exact translation and concluded that he "would do the bombing again in good conscience". I was shamed, the mayor was shamed, and I was sacked when the guests had departed!

No sacking was possible when I represented my newspaper at the Lord Mayor of London's annual banquet. On that occasion the then holder of the title, as was his habit, gave his speech in Latin. I translated for the journalists around me. Then the time came for the Loyal Toast to the Queen. Everyone stood up and raised a glass. So did I, but in my haste and stress from the task of translation, it was the cup of fruit salad which did not pass my lips, but gushed onto my shirt front. People around me suppressed their giggles.

In my first job in London and while working under the infamous crook, Robert Maxwell, I was asked to have some shipping documents certified by the authorities. They were for embargoed goods banned from sending to the (forbidden) Soviet Russia, so the documents falsely claimed the goods were destined for the NATO ally: Turkey. They were destined for the Soviet Union.

After this episode and my refusal to do such nefarious deals again, I was almost sacked. When I finally left Butterworth-Springer and was without a job, I washed dishes in the underground kitchen at Lyon's Corner House in London's Hammersmith area out of need, and was fed free.

I found a job as assistant editor and production manager of a group of magazines.

Every year there are many printing exhibitions round the world, but one is pre-eminent: Drupa in Düsseldorf. Theodor Anton and I have attended these shows since the 1950s and I was glad to visit the 2008 show. Drupa shows have indeed set markers for the technical developments which have changed the face of the printing industry. An innovation is the co-operation of rivals through the concept of Print City, which aimed to demonstrate that different aspects of new technology were applicable to many different answers.

On my first visit to Japan I came to Osaka, the Japanese business city. My hosts, Fuji Photo Film and their main agents, had put banners all over the town – very embarrassing indeed – with my portrait looking strangely eastern.

I had thought I would be addressing a group of some thirty to forty local printers. Then I stepped onto the speaker's podium. There were more than two thousand expectant people, with smooth straight black hair, intelligent and searching for knowledge, staring at me in the futile hope of learning something.

Everybody seemed to know me. On arrival I had been greeted by polite smiles and the inevitable: "So nice to see you, to see you again". Well, – I was certain I had not seen any of these faces ever before. They had seen my picture, though – and responded. So a picture had made the introduction simple. That was a long time ago. I was taught a lesson and got myself visiting cards with my picture on them. That was some time ago in Japan where life without a business card to proffer whenever meeting someone, one is simply lost.

Back in London a tall man came unannounced into my office, looking for me. He was obviously American. Distinguished looking – a typical East Coast man and New Yorker. A friendship of many years developed between Edward McSweeney III, his wife Mary and me. Edward McSweeney was a consultant, advising printing corporations and those with some interest in printing related matters. He made me an associate and I benefited from this link. Edward gave me free room in his office suite at the Marine Midland Building, at Park Avenue in Manhattan right next to the PanAm – now Metropolitan Life – skyscraper with its rooftop helipad.

Edward McSweeney's son, Dooley, worked downstairs in the bank. I became an associate member of various posh clubs and even addressed the American Legion at the Metropolitan Club on military oddities. That speech did not seem to go down well. The audience at first was reserved, if not hostile, but gradually softened attitudes during questions and answers time. I eventually got on fine with the veterans, many of them had been in the fierce battles after landing in Normandy and had suffered in Africa, Italy and finally in Germany.

It was the first time I experienced the tolerance of the ordinary people of America. They accepted me.

Whenever Edward McSweeney and his wife Mary came to London, often several times a year, he came to my home and when Edward left he would always dig into his pocket and have a billfold in his hand, from which he gave children a dollar bill. He was indiscriminate. At random one child was handed $100, another $1 and so on. After he had left, I collected the money, divided it evenly and paid the equivalent into the children's bank accounts, which I had started on the birth of each child. The accounts grew and were a sort of nest egg which the children could dispose of when they came of age. The older girls, sadly in my view, squandered the money. It was more wisely spent by the offspring of the second marriage and went towards home deposits or is still kept as a reserve.

Mary McSweeney died suddenly in Germany. Edward found her lifeless on his return to his hotel. He experienced the intricacies of flying the body back to New York. He remarried and was soon despatched to an old-age retirement home, where he impressed everyone by dressing up like a gentleman every day, spotless with polished shoes and wearing a good tie. We offered to take him into our home in London, but he declined and awaited his death calmly.

I presented an antique Chinese stone lion to Edward, and had brought it from London to New York as hand luggage despite its weight. On handing it over, Edward tried to lift it – and dropped it. An antique restorer repaired the damage, but the sculpture lost some of its value and became a garden ornament in his then home in Pleasantville in Winchester County. There I met the Dewitt Wallace family of *Reader's Digest* fame. I liked their collection of paintings, but was never enamoured by the magazine itself, where a former colleague of mine from London, Bruce Marshall, worked, living in the city and commuting in the opposite direction out every work day. Bruce later resurfaced in London.

Working for the publishers five of us in editorial and production went on to make fairly impressive careers. Bruce Marshall went to the *Reader's Digest* in America. David Jones (Taffy to us) became head of information at the British Travel & Holidays Association (the tourist board). Muriel and Philip Burton started their own publishing company. I too moved ahead.

I had attended an exhibition in Chicago and had included work visits to New York City and Los Angeles, taking a friend with me and paying for his ticket. He wrote rather beautiful English, was very handsome and a ladies' man, the envy of my circle. In New York he immediately gathered round himself a bevy of glamorous young women, mainly from the advertising world. He set up temporary home on, I believe, Long Island with six or eight of these young ladies and formed a rather more long-term association with one woman. That lady made a fatal mistake which cost him his marriage relationship back home in London. His girl in America, after he left an expensive lighter in her car on departure, (the lighter having been a present from his wife), wrote to thank him for the present. His wife saw the letter and threw him out. One evening in north west London's Hampstead I was going out when it was pouring with rain. While I was walking down to the main road I saw a bedraggled figure of a man carrying a plastic bag stuffed full with something. It was my friend, just having been thrown out by his wife and told to take his pyjamas with him. He asked me whether he could stay with me, but I declined and insisted he go to a nearby hotel. Sadly, I had to break off relations with him. He became aggressive and frequently very drunk.

While working with Tom Margerison at London's *Sunday Times*, a non-editorial task was the setting up of one of the first British photoset and web offset printed newspapers at Reading. One day the managing director of one of New Zealand's major newspapers walked into my office and suggested a part-time job. I accepted the idea and out of it grew a non-official task of vetting printers and journalists to emigrate to that country under the then working assisted passage immigration scheme. I saw and approved, and sometimes turned down, hundreds of people, husbands and wives, and often travelled far up the country for interviews, involving the High Commission of New Zealand only in the police reference and the actual immigration process. I even expanded into recruiting non-whites from Canada and northern Europe. I did the work for almost ten years. It became too much and I had to fade out. I am still in contact with some of the former migrants. Among those immigrants was a reputable European publisher from the continent.

At one time I, too, was tempted. Attractive offers of varying employment in New Zealand were made. I spent several weeks a year in the country. I was in Christchurch on my birthday. I had just been offered a good and very promising position on a newspaper. I phoned home and stood in a glass-enclosed cubicle in the hotel lobby (telephoning from my room seemed too expensive). I heard my wife speaking and told her the news, and cried bitterly. I realized I did not want to leave and uproot the family and disturb the children's schooling and childhood. I turned the offered job down to the consternation of the prospective employers and returned soon after to London.

Will nothing ever change? In the name of freedom the leaders of America and Britain tolerated for some years the aping of Nazi atrocities, like the wire cages of Guantànamo on Cuba, the bombing – one year after the *Pax Americana* war against Iraq – of the city of Fallujah, or the humiliation of hooded prisoners by the American liberators. In Hell they have learnt from the expertise of the Gestapo and the people of Abu Ghraib. Though the old practices are kept alive. Even Hell-Speak has been updated, The Damned are now called Customers of this eternal Club of the Former High and Mighty.

"*Stuff Happens*", as Donald Rumsfeld remarked and David Hare dramatized. During the Second World War, I hid successfully for almost a year. But the sleuths finally caught up with me and I reluctantly joined the German Navy. My younger brother had escaped to Spain. I was a POW in 1945. My (late) mother was then in Berlin and provided accommodation for Soviet troops and then later for American army officers. On VE day, I had tried by then to volunteer to the US Army (I was then a POW with the Quartermaster corps), but this was not possible there and then under Red Cross rules, though later I was later accepted, but the war was soon over by then. Bizarrely, I was made a prisoner again, and was discharged via Dachau, the former concentration camp, although I protested as my (non-Jewish) father had been murdered in just such a camp. On VE day some of us (trusty, and, more importantly, able to play some marching tunes.) POWs were for a few hours put into GI clothes and marched in the French town of Nancy to celebrate the allied victory. That was before we discovered the horrors of Stalinism.

We celebrated the end of evil and the "fact" that the liberators would never perpetrate atrocities like those of the Nazis. Since then we have learnt that offences against humanity have been repeated in Indonesia, the Congo and Yugoslavia. And now America apes the Nazis' use of wire cages. A friend of my mother was in 1936 held for some weeks in such a cage in Frankfurt until freed by the combined efforts of her later husband Whateley Carrington, British consular staff and head of a department at Oxford University. The Nazis still cared about foreign opinion at that time and she travelled to Prague just before the Nazis marched in, and went on to England at a time when such travel was almost impossible.

Now I read that in Iraq there are ten thousand new prisoners (suspected terrorists), among them children of eleven years of age! Nine hundred people in Iraq are on Death Row. Democracy at work, indeed! The world has not changed, but America – the hope of mankind – has changed.

I have to report sadly that an offence I committed in

1973 has now been designated as criminal. The British Rehabilitation of Offenders Act is not applicable under US law!

Democracy has many different faces. At one extreme end are the "democratic" republics like the former German Democratic Republic (the notorious DDR) or other left-wing dictatorships. In Britain or the United States the Prime Minister or the President are in name at least representing the people of their countries. So citizens feel free to write to the people or send them e-mails. The addresses are public knowledge. Some of these people have websites, too and most times get replies, even if they are fairly meaningless. Some of my friends or relatives did not think it proper to write to these leaders of a nation. Winston Churchill, I think, said that of all bad political systems democracy was still the best. I tried to explain that to a young Brazilian woman. She did not think it proper to write to these leaders of a nation. I am sure Brazilians can write to their President, even if it may be fruitless. My belief is that all these opinions, even cranky sentiments, are duly registered and considered. They give an indication of the mood of the public, as Britain's Prime Minister must have found out after the war against Saddam Hussein. Making war, however great one's outrage, does not condone killing innocent women and children or old people. The public does not like that unless it is badly coerced, like they were in

Soviet Russia or under the Nazis.

In America, security precautions after 9/11 reached silly heights. At Los Angeles airport I commented on the ridiculous requirement of having to take off my shoes in which a steel support was embedded. Three policemen came to interrogate me. I asked whether I looked like a disguised Arab. That feeble comment was received with deadpan calm and renewed search fervour. At Chicago's O'Hare airport I was asked to remove my belt. Having pointed out that I had been ill and lost forty pounds in weight and that my trousers would fall down, security staff (in full view of the public) told me to do as I was told. My arms were raised up. My trousers ridiculously sank to the ground. Some people managed to laugh. I was just embarrassed. I became an object of some ridicule. An airline representative saved me from further embarrassment by wrapping a travelling rug around me.

The then Secretary-General of the United Nations and winner of the 2001 Nobel Peace Prize, Kofi Annan, made his views on the death penalty absolutely clear when he said: "The forfeiture of life is too absolute, too irreversible, for one human being to inflict on another. Let the states that still use the death penalty stay their hand lest in time to come they look back with remorse knowing it is too late to redeem their grievous mistake".

I fail to comprehend why America has not yet abolished this barbaric punishment. Most, but not all, the civilized world has done so.

Saudi Arabia's official executioner has developed the technique of beheading and is teaching others. He believes he is carrying out "God's Will". President George W. Bush, when he was Governor of Texas, confirmed more death sentences than any other US Governor during his term. Then, in his moral indignation, he allowed bombs to be dropped on Iraqi targets in the year before Iraq was actually attacked. No count is given of the number of civilians killed in these actions.

But George W. Bush made friends, sort of, with the disgraceful Italian Prime Minister Silvio Berlusconi the sometime temporary head of the European Union – which had vociferously objected to the late Jörg Haider in Austria, a neo-Nazi – but kept strangely acquiescent in the case of himself. I had met him a few years before he acquired power, but was already in control of a media empire. He expanded into shaping the law to suit him.

I had been a member of the Labour Party since the 1960s. In 2003 I resigned because of the war on Iraq. In America and all over the world there were demonstrations, the largest since the Vietnam War, against the so-called justified war and bombings of Iraq. True enough, the country's ruler was less than admirable, but did that mean killing people? Worse governments had enjoyed the support and monetary aid from America. President George W. Bush and his sidekicks in Britain and Spain had agreed to relieve American soldiers from international justice. Like at Mai Lai, allied troops could in future commit any atrocity, without opposition, though still facing American justice. It all reminded me of Oliver North, who had done his nefarious work in Nicaragua and went on the public speaking circuit in America, a free man, even admired by some souls. Now Iraq is providing rich pickings: like oil and reconstruction contracts for American business. Thus is democracy being saved?

"Needless to say, the President is correct. Whatever it was he said". (US Department of Defense briefing 28 February 2003).

I, like so many people, am shocked. What feelings must any Arab have? Shock, outrage and hate at the humiliation of their fellow men and women? The hate will live a long time like that of the Irish who still remember Oliver Cromwell and the Black & Tans. The West will not easily live this down after a long history of occupation, of boundaries drawn after the First World War in straight lines by generals, and imposed regimes. Why were people like Donald Rumsfeld, who quite obviously ordered these interrogation techniques, allowed to continue in office while some soldiers who were obeying instructions are punished? Harry S Truman said "the buck stops here". It's something that George W. Bush does not adhere to. In *Stuff Happens* David Hare accurately pictures Rumsfeld and lets America's answer to East Germany's vicious red Hilde sit and idly cross her shapely legs. The forceful introduction of the *Pax Americana* has alarmed and shocked the world. Worse might still come. Some people are bored by Michael Palin's writings. The thoughts of Sarah Palin could scare the pants off them, if that lady ever reaches the top.

Donald Rumsfeld and Tony Blair in Britain have had no success, it seems, in locating weapons of mass destruction (WMD). Perhaps the answer is there. Before the cleansing operation on Iraq there were mysterious reports of Iraqi warships carrying these arms, circling in the Indian Ocean. A theory is being offered here which could save the faces of the warmongers. These ships may have created their own maelstrom, sucking the WMDs to the bottom of the sea. This theory is derived from the tales of the sad fate of the twisters sucking dancing dervishes to their frenzied sudden death.

Why is it that I can still smile to myself reading a story by Damon Runyon or seeing a film with Peter Lorre as a vicious butcher in an old movie, but am put off by the modern thrillers of James Lee Burke or Joseph Wambaugh and the sadistic goings on as described as going on in jail, denigrating despicable criminals? In the good old days crime and punishment were cleaner and morally justified.

Like millions of other people, I had welcomed the creation of the state of Israel. Jews had gained the right to their own home, free from the persecution of thousands of years that had culminated in the unspeakable indignities of the war and the holocaust. That this freedom from fear was won with a good deal of violence was well understood. Why should the oppressed not fight back? I applauded the rescue of the terror victims at Entebbe by the Israelis. I approved of the capture of Adolf Eichmann in Argentina, an anti-Semitic society of the modern age. But then doubt began to rise.

Mordecai Vanuatu was kidnapped illegally, imprisoned and often held in solitary confinement. The Palestinians, no angels themselves, were brutally held down and treated like sub-humans. Israeli behaviour began to resemble that of the despicable Nazis. Sympathy for Arab causes developed, although suspicions of fundamental Muslim thought lingered on. The American wars in the Middle East and perhaps still to come elsewhere, and the US unquestioning support for Israeli misdeeds promoted anti-Israel feeling (and also anti-Americanism). Another failed dream and illusion of goodness and right had gone.

At some time in Munich in about 1949 local

inhabitants were forcibly herded into a local cinema to see a showing of the French film *Les Maudits*. In it there is an episode where Nazi high-ups try to escape to South America in a commandeered submarine. The submarine is spotted and the boat is sunk. The Nazis, to make their tracks vanish, machine-gun the survivors, including the apparently homosexual cook and pet boy. The stolid citizens of the Munich district protested and walked out. They were herded back by volunteers, including my friend Wolfgang Steinhardt and myself.

Actors in movies become presidents, first they become Governors, usually of California or Minnesota (having perhaps been professional wrestlers). Or, like in Texas, other mortals make the world record in having death sentences carried out and at that beating almost every democratic oligarchic like Saudi Arabia or the People's Republic of China. But they become president not because they deserve it, but because it is so ordained and they are mega-rich. After all, perhaps also their father was president, so it is only right (and feudal) to have another president when your dad failed and was not re-elected. This is apparently democracy at work, or so we are told incessantly.

The effects of the terror attacks in New York of 11th September 2001 proved devastating to the world's economies. The fanatics having been sent to their death and the planners behind the attacks, even years after the mass killing and destruction on the world capital of New York City, succeeded beyond their wildest dreams.

Heralded by the collapse of the dotcom bubble, they caused whole industries to shrivel and at the same time enforced countless redundancies. Industry downsized beyond reason. Salaries of top managers and football or film stars reached obscene heights while ordinary people were in fear of losing their jobs and mass sackings of people came about in countries where unemployment was already rife. Profits slumped and household names in business disappeared overnight or just ebbed away. Even years after the attacks repeat disasters were feared. No city felt safe. The hidden attackers could strike again and even the Afghan and Iraqi wars could not stop the decline of industry and trade worldwide. Politicians and governments could no longer promise protection whatever the cost.

Laura Schlessinger ran as a sort of agony aunt on an American radio show. She dispensed advice to people who call in. At one time she pointed out that, to an observant orthodox Jew, homosexuality is an abomination, according to *Leviticus 18:22*, and cannot be condoned under any circumstance.

An open letter (US spelling) to Dr Laura, penned by a US resident, was posted on the Internet. To me it seemed quite funny:

"Dear Dr Laura, Thank you for doing so much to

educate people regarding God's Law. I have learned a great deal from your show, and try to share that knowledge with as many people as I can. When someone tries to defend the homosexual lifestyle, for example, I simply remind them that *Leviticus 18:22* clearly states it to be an abomination (end of debate, but continued). I do need some advice from you, however, regarding some other elements of God's Laws and how to follow them. *Leviticus 25:44* states that I may possess slaves, both male and female, provided they are purchased from neighbouring nations. A friend of mine claims that this applies to Mexicans, but not Canadians. Can you clarify? Why can I not own Canadians? I would like to sell my daughter into slavery, as sanctioned in *Exodus 21:7*. I know from *Leviticus 11:6–8* that touching the skin of a dead pig makes me unclean, but may I still play football if I wear gloves? I know you have studied these things extensively and thus enjoy considerable expertise in such matters, so I am confident you can help. Thank you again for reminding us that God's word is eternal and unchanging. Your adoring fan, Homer Simpson-Caldwell".

Soapbox

IF I were asked who the greatest influence on the Western world was in the twentieth century, I would nominate Adolf Hitler, the monstrous spirit of that age. This destroyer of families, countries and cultures changed Europe from an individual-centred and basically considerate society to one of intolerance made commonplace and callousness. Even America, not affected directly by his and his followers' actions, became violence-centred though it gained by the admission of many refugees. Albert Einstein or Winston Churchill did not change the world as much as Hitler and his cohorts did. They opened up new vistas, but essentially defended the human spirit and the world we knew.

Hitler changed all our lives, cruelly and viciously. His hellish deeds must never be forgotten – they have affected all of us, bystanders or victims and their descendants.

I was one of the passengers on PanAm Flight 103, on the leg from Frankfurt to London, to join the Christmas party at home in Hampstead. There I first heard that there had been a crash, but it was not until I saw the newspapers next morning that I realised the full extent of the disaster. Across the aisle from me, I remember, was a honeymoon couple on their way to New York, and next to me was a Lebanese student on his way to university. I telephoned Scotland Yard and PanAm's security officer in New York but could not help.

"Evil", wrote Marcus Aurelius more than one thousand eight hundred years ago "is the same old thing. It does not matter whatever happens. It remains the same old thing throughout the world. It fills history books, life around us and even the houses we live in. There is nothing new about this. It all is too familiar, but also transient".

The abomination of the Nazi targeted killings of selected groups of people and whole races justifying this policy based on their insane discriminating fanatical beliefs was sometimes matched in scope by Stalin's and his henchmen's determination to destroy the opposition. However, is the arrogant bombing and indiscriminating killing of millions of people in the name of spreading democracy that much preferable? The victims were never asked.

Sadly, too many people around me are dying. Some because they are of the previous generation, others only slightly older than me. Then there are the younger ones. one such, mature woman of great beauty and spirit and whose views I found rather irritating and disturbing, had the most beautiful children I have known, apart from my own offspring, of course. This woman died almost suddenly and I have to admit that that was perhaps some blessing. Those left behind are the losers.

I am surprised by the change of vocabulary. In my youth swear words were rare. Even young ladies nowadays use swear words freely – and meaning them. One of my mothers-in-law taught me to say "oh Fudge" instead of the now so popular f-word. I liked that advice.

London's former mayor, Ken Livingstone, not just liked newts – a sort of salamander without spots. He was successful in bringing the Olympics to the capital. Fares went up immediately to pay for the future event. The whole scheme strikes me as a very risky undertaking. It may bring money to traders and landlords. Experience – I lived in Los Angeles at the time the city staged the event – showed that simple things (like the price of a cup of coffee or snack foods) went up. That, however, does not improve a city's finances.

In these days of the cult of ugliness people dress truly sloppily and yet wear designers' clothes and carry – for free – advertising slogans for fashion houses stencilled or screen printed on the backs their simple fashion outfits.

Life is a great teacher. The school days and later working in Switzerland brought love for the landscape and the mountains, the rich colours of fields and meadows in spring, summer and early autumn and the wonder of the white snow in winter.

"Big Brother is Watching You". In the war on terror administrations everywhere in the so-called free world control freedom and peoples' normal life beyond even the most ambitious expectations of any terrorist. In fact, the protective measures being taken are a victory for the terrorists changing our society. Donald Rumsfeld put it succinctly: "Death has a tendency to encourage a depressing view of war". Obviously the former US Secretary of Defense likes war. The Pentagon people should have taken heed of ecological problems. The oil spill crisis in the Gulf of Mexico was forecast by the Austrian writer Gustav Meyrink in 1903. He wrote his famous *The Golem* and – more importantly these days – *Petroleum, Petroleum.* Even German BP apparently had knowledge of this story! A writer of a quite different kind was Hans-Heinz Ewers, a friend of Papa's. I still have his *Alraune* (Mandrake) volume. I remember from my childhood mysterious and magic stories he told Jürgen and me.

More peaceful was the statement by the German comic, the late Karl Valentin, who said that "art is beautiful, but makes for a lot of work".

Karl Aloys Schenzinger, once a quite fervent

communist, lost my father's friendship when he turned Nazi propagandist. He wrote the script for the insidiously influential and sentimental *Hitlerjunge Quex* film. The film influenced me for a while and I begged my parents for a uniform and to be allowed to join the cubs. I remained with them for a few weeks and the parents had difficulties to explain this. That, I believe started the authorities' suspicions of them.

More than two thousand years ago Socrates thought that "children are tyrants. They contradict their parents, gobble their food, and tyrannize their teachers". Maybe, but the Greek sage overlooked devotion.

Will It Last?, an address by me to the Wynkin de Worde Society in London in 1986, asked why do we, as a society, put up with functional illiteracy among young people, and not just those immigrants who are being blamed for so many of today's ills?

The illiterates come from communities with good education authorities. Ask any head of a secondary school and you will hear of the need for remedial classes to bring twelve-year-olds to a semblance of literacy. If we are going to pay more than lip service to the idea of a free society, then the spread of literacy – and the inherent freedom to disagree with authority – must become of prime concern to give education back its role as a cornerstone of social advance.

Pubs have great advantages. I listen in to

conversations and find I am getting interested in some of the people. I get to know them. Thus I strengthen my liking for the Irish. Is that because my father admired them so much? Did he like their brawling and hidden fury – and their poetry and gift of the gab?

A sort of "Big Brother", as in *Animal Farm*, thinking is coming into our free societies. A British Sunday newspaper published a picture taken outside the US internment camps at Guantànamo on Cuba and carrying the message "Honour-Bound To Defend Freedom". How reminiscent of the Nazi concentration camps' "Work Sets You Free"!

Heinz Höhne in his *The Order of the Death's Head* – the story of Hitler's SS – wrote that "on the road to absolute dictatorship maintenance of law and order can conceal an assault on civil liberties and historical necessity can be used as cover for the possible crime".

The requisitioning of the good and established term of "gay" annoys me and fills me with regret. The term homosexual strikes me as too clinical. I prefer the tolerant reference to a 'pooftah'.

Sometimes 'political correctness' has gone too far. In Hollywood I tried, years ago, to buy a copy of Joseph Conrad's *Nigger of the Narcissus*. Eventually I obtained it after being quietly taken to a separate room normally reserved for customers of pornographic literature. Anyone wanting to obtain Helen Bannister's *Little Black Sambo* children's books would probably be treated similarly.

The newspapers had a field day in London, calling the mayor Ken Livingstone a racist because he had condemned uncaring people, some of them of different skin colour or religious background. Anti-social people and yobs are an element and part of every society. The mayor was not racist in his comments. Not being able to speak one's mind recalls those days when people in the Soviet Union, asked their opinion, would fearfully answer: "I think the same as Joseph Stalin thinks".

Democracies have their faults. British governments in their rampant nationalistic and xenophobic arrogance refused to sign the Schengen Treaty which gives citizens of the European Union the right to pass frontiers without cumbersome controls. Britons travelling in Europe are being subjected to cumbersome passport controls, even when returning to their own country. In the folly of not signing up to the euro currency, and in the follow up to the adventurism of the Iraqi War and the mad borrowing spree of 2008 that British currency lost its value. Formerly weak currencies like the Italian Lira or the Spanish Peseta were supported by the European central Bank. No such relief yet for Britain and her people holidaying on the Costa Brava.

The world of high finance appears to have gone berserk and unbelievably greedy. Wild gambling bankers have wreaked havoc around the world.

Governments and the taxpayer rescued them and even gave them obscenely huge financial rewards for their doomsday recklessness or outright dishonesty. They continue to receive obscene bonus payments.

Life gets increasingly confusing. At one time I phoned my bank in England. The call went to a call centre. The lady who picked up the phone seemed to have a Welsh accent, rather attractive. It turned out she lived in Bangalore in India. We chatted briefly, and then she put the call through to the actual branch nearby in London! Years ago I suddenly had serious income tax problems. What could possibly have happened? I worried for days. Then I had an interview with the Tax inspector. All went well. It seems the Indian clerk had misread my file. There was no huge tax debt. Instead, a huge refund was on the way.

Since infancy, *Pears* soap was used. It also came in semi-transparent round balls which only some chemists stocked. There was a time when – somewhat sickeningly – "sweet-faced" little girls were chosen as *Miss Pears*. As a boy no such fame came to me. Today the no longer British-made soap is probably made in India for its American owners.

My Flat

ANDREW HERXHEIMER, with his wife Christine and her mother Gaby Berneck, gave me the use of a small flat in posh St. John's Wood in which I lived. I paid (a fairly modest) maintenance contribution and enjoyed the environs, as I have said earlier, especially the comparatively easy (and free) access by public transport. There is a very pleasant, elegant pub, The Clifton Hotel, one of the places the Prince of Wales, the future Edward VII, entertained one of his mistresses, the actress Lily Langtry. American tourists seemed fascinated by this spurious bit of British royal history.

My new flat overlooking the Grand Union canal and facing a small park is, I am sorry to confess, a mess. It needs tidying up. My children came and brought some initial order and since then I have felt able to do more by my own efforts.

I have sold some books. I had to create space. But experience has taught me to distrust dealers. When my second marriage had broken up, I had sold my collection of model cars – and got nothing for it. The dealer simply went bankrupt after getting the collection – for free. This man, Jeffrey Knight, had sent a handwritten promise to pay an amount of money which, though it fell short of the value of the model cars, seemed acceptable. But I have never received even that sum. It was the same situation again. My second wife negated on the promised £1,000 contribution to "residual expenses" after we had sold the former apartment and now the dealers were out to cheat me after I had agreed to the reduced payment. On top of all that, my third wife suggested I should pay a share of the costs of the dissolution of marriage.

Londoners have a real disadvantage in that they get the same pensions as anybody anywhere in Britain. There is London weighting for some civil servants, firemen and many other jobs. Why not pensioners? Beer in parts of London can cost up to £3.80 a pint, in Highgate a pub has the same drink for just £1.80. Bangers & mash cost up to £8 in St. John's Wood, but a mere £4 in some boroughs.

Unfortunately, I occasionally have a tendency to pontificate. I hold strong views and like to expostulate on them. Generally I say things calmly and politely. Sometimes I am bullying in stressing that these views have to be accepted by others.

A good friend died. Niels Christian (N.C.) Nielsen was Danish, the son of a butcher. He fled the country, and lived and married in Sweden. When the Nazis invaded Denmark, he had joined the student resistance, was found out and tortured. The Nazis crushed his testicles. His first wife gave birth to a child. My friend was overjoyed. He thought of himself as a man, after all! His then wife told him spitefully the child was of her lover, an airline pilot. N.C. was crushed and divorced her. Earlier fate haunted him.

He married again. Gunilla, a fine woman and a librarian. Unfortunately he drank too much and when very intoxicated would take out his violin and play his scratchy instrument, maudlin and remembering women he had loved and lost. He died drunk. Fate had been cruel to him and let him down.

I love New York. My son Augustus shares the love of this city and at one time wants to live and work there. The first sight of the skyline when one arrives from Kennedy airport fills me with awe and pleasure. The museums and their coffee shops are good places to visit after admiring the fabulous treasures of the Metropolitan, the Frick Collection and the Museum of Modern Art (where Thomas Bittner at my suggestion gave an after-dinner reception, at which I mimed a German Dada poem (*Nightsong of the Fish*), only to be reprimanded sternly by an elderly refugee lady that my rendering was inaccurate!) and so many more galleries and museums.

In New York I never failed to visit the Strand and Argosy bookshops. I visited Brentano's on Fifth Avenue and in former days Scribner's was there, too, almost home to some notable American writers and now no longer.

Inventions and innovations have made life more pleasant and easier. There is one exception. The mobile or cell phone, sometimes and mainly in Germany referred to as 'the handy'. It is the bane of modern life. People shout into it, warn their partners that they are on the train (perhaps so that lovers can escape discovery in time?), ruin dinner on an evening out in restaurants, even on the toilet, and so on. Only a few restaurants successfully bar the use of these instruments of communication or some telephone user letting the whole world know his problems, shouting them out loud. Concert halls or lecture halls offer no respite. La Scala in Milan tries to stop the nuisance. A very few places take phones off people, but some passengers even on security-conscious airlines insist on talking mobile while sitting down. Drivers seem unconcerned by the danger they pose to others while telephoning and driving their vehicles. One even sees people running to catch a bus and unable to stop using their hand-held devices.

In his *Paris Peasant*, originally published in the mid-twenties of the past century, the French writer Louis Aragon wrote: "The telephone is supposed to be useful, but, of course, it is nothing of the kind. See how man is seized with convulsions as he screams "hello" into the receiver. What is he (or she) but an addict of the dope called sound, dead-drunk with conquered space and the transmitted voice?”

Same or Different?

JOHANN WOLFGANG von Goethe described randiness eloquently. So help me, I was randy and eighteen years old. Only decades later I discovered that randy in America is a quite respectable forename, short for Randolph. I was undoubtedly randy in the British sense.

During my life I went through periods of unexpected shortages of money. I thought of having to take out loans from the bank on somewhat shaky pretexts. To my pleasant surprise friends came to the rescue and bailed me out without my having to beg or even mention the subject. Andrew Herxheimer, my friend from elementary school, spontaneously sent me £10,000 on loan. I repaid it after my second divorce.

I have all my life spurned hire purchase or loans for unaffordable extravagancies. I had paid cash for the apartment in Swiss Cottage and made half of that property over to my second wife, who had contributed to its purchase. Opposite that long-lost family home was the Tavistock Centre, a day hospital for disturbed people of all ages. It stood in its own grounds with neglected gardens at the back. Willem (ten years) and Augustus (aged eight), persuaded the hospital porter to let them use this area as a "nature reserve". They tidied it up with the help of some school friends, including neighbours, Rowan and Holly Reiss, today very capable musicians, and grown into beautiful women. They and the boys all graduated with First class honours.

Both Hampstead weeklies carried reports and pictures on the project. The plot thrived for a while, but then had to make way for an asphalt parking space. Progress came and a spot of nature in town was lost. Money was made.

As Gail Tsukiyama says in *The Samurai Gardens*, "Life is not just from within, it extends all around one, whether one wishes it or not."

The records of the 1940s and '50s by singers like Anne Shelton or Ella Fitzgerald are not aggressive or arrogant, like today's rap or other music. The same holds good for recordings, I feel, of Benny Goodman or Glenn Miller, Hoagy Carmichael and even Cab Calloway.

Even the serious compositions like *Rhapsody in Blue* or *Porgy & Bess* bear this sign of innocence and wonder, anticipation and expectation.

Books are the same. There was an innocence, not today's violence and perhaps America is just experiencing the unjustified superiority of the

Victorian times of the British Empire before it faded.

There are a number of films that made a deep impression on me. I go to see them again and again, pressing family and friends to accompany me. Most of all I love Jacques Tati's *Les Vacances de M. Hulot*, a film which needs no words. Then there is the zany *Hellzapoppin'*, with Ole Olsen and Chic Johnson. Two French films are Sartre's *Le Jeux Sont Fait* and *Beauty and the Beast* with Jean Marais. Another, also French, is *Les Maudits* about claustrophobia and man's cruelty to man, so appropriate to the Götterdämmerung end of the Nazi era.

There are other, perhaps equally notable films, like Vincent Price's *Dead of Night*, with Googie Withers, or *The Best Days of Our Lives*, the Billy Wilder production.

Just before the Second World War began, I discovered art. I was first interested in the French painters of the impressionist school. I bought myself a book on Gauguin, and then more illustrated tomes on Derain and Matisse, August Macke and Franz Marc. The classicists came later when I was perhaps more mature.

When I was fourteen years old I bought with my pocket money a book on Goya's *Los Desastres de la Guerra*. I still have this. My father had a much-admired picture by Claude Lorrain. I liked that but it was burnt when the house fell victim to allied bombs in an air raid one night. With the picture went a huge canvas by Rafaello Busoni – a bucolic scene in Italy – and a commemorative set of Edward VIII gold coins.

Yasuko, Ken Terada's daughter, was to be married. I was in Tokyo and had a brain wave. I phoned my second wife and asked her whether it would be alright to invite the Japanese girl for a few months to London, thus giving her a last look at independence and freedom and the chance of further improving her English. My second wife readily agreed and mentioned that the large flat in London's Belsize Village was just about big enough.

The question of chaperone was solved because her brother Masami would accompany her. My boys agreed to share the accommodation, and Yasuko's English improved phenomenally. She now translates books. Masami learnt to cook and be a future house-husband, though he quickly dropped his acquired skills when he returned to Tokyo. Yasuko got married and has two sons, now grown up. I gave a speech (in English) at Masami's grand wedding.

There is a memorial arbour in Israel which commemorates the men and women who helped Jews during the Nazi era. I tried to get my father honoured there but failed although his contribution was verified by people at the former Yugoslav Embassy.

The family protected and even rescued persecuted Jewish people. I am glad that a record of these activities is now lodged with archives in Jerusalem and Los Angeles. Not all Germans were evil! Future generations must understand this.

I derived enormous pride from a short piece I wrote for the Simon Wiesenthal Center in Los Angeles in 1998, which was published to commemorate *Kristallnacht* (the night of the smashed Jewish shop windows and desecration of synagogues). My contribution to the booklet was the only one by a non-Jew remembering those terrible events faking the outrage of ordinary Germans at the assassination of Ernst von Rath in Paris by a young distressed man from Poland. The representatives of the German and Austrian consulates attended. Barri was there, but I was in London. It was too warm for my wellbeing in Los Angeles. The invitation to the event had arrived after my departure across the Atlantic.

I cherish some cartoons from the *New Yorker*. In one there is a picture of a dog approaching St. Peter's desk at the gate to heaven. It asks plaintively: "Please, can I have my testicles back". Another has a factory owner overlooking his property. He says to his small son, "one day, all this will belong to your mother". Another cartoon just announces "Books on Paper" (there is a notable absence of a television set) and in another two tormented souls in hell are cowering in a cauldron, while two devils stoke the fire. One of them turns to the other and says, "We do not call them the damned any more, we call them customers". Or take those two men dressed in renaissance costumes standing by the bedside of an old man, with one of them saying: "Signor Vivaldi's dying wish is for the *Four Seasons* to be inflicted on as many people as possible".

I am an admirer of the limping George Gordon, better known as Lord Byron. Apart from his work I only read and remember a few poems by such people as François Villon, some sayings of Goethe (though I do not fancy most of his rather pretentious stuff, but like his *Italian Journey*, which was one of the first adult books I bought). I also like other Germans and the moderns like Christian Morgenstern or Joachim Ringelnatz. Lord Byron wrote a wonderful epitaph, declaiming:

"Posterity will never survey,
A nobler grave than this:
Here lie the bones of Castlereagh:
Stop, traveller, and piss".

Nevertheless, I am in tears. The past years have been years of disasters. In 2002 at the time of my stroke I narrowly escaped death. I had prided myself on my health, achieved without exercise, which I still loathe. The stroke reminded me of a cartoon in the *New Yorker* which showed a gravestone with the inscription, "Never ill – and now this". That was my old self and I am almost back to it.

I am mending. I am surrounded by love and yet feel lonely. My third wife has left me (come to think of it, so have the first and second). It would be churlish, though, not to recognize that she was constantly at my side in hospital when I was near-dead and when I was recovering against all odds. She was much admired for her devotion by nurses and patients. I was proud to have such a wife. But then she dropped me, suddenly. I feared this subconsciously, but was lulled by her ongoing protestations of love. I had to learn and am still learning that appearances deceive. I was too much for her, it seems.

For many years I had a girlfriend, a grown up woman almost my age. She lived far away. We wrote each other letters, e-mails or talked on the telephone. Far too rarely we also met. Fate was cruel and depressed her. In the end the relationship broke down. She is alive and I hope very much that she has many years to live. I shall not give her name and would hate to embarrass her. Really, we should have come out in the open. The past reared its head. I rushed into my third marriage and have since promised the children not get entangled again so soon.

I am full of guilt. Sometimes I think it could be due to my Calvinist (though not religious) upbringing. I ask myself why I should feel guilt. My parents and their families were decent Germans. They disapproved of the Nazis, helped persecuted people, and my father was eventually murdered in a concentration camp. I, and to some extent my brother Jürgen and my oldest cousin, Helmut, had an inkling of what the Nazis really were and how amoral they behaved. My other cousins were all too young to know, they are – I think – still puzzled and want to find out what it was that made Germans and Germany become so madly and insanely disorientated and criminal. Only one tiny branch of the family believed in the Nazis. The others helped victims and were, in part, rewarded for this after the war.

We, all of the family, did not get any substantial monetary restitution, and instead were rather neglected by the reparations, being non-Jews. I ask myself, for instance, why a late friend of mine, whose father was Jewish and had died before the Nazis usurped power, but who did not himself claim to be a Jew, received a rather lavish compensation settlement, while we got a pittance.

Since my stroke, I cry easily. I am told that is not so unusual. I am also told by my children that I had always been a sentimental softy and easily cried even in the old days. So I cry easily, oddly enough sometimes with happiness. I am really quite happy, even if low down. I must accept that I am a softy.

Things that make me cry with happiness are all in my mind. I cry because I see how one of my daughters and her husband love each other or my grandchild. I feel a bit ashamed when in public and I am asked why I cry when everything looks so fine. Nobody understands really, but my crying is joyful and content.

Men do not cry – that's it! I have always been rather proud, even arrogantly so, of being different. People in general are different. That is the way they should be. If they were all the same, that would be really boring. Good and bad (and mediocre), they are like beautiful and ugly, or mediocre. They are great. Why should an ugly person not at the same time show real beauty? When I was a young boy one of the nicest men my mother befriended was disfigured. I liked him, once my mother had explained how a grenade in the first war had destroyed his eye in his patchily reconstructed face. He was a very nice man. I saw that through my child's eyes and know it even now. It makes me cry and not in sorrow, but with happiness and even gratitude. He was different – good.

After my stroke I am not just weepier, but also notice more about the people around me. In this I am like those awakening from the slumber of death. I feel luckier than many others. I was supposed to be dead within two weeks, but my pigheadedness won over that forecast. Albeit, I notice how so many others, especially black people, and old at that, are crippled worse than myself and drag themselves through life. I look at them and am thankful that I am so relatively up and well. Since my stroke I have been on Warfarin, the rat and mice poison which thins the blood and thus kills vermin fairly painlessly. It prevents blood clots.

I am reminded of a House of Lords debate on

exterminating vermin. Then a noble lord spoke and explained that he and his lady wife knew that it was not necessary to poison the little pests. In his manor, he explained, they put out food and watched the mice at play while sitting before the fireplace. When the little animals are no longer shy, his lordship explained, it was time to tell the mice to go to the neighbours' castles. They had had their times in his, he said. The mice, of course, took the advice and promptly departed. Crazy perhaps – but a case here for the retention of reason and two houses of parliament, letting unelected experience sit in judgement of elected expediency.

I had an ambitious plan and intended to take a hiking tour from Wüstrow on the German side of the Baltic, a small resort between Rostock and Stralsund. I recalled my childhood days in Berlin and the holidays at those cities, the island of Rügen – where the Nazis thought the Aryans had come from – and the marzipan city of Lübeck. Augustus, my youngest son, was worried and decided to come and join me to check on my well-being. He arrived two days after me to keep me company after he went for a job interview, where he succeeded and instantly doubled his salary.

While he was on his way I tested my strength and stamina. Alas, I soon had to admit I was not up to long walks. I was too wobbly. His hire car would take me, and so we set off on a trip of togetherness, talking all the time. We got to know each other really well. It was marvellous.

How different people are. A daily bath or shower is routine for me. I know, of course, that some people have this need, and I am also aware of "the great unwashed". Thus it astonished me, and I am still unsure and do not dare ask. A woman of whom I am very fond mentioned that she would take a bath. Did she not take one every day, I asked myself, and thought whether there are days she really did not bathe.

Nevertheless I am frequently saddened by the ugliness of so many fitness freaks (though there are notable exceptions, such as my daughter Anna Cocca-Jaspert, and my former wives). These ladies – and men, like that persiflage of an idealized, but rather misshapen and supposedly perfect, Charles Atlas replica of the body-building almost artificial creation for Hollywood, the governor of California Arnold Schwarzenegger, are not being considered here for their beauty or grace – express more than joy-through-health, but rather a grim determination to be fit. It shows in their looks. Hilde Rosbaud, the widow of Paul, was a sobering example of that fitness craze. A stunning beauty when younger, she in old age had tanned to a parchment-like skin and an emasculated wiry body without feminine roundness anywhere. Wiry, frizzy and dried out.

Getting somewhat long in the tooth (lacking a few teeth now) I still travel, but mainly in Europe only. There are the children in Spain and Switzerland, and my brother in Spain, as well as relatives and friends elsewhere. Travelling almost annually to Provence, my friends Gerald Clark and his French-born wife Benedicte brought me back to life after the depression caused by the burst pipes disaster at home. They saved me from the brink of madness.

I am constantly amazed and pleased by the close contact with my children and the really good friends. Right within hours of my coming out of hospital suddenly after a minor operation, which irrationally I had feared, my eldest son came to have a drink and snack with me. My children phoned immediately. My friends called. Amazing to be surrounded by so much love.

Since my stroke I have constantly admired people rallying to me. Impressively, acquaintances give me support. I was shy at first. I was also helped with the computer intricacies. These friends contributed importantly to my recuperation and return to society. So did my editorial colleagues.

How things change. Since adulthood I was in the habit of a dozen mugs or so of tea daily with sugar, but after my stroke I developed a sudden aversion to the sweetening. Now I am told to drink water, and that tea is not giving me the needed amount of liquid. So I drink water instead, even preferring it, adding effervescent vitamin or magnesium (to avoid cramps in the night).

It irks me that I must have seemed to others like an old man with a young wife or rather like an old fool with a younger woman.

Nowadays I feel weepy when people are nice to me or when in happy surroundings. I am happy when I am with the children. Beatrice has much of my furniture, books and pictures. I feel comfortable in her home. I feel at home and weepily happy at Anna's with my dining room table and chairs and the books about Switzerland, Zurich and Gottfried Keller's *Landvogt vom Greifensee* – surely nobody ever again wrote such beautiful German?

Sometimes, but not always, I get a bit nervous living on "borrowed time" – so to speak. Like most people getting old, I have some unfinished business and rack my brains to think what must still be done, or worse still, knowing that this or that is waiting to be tackled, for I am often lethargic and put things off. There are thousands of photographs, and nobody but me any longer knows who the people on the pictures are. I can still identify the faces. My children cannot. Such records should not be lost. They are a record of life and the travels and events of generations of people – coming from czarist Russia, various continental countries, Britain, North and South America and Australasia and India and the Near East, as well as the Far East.

Looking back during these remaining years of

life, I feel gratitude to my parents, Willem and Isolde Jaspert. I thought I had a difficult and somewhat lonely childhood. I thought until after my stroke that my most difficult years were after Papa was murdered and I had to fight my own way. I became a loner, perhaps difficult to live with, some say impossible. Even so, I survived because my parents were decent people who believed in doing right even at the cost of not seeing their children. We were sent abroad so as not to live through Nazi-dom and its atrocities. We knew of the Nazis, saw them, but knew we were not part of this nightmare. This gave us strength to survive and be alone. When I think of the sacrifice my mother made to lose her sons for so many years I cry, but I am also proud she spared us from being the sort of people we would otherwise have been highly likely to become. Tall, blonde Aryans carrying the Hitler flag, like that awful creature *Hitlerjunge Quex* whom the renegade Karl Aloys Schenzinger had glorified and made into a martyr, prey on communist hordes.

I fervently believe in what the Chinese-American writer, Adeline Yen Mah wrote: "The most precious gift we can leave our children is not money, but knowledge".

I suffered a lapse in my rehabilitation from the stroke after the shock of divorce (again!), and became, once again, unsteady on my feet, stumbled and fell, did not sleep well and became listless about eating.

Only in company did I eat proper (restaurant) meals, and I did not have the stamina to cook. Eating alone or even preparing meals became a hated task. Friends were different. They could share, although I would have liked to be affluent and invite all round. When it comes to the necessary dreaded meals I tend to buy ready-made foods for the microwave. Occasionally there would develop great hankerings for luxury foods – lobster, oysters – or for simple things like bangers-and-mash.

I loathe those medicines in blister or individual day packs and long for the days when they used to be dispensed in bottles, which would relieve me from having to struggle to empty the individually packed pills into the receptacle I preferred. As if I did not already know what day of the week (as indicted on some packs) it was: Sunday, Monday, and Thursday or whatever. Sometimes I would forget the date, I always knew which day of the week it was. Now the chemist around the corner dispenses medicines into bottles for me.

Gradually, I have come to accept my lone situation, but realized it was too difficult to face a future all alone, despite the care of family and friends. I applied for sheltered housing, and have found a suitable home for my dotage. And yet, I was determined to carry on working, though I was enough of a realist to know that the call for my services would rapidly diminish, especially as the effects of my impending divorce played havoc with my efficiency. I had to reluctantly accept reality.

Being treated by my third wife like a piece of discarded rubbish made me strangely aware that, after all, I was perhaps quite worthy in attitudes and views. I missed the comfort of women, the *Kindness of Women*, as J.G. Ballard has called it in another context.

I learned to talk to others, English or foreigners. Of course, I had talked in the olden days, but this was different – involved and full of real life.

There came a new-found courage, because I was lonely, to expound views on literature, paintings, music and even historical roots of politics or languages and nations, understanding relevant causes – and effects. I felt able to voice views on, say, Dostoevsky, although I could read his work only in good (or bad) translations. I suddenly saw my father's importance and relevance as a recorder of Watchiwoke Bantu languages of Africa and their influence on other regions, mainly the south of the huge continent. I "felt" music, previously only liked or disliked. Gershwin or Piazzolla moved me, as did Beethoven or Bach. The seeds for this receptiveness had been planted by Mama and my wives. Now music is an ineradicable part of life.

Once, in London, a woman gave me a friendly kiss. That made me sleep peacefully again during the night after two weeks of sleeplessness.

I have inherited the forebears' wanderlust. I have travelled virtually everywhere and liked to stress: "not to Antarctica or Mongolia and not to West Africa". I had hardly ever travelled with more than one bag, preferably carry-on. That way I passed quickly through immigration and customs. Of course, being in a wheelchair after the stroke – and once after food poisoning from eating a raw fish dish in a posh place in Brazil, which debilitated and forced me into asking for assistance – sped me through immigration and customs. When I arrived in Los Angeles after the Brazilian event, my third wife was upset seeing this on arrival.

I was queasy about some food and, since seeing a factory farm in Northern Ireland, did not eat chicken or pork. Doctors advised against red meat. Sometimes, in flying on my travels, I would readily forego the meal service. Occasionally a kind purser brought something from the First Class.

The children had sometimes gone along on even quite exotic trips, worried about my dislikes of some foods and occasional anger at having no alternatives to food refused or I was not to eat. The children had no objection to chicken, but some of them did not eat fish or tomatoes which I loved, although they were red, too.

Life is stranger than fiction: a man I interviewed so many years ago for a job in New Zealand and who returned as one of my "failures" after four years there and came back to England, was instrumental in the first step of getting this book printed.

The newscaster and anchorman, Walter Cronkite died. I had met him through Edward McSweeney and we had dinners in Chinatown in New York City, unencumbered by discussion of politics. I felt that he was trustworthy – a sort of American version of Alastair Cooke of the BBC.

Some twenty-odd years ago I had lunch in the posh Royal Yacht Club in Stockholm and had to rush off to the airport at Arlanda. In the evening I was searching for a place to have dinner near Golden Square in Brussels. Lo and behold: my lunchtime host was strolling down an alley. We greeted each other and shared dinner.

Another time I was travelling from Barcelona to Madrid on one of those fabulous articulated Talgo trains. The aged man sitting opposite me studied me and kept frowning. Finally he asked me whether I knew Dr Walter Anger, who was my maternal grandfather. I had never met him. The old gentleman from South Africa told me that I looked like grandfather's spitting image.

As often as was feasible I took the children and family on my travels, some such trips were enjoyable but the family also experienced some bad influences. Once, in Monte Carlo, they were given free "play money" – chips. A daughter gambled, won and then lost her winnings. I myself did not gamble, but feel it is right to support good causes by playing the lottery.

At one time it was customary for suppliers at Christmas to give gifts to the people who gave them work. Printers and blockmakers (the people who made printing plates in those days of letterpress) presented gifts, mostly wine or spirits. One blockmaker gave me a bottle of Krug champagne. I knew a very good looking girl who loved champagne. Usually I bought her a bottle, one I could afford, and we opened and drank the liquid. At shortly before eleven in the evening she made me take a taxi for the last train home. I left, frustrated, but on time. We had the Krug champagne, but she then called the taxi and I caught the last train to London. Next morning I had a phone call at the office. "If only I had known what we were drinking" she said, "You could have stayed the night." I broke off the relationship, but returned to it years later.

Some People

I MET Caroline Aubrey-Caradec at Heidelberg in Germany in the hotel where we had been lodged on the shores of the Neckar River. The rest of the party thought we had shared the same room. However, it was not so! We remained just good friends. I never tried to speak French to her again. She had told me I was massacring her language. In 2002 she relented, and sent me Henry James' *Daisy Miller* in a bilingual (pedestrian) translation and knew I would be able to read French.

Her late husband, François Caradec, wrote about the Victorian performer, Le Pétomaine, whose performance had amused Queen Victoria, and published a volume on *Mon Chien*, his beloved sad-eyed dog, and much more. Once Caroline Aubrey had been invited with me to dinner by the Swedish publisher and printer Albert Bonnier, Jr. he taught both of us that a Scandinavian custom demanded that one always looked into one's table companion's eyes when toasting. We drank rather a lot and I thought we had fallen in love. In the morning I realised I had proposed.

I begged forgiveness and retracted. I collected hotel notepaper for Caroline's collection. I bought a book in which a German artist had published drawings done on hotel letterheads from around the world. I have good memories of some of the hotels where I had stayed. At one, Villa d'Este, the former cardinal's place on the shores of Lake Como, my son Augustus, then only a few months old, and I lovingly slid down the marble banister of the splendid staircase.

On another night in Stockholm, Albert Bonnier recounted to me the losses incurred in launching a failed weekly. That was when I bemoaned that my wallet full of French currency, my passport and tickets had been stolen at Berne in Switzerland, where the police informed me politely that it could not have been a Swiss who stole them! Apparently they believed it inconceivable for one of their countrymen to commit such an act. Albert Bonnier just said that what had been a big loss to me was just a trifle to the money he had lost with this ill fated venture. In an odd way it reminded me of my second wife's nominal uncle Mac who was one-hundred-and-two years old. When he reached a hundred he asked to be excused from receiving the (at that time) usual telegram of congratulations from the Queen. He did not approve.

A friend of my first wife from her days at university also became my friend. He was married and had a beautiful son. His wife had been one of the last Jewish children before the outbreak of the Second World War to reach England by *Kindertransport*. She was a passionate woman. I was, and am despite appearances, very shy and was incapable of responding and remained so. Later the couple were looking forward to the arrival of the second child. When the day came, the husband went to see his wife in the hospital in Kensington and meet his new son. Imagine his surprise at seeing a lovely black boy – the son of a West African lover. How must the mother have felt during her pregnancy, dreading the arrival of the evidence of her affair?

The couple were divorced soon after and unusually the marriage was annulled by decree of a Roman Catholic court, with "judges" having come from as far away as Rome. I was dragged in as a reluctant witness to the non-existence of a real marriage, despite the fact that a child was there already before the surprise events.

My colleague Roy Brewer and I were in a hotel in Stuttgart in Germany, standing at the bar before dinner. Next to us was a very loudmouthed German from Brazil, who was praising the Nazis and their heroic deeds. My friend, who falsely claimed to have been an officer in the British Army, pointed out quietly that he spoke German and that in his army days he would have arrested the German. An altercation ensued. We were told to instantly leave the bar, to which we replied that it suited us, as we were going to have dinner now.

The German objected. He, too, was going to have dinner in the hotel restaurant and he would not sit in the same room with us. As he was a rich and important guest, a special table was set up for the two of us and we had complimentary wine and dinner in the hotel lobby. We did not care, but complained for some time of the better treatment for the rich.

Early in life I had realized that a really good story always should contain an element of telling against the one who tells the story – usually a joke. That self-effacement makes people really laugh. It was true: best of the infamous anti-Semitic jokes were always told by Jews, commiserating really with their fellow Jews' plights. The "Caruthers" jokes, crude as they are, were mostly better appreciated if they contained "real life experiences" and showed the hero of the story in a pitiable light, *viz* "but everybody's sits on Caruthers" like. There was the old prison chestnut: its social hour in prison and the inmates gather round, telling each other old familiar jokes they all know, so they recite by numbers only. A new arrival wants to join in the fun. He says, say, "67". Dead silence results. Finally the prisoners' trustee speaks up: "You told it wrong". End of story and a long face.

Once I had a sneezing fit, and this was funny really– my dentures flew out in the taxi taking me across town. I did not notice. Only after the taxi had driven away did I realize that the plastic teeth were missing.

Too late, I had to be measured up for a new set – at considerable expense and waste of time, of course.

On holiday in Spain one year, a friend had joined us with her children. We had sat by the pool talking. The children, hers and ours, were crawling about. Suddenly I noticed that her younger son had disappeared. I saw him lying stiff and still at the bottom of the small swimming pool. I jumped in, fully clothed, brought him up and gave him the kiss of life. He survived.

Many people wonder at my differing reactions to cats and dogs. I love dogs and am literally scared of cats, which nevertheless tend to show me affection. That frightens me; they are not content to sit on my lap and across my crotch. At one time visiting friends in Berlin, we were having dinner. Just as carefully lifted the forkful of spaghetti to my mouth, the cat jumped on to my shoulders. I screamed and the pasta and rich tomato sauce was all over me last clean shirt of that trip. I was forced next day tom wear the soiled shirt on the plane back home.

When there was a miners' strike in Britain, the street lights were off. It was dark in the evening I was mugged. When the police came I was still trying to find my knocked-out front teeth, I told them that I had heard running footsteps "like a black boy's". Well, the police were not allowed to take that as even a suspicion. Race reared its ugly head. My statement, when read to me, simply stated that I had thought to have heard running footsteps. Everybody "knew" that they were a black man's – but nobody could say so. I even began to doubt that I had heard anything at all.

There once was a prolonged postal strike in Britain. I personally suffered, because the payment demand notice from an American life insurer was delayed for six weeks. All my premium payments were forfeited and became worthless. The insurers were adamant and insisted that I should have been alert to the situation. But there was a funny side to this, too. The director of a London mail order firm for erotic literature in the city's Soho area said the situation was "desperate". His company used a good area accommodation address "because it gave their mailings that mark of respectability". The strike brought disappointed customers "champing at the bit", (according to the London *Sunday Times*).

I liked to fancy myself as having assimilated English life. However, in my heart I knew that I had not totally achieved this aim. There was the accent, slight normally, and sometimes odd, making telephone callers think there was a trace of Irish (which suspicion I appreciated and rather liked their boisterousness. I applauded it. Had not the Irish reclaimed English literature for the English in the late eighteenth and nineteenth century? But the Irish, erudite literati as they might be, were also conceived as brawling navvies by the English.

Many of the Irish people I knew at one time were capacious drinkers. The late Peter Walsh, who had spent some time in jail after the Selfridges bombing, had a beautiful wife, Denise. She at one time had been the girlfriend of Brendan Behan, the *Borstal Boy*. Later she lived in Spain and rejoiced in telling me the plausible story of Behan being routinely arrested for intoxication when leaving the pub at closing time. One day, so she claimed, he was determined no break this vicious circle. He stayed sober, but provided himself with a packet of Donnelly's sausages. Pretending to urinate on the grass outside the pub, he was pounced upon by the constable who fainted when Behan pulled out a knife and cut a sausage which he had held in a strategic place.

Many people also suspected me of having a South African or sometimes Dutch inflection to my speech. The former view was encouraged by me. There were obvious links there. My maternal family had actually lived in that country. The country was – even if formerly only – still thought of as part of the British Commonwealth. Dutch also had some snob value. There was the affinity to Afrikaans and South Africa. There was also the connection to my father's family and the Flemish ancestry, which I could lay claim upon. Furthermore, the Dutch were reputable allies, invaded by those "beastly Germans", with whom I wanted to avoid any association.

What is called the wit and wisdom of Hollywood is exemplified by Bob Hope, who said "that people who blow kisses are mighty lazy". Of another Hollywood actor, Cary Grant, who like Hope was British-born, according to Dr Henry Gibbon, said, "A kiss is the anatomical juxtaposition of two orbicular muscles in a state of contraction".

Every four or five years the world's most important print exhibition was held in Düsseldorf. I rented a roof top flat in the centre of town for several years. Sometimes I let friends stay there, too. One night a friend called me out of bed. He had field glasses and came to observe a couple, in another home on a high floor, making love and undressed as nature demanded. He had seen them performing antics the evening before. He stood on the roof terrace and invited me to join. I could not help watching.

This friend also drank heavily. I bought some schnapps on my way home from the exhibition and put the bottle in the fridge. Every night when I came back to my base, I wanted to pour myself a drink. There was no drink. My friend had drunk it all, though he bought a replacement.

Another time in Chicago, where I was doing exhibition reporting, an editor with his secretary came to our hotel. We went to the hotel bar, which also had music, but no dancing. Nevertheless, my friend and I found partners. Eventually my friend got to dance with the secretary. She told me she had never met anybody who danced as beautifully as my friend. I concluded therefore that my friend who had told me that his first wife liked ballroom dancing was himself an accomplished ballroom dancer. I was wrong. My friend, though, took the secretary to London, where she also took her children. My friend arranged for riding lessons for the children on Hampstead Heath. Then, one day my friend's real wife asked me to help sort their marriage out. They stayed married until he died.

My second wife and three daughters, on our way to Sweden went to see a maternal great-aunt Ollie Kalmerten near Husum on the flatlands of the North Sea and then travelled on to Niebüll near the Danish border to visit Emil Nolde's house and garden, where he had painted gorgeous flowers. His pictures aroused the violent dislike of Adolf Hitler and were held to be "degenerate". Nolde's work was banned from public showing. To think of such destruction of a man's life is too terrible to contemplate. His paintings live on. I have a souvenir of his gardens on the wall of my flat, my daughter Anna, then a toddler, standing grinning in a mini-dress amidst the flowers in glorious colour as he had painted them.

An acquaintance was press officer for an important trade association here. He came from an important family. His father had been Lord Mayor of a big city. He himself had been an aide-de-camp of Field Marshal Montgomery.

His principals gave a gala reception with drinks at the beautifully located and impressive British Embassy in Paris. Waiters serving drinks and canapés were dressed as flunkeys in baroque costumes and wearing powdered wigs. An impressive event, it was. The champagne being served seemed not to agree with my friend. He was sick all over a serving tray. He handed the tray back to the flunkey, who had not batted an eyelid, and asked for a fresh glass of champagne, which was duly brought by the good man.

After a mainly business trip to Japan, accompanied by Julia and my youngest son Augustus and daughter Anna, we were joined in Hong Kong by Willem to fly on to a holiday in the Philippines. We had taken up a special offer by the Manila Hotel (refurbished after having earlier been used in the war by General Douglas MacArthur as his headquarters). Anna, still a teenager, was much admired by the hotel staff and befriended by a page boy. I mentioned earlier that my wife's necklace was stolen I later gave my wife a replacement, since bought back from her and given to my granddaughter Poppy, of gold nuggets, each worth a few hundred pounds sterling, which I had collected over the years on six continents.

Crime has its funny side, too. My then wife and I had spent a holiday in the city of York and in the vicinity of its wonderful cathedral. Again, we had a nice time. On return home, with Julia entering first, she recoiled and told me to be on my guard. Burglars had been and created visual chaos in the home. They had taken prized possessions, a small Rembrandt etching and my beloved childhood treasures: die-cast model cars, some of them my parents had brought back from the United States. They had stolen some of our suitcases to carry the loot off. The police came while I was sitting by my typewriter.

They saw me and exclaimed that they could believe my tale of finding our home in chaos. I had to point out with some embarrassment that the burglars had not entered my workplace and that chaos was a usual feature of that room. Visitors and cleaning ladies had been taken aback by its appearance in the past. However, again – the insurance paid.

One of my maternal aunts lived in Kiel in Germany near the shores of the Baltic. Below her home was that of the inventor of the teletype and the forerunner of the scanning machines used in reproduction for printing. I knew Dr Rudolf Hell and had interviewed him and later visited him in Zürich where he spent much of his late years. He died a hundred years old. I mention him and John Crosfield elsewhere in the reminiscences. Both had the same background and were on opposite sides in the war – each knowing how to counter the other's stratagems.

In Zürich I celebrated twenty-five years of my second marriage. We had a suite in the Baur au Lac overlooking Lake Zürich. The hotel's files showed that, to my amazement, I was known to the hotel. The files showed that my mother had stayed there and that I attended *thé dansants* in the 1940s – as an unwilling schoolboy having to learn dancing and social manners.

Travel in the olden days brought special rewards. Going by train and ferry I bought freshly landed fish at the quayside in Ostend for just a £1 or £2 and we ate it at dinner and introduced the children to novel tastes. Once my plane was re-routed via Atlanta in America when I had with me a basket of tropical fruit from Barbados. Sadly, US agricultural rules – although we were clearly in transit – enforced surrender of the exciting hand luggage. After that I brought fruit back from Malaysia or Brazil or India, lamb from New Zealand and rice crackers from Japan. America offered other things. The children developed their tastes and still like some specialities which nowadays they can get at their abodes. Today you can get most tropical fruit in London. The city offers practically everything from anywhere. In the world outside the metropolis and its counterparts around the world, the choice is big.

A Danish friend drank too much and died. I liked him and spent holidays – with the family – in his country home near Norrtälje. One night in Finland in the Arctic Circle he rescued me from the arms of an amorous Eskimo lady – only to ask me whether I had anything to drink when it was well past midnight. He thought that question, answered in the affirmative, was the occasion for a party and knocked on the doors of colleagues' rooms, waking them up and telling them to bring tooth mugs along, to partake in whisky. He died young, always a good and lovable man, and a staunch friend whom life had treated rather badly. He had pioneered the so-called Polar route of SAS, the Scandinavian airline, to Japan and knew places like Gronland, and – of course – Alaska's most remote regions.

I am told that the Red (American) Indians, whom I admire for their close feelings for natural things like the growing of trees or renewal of life in, say, a herd of buffaloes they hunt, feel that white people are mad and misguided. The say Whites think with their heads. Indians feel that is wrong. Real people should think with their hearts. Then they will fully live.

At a party in London I met the then very young consul of Fidel Castro's new Cuba. He was much taken with Pippa, the mini-skirted, beautiful wife of a dissolute, but witty friend of mine with whom I have since broken. The consul invited me to Havana and I travelled to Cuba via Madrid on Iberia Airlines. I worked for the *Sunday Times* at that time, when currency restrictions were still in force.

I travelled with almost no luggage, but about $2,000

in cash. At Heathrow the customs officers stripped me down to my underpants and I almost missed the plane to Spain. There I borrowed summer clothing from my brother in Madrid. In Havana the immigration officers queried my entry permit, but allowed me to take a taxi to the Hotel Naçional, formerly, the Havana Hilton and a haunt of gamblers and tarts. Foreign currency secured excellent food and lodgings. In the morning my visa was duly approved and the charming officer-in-charge invited herself to lunch in my hotel. She graciously allowed me to buy the food and drinks for herself and lady companion.

A photographer had come with me to Cuba and took hundreds of photos but only one picture and a few sentences of mine were finally used in the paper. My story was spiked to make way for reports of the death of some famous person. The visit, however, bore unexpected fruit. Later in Leipzig in East Germany I met two Cuban bodyguards who invited me to an official Cuban government party.

Great are the wonders of modern technology. I depend on telephones and computers. But why can't they be made simple to use? Voicemail is the bane of my life and why on earth cannot computers be simplified to operate like model trains, which function effortlessly whether they are made in Europe or America or Japan. Instead, one has to obey some rules seemingly worked out and formulated that complete nerds, of whom I am one, are thought to understand, but cannot cope with.

I am starting a new life and embarking on new ventures. Will I have time? I'll never know. The end will come, as things accomplished or life's tasks unfinished. Never mind: let the adventure starts, late perhaps, but let it start. Completed or incomplete. The start is made.

Viagra and then later followers, designed to restore the youthful penile rigidity, did not impress me. Most of these drugs gave me headaches and I desisted from taking them, though indeed they helped overcome the problems of old age inability or insufficiency. Alas!

A friend of mine sits up late, well into the wee hours of the morning. He watches television or listens to the radio.

In the morning he is tired, naturally. I say to him that I have an advantage in never watching television in fact, I do not have television and as I am well over eighty years old could have the licence fee paid by some government office. I know because I wrote to the Prime Minister at Downing Street whether I could have theatre tickets instead of television money. I got a clear reply which simply said: "no way".

My friends think that having no television deprives me of learning about things not known before. Well, but I probably do not want to know, thus my loss is at the same time my gain: my peace of mind is left undisturbed. There are already too many memories of past times that perturb me. Why add deliberately to this burden?

There are irritating fashions in food. When I was young, they said "Go to work on an egg". Today they warn you of eating more than two eggs a week! Similarly, liver, cooked as blue or rare as feasible and edible was supposed to be good for you. Building brain power by eating brains is almost unobtainable since the outbreak of Mad Cow Disease. But Italian scientists – who else – have found that pizza fights the growth of cancer.

Less confusing is the British discovery that lasagne was known to Britons in the sixth century long before Italians were told by Marco Polo – the original conman and author of *Il Milione* – of the Chinese invention of pasta, or the Chinese were told of the Italian invention of pasta, whichever country came first.

Things change all the time. They do not necessarily change for the better. Hardly ever does one get a reply to a letter to some corporation. Sometimes, with luck, a telephoned reply is received usually from someone who is clearly illiterate, for explicit points of the original letter are not considered. The very occasional letters are inevitably misspelt.

Here is inflation: The children now earn more in pounds sterling than was ever paid to me, the father. I had started work in London as a foreigner. The wage of £450 a year was more than the average grammar school teacher's salary then. Colleagues then were jealous, but the explanation for the better rate of pay was easy. The schools in Vienna, Budapest and Switzerland had been rather famous internationally and posh. I knew the right people and spoke Latin, German and a sprinkling of Spanish – all were useful. Understanding some Dutch and Swedish was a plus. Close relatives were or had been in the governments of South Africa and – also – the German Navy (quite high up). Life was made easy.

One changed jobs by simply picking up the telephone and indicating that a new job would enhance employment skills. It worked for a person with the "right" background. In a way it was shameful. Merit had little to do with advancement. Friends got jobs, for instance, running the East Africa section of a well-known corporation just because they had been officers – like their fathers and had been to a good public school. The joke went thus: "he is only twenty-three years old and is already in charge of international activities of this company. His father though, remains chairman."

Some young men just had it made. The old maxim of mothers forgiving all remained valid: "Oedipus. Shmoedipus. As long as the boy loves his mother"!

I have become a somewhat grumpy old man. While I think I am tolerant, I loathe mobile telephones. For some unfathomable reason their users seem to want everybody around them to hear what they are saying.

While I like women very much, I do not like the current fashion for bare midriffs. Apart from the bigger cities in Italy or Spain one does not see them there – or rarely in places as far away as Japan. When Japanese girls, though, are in Britain they do as the English do and wear those ungainly skimpy T-shirts or blouses knotted at the stomach.

They used to say that Mussolini was not all bad! After all, despite his evil reign, trains in Italy were on time. Equally, the evil and demented monster Hitler had the autobahn motorways built and gave people like me the opportunity to be relatively tolerant, though at times I no doubt am quite narrow-minded. But I got to know other cultures. Perhaps the positive points of Stalin and Mao-Tse-Tung will be known to me some day soon. There is also the undoubted fact that Hitler brought back full employment – even if by dubious means. Two of my uncles – both on the paternal and the maternal side – suddenly found good jobs. One of those uncles was so grateful that he became the family's black sheep – the only Nazi believer among relatives!

Now they want to introduce identity cards. They are used in most countries outside those under former British rule. They were used in wartime Britain, too. The Nazis, in the then occupied Channel Islands, made British police (who did not envisage the inhuman crimes planned against these people) round up Jews. After the war in London we followed the call to burn our cards in Trafalgar Square. Police looked on, smiling benignly. The question should be: would some future rulers misuse the data on these card files to pinpoint supposed enemies of their policies?

Daniel Ellsberg, of the Watergate scandal, wrote: "the day after the next 9/11 (New York World Trade Center terror) our freedoms are gone".

I count myself very fortunate in spite of all the upsets. I know that – without any of my doing – the decency of my family and their good friends has been recognized. Several of these people were honoured by the major Western allies. They awarded some of the first publishing and broadcasting licenses in the British-, French-, US- and even Soviet-occupying Zones in Germany after the War. Some of these people were even allowed to set up business partnerships in Western countries. I am grateful and not a little bit proud of this and my background. I was enabled to remain a proper human being.

A Rather Long Epitaph

WHAT DO they call it so often? The University of Hard Knocks or simply the University of Life?

I realized that I must embark on reshaping my life, lived until now through marriages, and three times failed, though blissful changeovers. Fragmented as my life was, I have become dimly aware that there is more to life than living through others and the past. Painful as the new experience will be, it is also a good one, giving me a new-found total freedom, to be marred by occasional retrograde longings for past dependence and affections.

I look back and find myself somewhat naïve in generally trusting too much in people. Should I not have learnt from my father's friends betraying him? I have good friends whom I cherish and even admire. However, I trusted some and even long after the Nazis and no longer in danger or even unaffected by those evil people, undreamt of betrayals have occurred.

Is there time enough to grow into a new man or will I die all-too-soon?

What has been done has been done. There is no

way anything that has been done could be undone. It has certainly happened.

One may apologize or bask in a success, regretting or rejoicing. It is always certain that that which happened or was done remains certain. In turn this leads to what Allan Watts, who popularized Zen Buddhist philosophy in the West, described as the *Wisdom of Insecurity*. Roy Brewer introduced me to all this. Any forecast is just an attempt at foreseeing future events. It is only a guess, albeit sometimes an inspired one.

What is the use of "crying over spilt milk"? Once spilled, it has been spilled. Thus it is futile to keep secrets. They are protection of oneself or others. Pointless. Why bother to set store by them?

All throughout my life and from the time I was six weeks old and went by convict boat from Europe to Africa I had been possessed by wanderlust. I had been lucky and my work took me everywhere in the world. I wanted to carry on. After my release from hospital and since my wife left me, during the first nine months after the events, I twice visited my daughters Anna and Beatrice with their small families, as well as my brother Jürgen in Spain, Switzerland and Mexico (where my son Willem then began his career as a photographer on *Harper's Bazaar* and *Elle* magazines' Mexican editions, thus following in my mother Isolde's footsteps.

For some months I did not really want to believe that

I was without my wife. I hoped against hope that she would do an about turn and return to me. Gradually I began to face facts and accept separation. I decided to bring back my belongings from California, leaving my presents and items of furniture except an armchair and a picture – a large original print by Matisse – there, my son, Willem, then in Mexico, promised to come with me. I had already sent my wife's belongings to her without asking her to pay. I flew to America via Washington DC, planning to reach Los Angeles via Mexico City. On arrival at Dulles (Washington DC) airport the immigration officer gave me a hint that my wife, without telling me first, had filed for divorce. I had a Green Card but was only allowed to stay a short time. Under the circumstances I was not worried, but perturbed. I telephoned Barri from my hotel near the airport and was told that indeed, she had petitioned for divorce and that I had some papers to sign when I got to Los Angeles where my son and I booked a room in the Beverly Plaza Hotel, where I had had an occasional glass of rioja wine and tapas in happier days.

My effects got to London eventually. Barri had been decent and prepared them for shipment and they had needed only packing by my son. The velvet-covered red armchair went directly to my son Augustus' new flat, where it looks very nice.

The shipment of effects cost a lot. Barri, after some months, paid for only the cost of shipping her belongings. I, on the other hand, was out of pocket to the tune of thousands … and on top of all this was invited to equally share the cost of the divorce I did not want. I declined, but paid my share of the court costs only.

Leaving America, I was briefly arrested for giving a false address. The "gift of the gab" saved me and brought a speedy release to fly to England.

A former school friend of my third wife and her husband were the first to re-establish contact. I was mightily pleased and liked her friends, but few others responded to pleas for maintaining contact. Some of these temporary friends suddenly heaped abuse on me.

Eating alone by myself, or even preparing meals, became a hated task. I knew that one has to eat by sheer bodily necessity. I hated the time needed and the mere activities involved, though I liked food in company of children or friends. I appreciated being taken out and was pleased when my by then grown-up children invited me, normally I took it for granted that even in my olden days I should invite my children … and former wives.

Occasionally there would develop great hankerings after luxury foods – lobster, oysters, or simple things to eat like bangers-and-mash or fish heads – and I carefully collected the fish eyes the youngest son had once at a tender age, but no longer, wanted (although I could not understand this reluctance, being a compulsive collector of everything under the sun). What I wanted to be from time, was to be a true gourmet and *bon vivant.*

I craved the sharing of lives, but also the softness and warmth of a body next to me. It was not the urge to have sex – although that was there, too – and sex would and should please both parties, in mutual giving and taking of love and pleasure, sought by both.

Anna, my daughter living in Switzerland, came to London. She has developed an interest in things Japanese, mainly woodblock printing. I am pleased. I gave her most of my books on the subject, including some rather valuable old volumes from Japan. Now I can feel really "at home" when I visit her, or my other daughter Beatrice in Spain or Augustus and Willem here in England.

Lost Times

THE FRIENDS of the parents were a varied lot. Too many of them suffered a cruel fate. Otto Linnekogel's face was destroyed by shrapnel in the First World War. Victor Kunstely survived the Nazi concentration camp, but was blinded. Some disappeared.

Sometimes I indulge in fanciful daydreaming, a sort of "Walter Mitty" thinking. I fancy myself as a good spy perhaps; I cannot help listening in, for instance, to other peoples' conversations.

The decision had already been made. On a plane to New York a few days later after my 'study' had been submitted, I happened to sit next to the manager of the weekly. I had the grace to tell him that I could not help but seeing the papers he was studying about the setting up of a satellite printing operation (about which I knew anyway).

I think the coming Olympics in London are a waste of money. Far better to give the vast funds allocated to this prestige event to deprived areas.

The Swiss writer Friedrich Dürrenmatt stipulated that administrations are self-serving. They are managerial about "terrorists" but no more explain their so-called protective and illiberal control over their own "subject" people and their rightful privacy. Even beautiful Switzerland will control the people excessively.

Those who fight monsters must take care not to become monsters themselves.

The roller skating circus horse Negro Caballo was in the habit to nibble at flower pots on the window sill, which it then dropped on the heads of passers-by on the pavement below.

Regrets

LOOKING BACK over my life, I find regrets for impetuousness.

I meet my first wife Hella roughly every fortnight, until recently when she turned into someone like a recluse. She looks good and we have much to share in thought and attitudes. I see Julia – my second wife – almost weekly. She, too, has kept her good looks. We get along fine. She gives me real support. I could again live happily with either or even both of them.

Sure, in my view I think they made big mistakes when they divorced me. I, admittedly, was stupid and did not fight that or tried to make my behaviour explained as – albeit enjoyable – aberrations. I even contemplate today to invite one of the ladies on a trip abroad. Nevertheless, although I hanker after the renewal of past love, I was until recently in daily contact with one of my old flames – seriously so. While I feel that I am – contrary to appearances – rather steady, I have to admit that I am reckless without meaning to be.

Today many people are so lonely – even in company.

There I was in a restaurant. A husband and wife couple, I assumed, were taking out a woman friend. Both hosts had mobile phones and used them incessantly. Their guest (like a dumdum) stared vacantly around, waiting for the food to be served – probably to just have something to do.

Ignorance is said to be bliss. One of my daughters came to meet me at Ostend while I was in Germany. On the train when we came to the River Rhine proceeding to Cologne, she exclaimed "is that the Nile?"

Peace-loving combined with national pride has become a terrifying obsession of many politicians. I had always believed that Britain was fair. The sorry episode of the Iraqi war disillusioned me.

I shudder to contemplate the coming identity cards. They state people's characteristics and background. Earlier that had enabled the Nazis to round up Jews from France, The Netherlands and even the occupied Channel Islands, for gassing. "Like people and trust them or lead a life full of pain and disappointment".

There was a time when good Germans were still known even if the Nazis' evil deeds and the war upset the civilized world. After the outbreak of the war Eric Ambler could still write a story about good Germans making it clear that the fight was not with Germany, but against the Nazis. In his wartime speeches Winston Churchill often distinguished between Germans and Nazis. All this changed very much when details of the

Nazis' atrocities leaked out.

A few years ago I flew to America my Green Card had been withdrawn, but I fondly imagined that as a British passport holder I could visit the country. On arrival at Kennedy the passport officer let me in, but said that I would have to report before a judge and would first have to go to jail, as I as one of those people who needed a visa. Fortunately this was a Friday, so I got my friends in Connecticut to pick me, stayed the weekend with them, and they then drove me to the airport bus pickup point. Once there a bought a new ticket and flew back to London via Canada. Only when we were safely over Canadian territory could heave a sigh of relief. There would be no longer any danger of having to go to jail!

Werner's son Michel married Colette, the daughter of an escaped French prisoner-of-war my uncle and the family of Werner sheltered in their garden shed throughout the war. Elsewhere I recount how the family and I tried to help and support Jews during the years of terror.

My maternal grandmother, who had at some time lived with her husband in South Africa, always told me what terrible things had been done to the Boer women and children "in the concentration camps". The Nazis never failed to point out that "it was Britain to protect the state's security to have created concentration camps". The South African camps were beastly, but never fiendishly planned death camps. Grandmother felt no outrage at the fate of the men. They were willing to die for their beliefs and took up arms to kill other men. Later that puzzled me.

Although I trained in the use of firearms I really rather preferred to lug Jerry cans. There is among several such sentiment German poems one by Wilhelm Hauff which tells of young men willing to die. It says:

"Heute noch auf stolzen rossen
Morgen durch die Brust geschossen"

(In rough translation it means that today we ride high, but tomorrow shots will have entered our chests).

In my dotage years I was invited to an officers' party at one of the great regiment's clubs near Buckingham Palace. Wine and canapés were served. A friend, who had done service in that regiment, but as an enlisted man, complained that he should have been invited. But to an Officers' Club?

Looking back I realize that (including my school years) I lived altogether in ten countries. That meant absorbing a little bit of many different cultures and mores. Undoubtedly this has shaped much of my thinking.

Abraham Lincoln wrote "it is not the years in your life that count. It is the life in your years!"

As my final hours will be approaching, I think of the story of Count Ernst von Gleichen – of hundreds of years ago.

I know I was privileged. I had love all around me. I tried all my life to return much love all around. I am grateful, too, for everything I was made to learn and what I learned.

Old age brings many regrets. I had fondly imagined that I would spend my final years in the comfort and familiar surroundings of my Hampstead home where I had lived for almost fifty years. Impetuous infatuation and self-indulgence put paid to those hopes. My final home is much smaller though rather nice, but in a somewhat bad area.

Know Thyself! But Who Does?

AM I indeed a lapsed Calvinist with some Jesuit leanings?

At eighty-two years of age, I realize how my youth and growing up have been influenced by Jewish friends and mentors.

Back in Germany I hid successfully for over a year. During that time my mother Isolde gave shelter to Erika, a young Jewish woman, who gave birth to her baby, a daughter who now lives in Austria. The father was a family friend, manager of a famous art gallery and rescuer of much "degenerate art", much of it now housed in a museum in Austria. The parents survived and were married after the war. As a teenager I assisted in the clandestine birth of the little girl – to prevent her from screaming and protect her and us from neighbours who might have denounced us to the Nazis. I still wake up terrified when I have nightmares about this.

I was in hiding, but the Nazi bloodhounds found me. Paul Rosbaud, an Aryan family friend, and as I later realized an important source on science to the

British Secret Service. While files on Frank Foley have been released by the British Secret Service or MI6, Rosbaud (notwithstanding *The Griffin* by Arnold Kramish, he remains an unsung hero of the Second World War) got wind of my impending arrest and warned my mother. I gave myself up and that saved my life. The draft board forced me to join the wartime services. Having an uncle who was a vice-admiral (I never let on where) I was automatically made an officer's candidate and wore a navy blue uniform with some sort of gold chain. Mama cried when she saw me in what looked like a little boy's sailor suit on her tall son.

Much later I came to doubt just one Jewish person: he maligned me and also did some twisting of a last will under which my former wife Julia and I stood to benefit greatly. Of course, this would never condemn all Jewish people. It is – however – very sad. Elsewhere I mention this regrettable affair in greater detail. As my uncle Werner, one of the last the last writers on the – then by the Nazis banned – *Frankfurter Zeitung* daily also reminded me: "all Russians are not all Stalinists, just as not all Germans are Nazis. There are always bad eggs in every country". My uncle Werner later, like Reinhardt (another of my fathers' brothers), was granted one of the first licenses to publish after the occupation of Germany. Other relatives were granted publishing licenses in the British, French and US

Zones of occupation, too. They were recognized as "decent Germans".

The married-on uncle Männe won the Order of the Iron Cross in the First World War. His life was spared in Theresienstadt. His wife had joined the public protest demonstration of six thousand Aryan wives of Jewish men in Berlin. Liberated after his horrible experience he did not hate Germans as such.

Paul Rosbaud later came to play a pivotal role in my life. His contacts with the Secret Service in Britain enabled him to bring me to England, supported by them, with a residence and labour permit, paid-for air ticket and some valuable currency at a time when Germans could not travel, unless the allies wanted their specialist knowledge.

In his acceptance speech of the Nobel Prize more than thirty years ago, the novelist Saul Bellow said that the people who lived through the crises and disasters to befall mankind since the First World War have learnt to shed some prejudices and become more tolerant. George Santayana had earlier stipulated "Those who cannot remember the past are condemned to repeat it."

What is going on in the United States of America? This Defender of Freedom has brought endless shame to the country. After the atrocities of Vietnam, Iraq, the sad saga of the Guantanamo concentration camp (and other places), now has the case of the demolition of the spirit of Private Bradley Manning, held in solitary confine-ment and forced to strip naked at night - on official orders. He had passed on de-tails of tor-ture in confidential and embarrassing messages between his govern-ment and legations overseas. A brave young man. It is a good citizen's duty to re-port abuses of pow-er. His treatment smacks of Nazi and Stalinist practices which America had earlier so valiantly helped to defeat. My last visit to Papa haunts me. His brother and I were allowed to visit him after 10 days incarceration at Ge-stapo headquarters. Papa was a dehumanized wreck by then, Has democracy reverting to barbarism? The pub-lic knows best. Finally, the U.S. Government bowed to pressure and seems to has eased his conditions of con-finement.

Looking back, I realize how lucky I was to escpe Nazi ideology and re-education. My super-Aryan looks also probably protected me, though I came to hate that very outward appearance. My looks and youth fooled the Nazis. Any seemingly blatantly furious utterance was simply condoned as eccentric and snobbish.

Now in my own dotage I intensively relive my past. In my fantasies I experience again the horrible experiences of the past. In between I have dreams of my working life and travels, meeting important people or raising substantial funds for various seemingly worthy causes.

Books are much of my life. On a very recent trip to Germany a bookseller gave me a shopping bag carrying the message *Lesen gefährdet Dummheit* (Reading Endangers Stupidity).

Index

C

Glossary

An update of Ambrose Bierce's *Devil's Dictionary*

abortion the right to life, exemplified by shooting the abortionist doctor
aerated literally 'filling with air', as in airhead or wind. A physiological phenomenon enabling anyone to blow bubbles under water, also a kind of chocolate bar
ally a satellite state, often reluctantly joining in a costly and needless war
arbiter a go-between, believed to stem from the Latin arbor (wood), e.g. "one who does not see the wood for the trees"
Arbeit macht frei a cynical German placebo phrase to cover murder
art a wartime permissible target of looting
aryan a self-delusion of believing in one's superiority
autobiography a written record of confused memories, *see* pulp

bailout the allocation of huge monetary funds to

save failed banks and investment houses at taxpayers' expense. This usually involves huge bonus settlements out of public funds, e.g. higher personal taxation and a drop in the value of the currency

banker a reckless gambler supported by government rewarding his profligate spending of other people's money, *see* pulp

beancounter an accountant or anyone able to juggle figures, *see also* sultana

berlusconisize boast of expertise in adultery and corruption to win widespread electoral support

blairite a humbug in denial, also a war criminal, *see* hypocrisy

blasphemy the blessing and prayers by clergymen that accompany bombs destined to kill non-combatants and destroy homes in enemy cities, *see* hypocrisy

bombing state-sponsored terrorism. In some countries clergymen bless the bombs to be dropped on civilians

bonus (*see also* banker) a reward for reckless gamblers and tycoons who have used other people's money to claim obscenely large "golden handshakes" and enormous pension payments as a reward for the mismanagement of funds entrusted to them

born-again a criminal who supports the execution of other criminals, but not himself, *see* hypocrisy

bushite a born-again person believing in capital punishment, a war criminal, *see* hypocrisy

calamity that which should befall others
catastrophe originally a natural disaster, nowadays any form of government
celebrity a person of little importance, but with few moral or social restraints, often found in the entertainment industry and much wooed by the media, *see* pulp
Christian *see also* born-again
claptrap a political speech
cleaning-up the planned annihilation of innocent civilians in war
collateral damage the wanton destruction of property (and lives)
commonsense nowadays bleating or an obsolete way of thinking, believed to have been a 'lost' faculty of early man before reason came
comprint to compose, comprehend and print, also a conference of conscientious and intelligent people from all over
conformity an aim of education, *see* mediocrity
consensus fear of disagreement, e.g. "I think the same as Our Glorious Leader"
consultant a person able to teach his grandmother how to suck eggs. Governments are in the habit of amply rewarding such advice
customer a human being who is always right, also a damned soul in hell
customer relations living hell

currency *see* financial centre
cyclist a noiseless road user freed from the irritating observance of traffic lights and allowed to silently ride on pavements at night without lights in darkness to indulge in the amusing sport of scaring streetwalkers, old ladies and handicapped pedestrians

democracy a form of political government thought superior to totalitarianism, but equally liable to corruption and self-righteous dictatorship
dictatorship the shortlived duration of a government for the people meant to last one thousand years
diplomat a smooth talker explaining the rights or wrongs of his country while always in the right, *see also* spokesperson
dissent a view that must be suppressed and severely punished
dong a legendary and silent male sexual organ

education a doomed attempt to instill rudimentary civility and knowledge in young people, *see* conformity *and* mediocrity
embarrassment being found out, e.g. sitting down and having forgotten to lock the lavatory door
enema a form of irrigation of the body. The plural of this term is also pompously known as emata
enigma a man's female partner or inamorata

ennui a lack of interest in any form of education
envy wishing for that which should rightfully belong to you

facetious any comment
fairies mythical and magic mystery workers, *see also* goblins, leprechauns and Zurich. In mankind, a single oriented sexuality usually of an aesthetic or muscle-bound person
faith *see* religion
financial centre gambling casinos sometimes claimed to be essential to a country's trade balance and currency
flatulence a sudden and unwelcome outburst of warm or hot air. A favoured electioneering stunt of the blind leading blind voters is to ask them to watch their leader's lips
fop *see* vanity
freedom an illusion which must be kept in check, *see also* democracy and hypocricy
friendly fire an accidental salutary execution
fudge an explctive five-letter word utilized by frustrated, but refined denizens of Pinner, Middlesex (England)

gambling *see* bankers
gentile a superior being, especially when Aryan
gibberish *see* whitewash

gnome *see* Zurich
goblin mythical sporadic visitor of one's house, also a household cleaning machine. *See also* fairies, leprechauns *and* Zurich
greed a mental and physical affliction largely affecting bankers, politicians and major public figures
gulag Soviet Russian re-education camp for opponents to the regime, *see also* holocaust

Hagens German pseudo-scientist and ghoulish defiler of plasticized corpses for display, a sort of modern-age Burke & Hare graverobber
handy (from the German) a mobile electronic instrument of verbal telecommunication which causes utmost irritation ito nearby people. A useless instrument as normal usage in a loud voice would suffice to be heard clearly across oceans
hell the residential home of damned souls
hero brave self-sacrificing foolhard or a military gent who courageously sacrificed the lives of those under his command
hoi polloi the general public, also known as 'the great unwashed' or 'muggins'
holocaust the legalized murder of six million Jews and one million Austrian/German opponents by Hitler's henchmen. In the former Soviet Union Stalin had another version performed
hunter an animal over respectfully dressing up

to kill before giving animals the opportunity to run for their life before despatching them to paradise. In human terms also known as *cherchez la femme*, also a type of fob watch

hypocrisy *see* 'blasphemy

immunity the license given to off-duty transport staff to disregard bylaws and always stand by the entrance to mainly privatized buses, blocking the entrance to all boarding passengers, obstructing the view ahead and talking to the driver in order to distract him. Both driver and standing colleague all the while gesticulating animatedly

independent lapdog

infidel anyone of a religious persuasion not of one's own who must be enlightened by man's brimstone and fire. In history the Crusades and the witch trials are examples of following this noble principle

irrigation a colonial term, *see* enema

jail a college for criminals

janitor a guardian of morals

language primarily known as alien, but much used by illiterates and based mainly on a limited vocabulary of four letter words

leprechaun believed to be an original tribe of Ireland, *see also* fairies, goblins, leprechauns *and* Zurich

liberation in wartime a violent change from occupation to oppression, occasionally called the dawn of democracy heralding the defeat of despotism and the coming of a dictatorship or tyranny, *see also* revolution

libido a natural impulse in the animal world, associated with some pleasurable feelings. In human relations frequently the cause of litigation

life has it any meaning or is it just a dream?

liquid that which is not solid

loot *see* art

maecenas originally a Roman benefactor, now a term used for a sponsor seeking to enrich himself

maelstrom believed to have caused the disappearance of the Iraqi fleet carrying those elusive WMD

mammon originally the false Babylonian god of money, originating the ever popular Dance before the Golden Calf. In modern times the term acquired the meaning of greed, as in bankers' bonus *(see under this term)* and Members of Parliament expenses or US Congressmen 'pork barrel' payments, also a profitable outcome of lobbying and influence peddling

March a joyous and expensive month of far too many birthdays

masturbation believed to refer to the self-abusive vice performed by Victorian teenager Master Uriah

earlier ascribed this affliction often thought to cause blindness to Mr Onan in the Old Testament and fully described later by the 20th century American writer Philip Roth. There is also some historical evidence of female masturbation in the early Roman story of Dildo & Aneas which lead to the Carthaginian War. In recent times healers like Dr Ruth Wertheim drew attention to the probably beneficial nature of the practice

mediocrity another aim of education, *see* conformity

mendacity another term for brazen greed of such worthies as politicians or bankers lining their pockets with public funded or taxpayers bailout monies, *see* mammon

naloptian name of a colour-dyed ice cream

nausea a by-product of education

nation a large group of people haphazardly thrown together

navel a relic of the umbilical cord, also known as Senior Service or maritime military affairs

nepotism elevation of family members linked to depotism

Olympics prestige-seeking folly and waste of money which would be better spent on worthwhile projects. In Roman times known as *panem et circenses*, a soporific for the masses

passport a faked travel document favoured by some governmental state-sponsored assassins

patriotism justification for the indiscriminate slaughter of defenceless women, children and old people, such as by the atom bomb in Japan or the bombings in Cambodia, Iraq or Vietnam

pork barrel the profitable lining of one's own pockets while claiming to secure benefits for the populace

poverty a generally lamentable relative state of financial shortfalls in third world countries, e.g. beggars can't be choosers. The wealthy, when confronted with a clamour for bread, will offer cake

public relations exaggerated claims for miraculous effects promoted by non-medical spin doctors and much utilized by nonentities

pulp a basic ingredient of paper on which to print

pushmi-pullyu a mythical beast with two heads (at either end of its body described by the English writer Hugh Lofting. Alone among the mammals nature had relieved it of the production of digestive gases

religion a mythical belief in powerful beings controlling earth, water, fire, love or war. etc. In modern times, skills are being attributed to just one almighty benign – and at the same time malevolent – split personality being, looks after mankind and visiting believers and nonbelievers alike with catastrophes, illness, pestilence, war and strife or earthquakes. Zealous believers seek out imagined nonbelievers and let them fight wild beasts, put them on the rack or gas millions of peaceful people. Suicidal male believers in some religions on death are met by bevies of an inexhaustible supply of virgins, others may have to be content with soporific harp music. Women get few rewards, but may just be customers – or what used to be called "the damned"

rendering letting others do the torturing while condemning it in general or Being Holier Than Thou.

retaliation the justification for the deliberate murder of innocent civilians in order to terrorize communities

revolution a bloodthirsty change of government, the change to another form of government, *see* liberation

robber baron a scoundrel with a romantic aura. In modern times an Italian statesman and friend or ally of other countries, presidents and prime ministers

sanctimonious moralistic statements of arms dealers or bankers when trying to justify their activities regardless of which country they speak of

satellite state lapdog ally

saving the economy the fiendish, supposedly brilliant scheme to use taxpayer's money to rescue bankers and banking from ruin and reward them for their greed

school a training institution for conformity

sex *see* libido

sincerity *see* politicians, such as Messrs Tony Blair and George W. Bush in self-righteous explanation for abominable happenings while claiming to bring democracy to Afghanistan or Iraq and other regions. Examples are Abu Ghrab, Falludja or Mai Lai in Vietnam

smite a favourite activity of a mythical almighty being in treating friend and foe alike

smitten defeated, also besotted and delusional in believing that the sun shines out of another person's rectum, *see also* religion

spokesperson someone who is always able to utter gibberish and whitewash

sport a competitive stressful pastime considered beneficial, *see also* Olympics

statesman say nothing more! *See also* spokesperson

stoning a popular public execution, mainly of females, who have transgressed some traditional Muslim rules. Normally a close family member is mercifully allowed to hurl the heaviest piece of skull-crushing rock, *see* religion

Stuff Happens title of a play by David Hare. A phrase much used by US spokesmen. *See also* sincerity

sultana a small, sweet dried grape, originally stemming from a sultanate. Also known as Corinthians and commonly known as the digestive end product of a miser's system, *see also* beancounter

taxation money for deserving causes, such as armaments or representatives of the public. A common hope is that there will be no taxation without representation

taxi a hackney carriage whose driver often can boast of an expert knowledge of the most scenic and circuitous route to any destination. Generally quite sheepishly appreciated by American tourists who – when going home from JFK – are all too often given yet another opportunity to admire the elegant calm of the beach villas of Long Island. Dr Johnson, it is said, stipulated that "When a Man is Tired of East Croydon (or East Finchley, for that matter) He is Tired of Life"

taxidermist similar to an embalmer (of animals). Modern practice of taxidermy no longer shows animals mounted, but – in the case of apes and monkeys – just holding hands

trivia the content of most newspapers, *see* pulp

vanity a vain, often mindless and usually shortlived attempt by politicians and so-called celebrities, but also many ordinary people, to claim perfection of body, mind and soul, frequently associated with deplorable manners

vomit (verb) to reluctantly enjoy one's food in reverse. In modern history a US President thought his Japanese host at a state banquet would appreciate such a gesture acknowledging hospitality. The guest from

America did not fully realize that different countries have different customs

warmonger a Kissinger (politician), *see also* Blair and Bush

Werner *nomen est omen* – a person's first name. A person burdened with being a warner, watcher or guardian

whitewash gibberish uttered with a serious face

WMD (Weapons of Mass Destruction) imaginary armaments, unlike anthrax, atomic or hydrogen bombs, *see also* maelstrom

wysiwyg mostly rubbish

zilch public spirited rubbish

Zurich Swiss metropolis and home of financial gnomes. *see also* fairies, goblins and leprechauns